COMMITTED

CRITICAL INDIGENEITIES
J. Kēhaulani Kauanui and Jean M. O'Brien, series editors

Series Advisory Board
Chris Anderson, University of Alberta
Irene Watson, University of South Australia
Emilio del Valle Escalante, University of North Carolina at Chapel Hill
Kim TallBear, University of Texas at Austin

Critical Indigeneities publishes pathbreaking scholarly books that center Indigeneity as a category of critical analysis, understand Indigenous sovereignty as ongoing and historically grounded, and attend to diverse forms of Indigenous cultural and political agency and expression. The series builds on the conceptual rigor, methodological innovation, and deep relevance that characterize the best work in the growing field of critical Indigenous studies.

Committed

REMEMBERING

NATIVE KINSHIP

IN AND BEYOND

INSTITUTIONS

SUSAN BURCH

The University of North Carolina Press

Chapel Hill

The publication of this book was supported
by a grant from Middlebury College.

Set in Scala Sans by codeMantra
Manufactured in the United States of America

The University of North Carolina Press has been a
member of the Green Press Initiative since 2003.

Cover photo by Alexanderportraits.com, courtesy of Jack Jensen

Library of Congress Cataloging-in-Publication Data
Names: Burch, Susan, author.
Title: Committed : remembering native kinship in
and beyond institutions / Susan Burch.
Other titles: Critical indigeneities.
Description: Chapel Hill : University of North
Carolina Press, 2021. | Series: Critical indigeneities |
Includes bibliographical references and index.
Identifiers: LCCN 2020037060 | ISBN 9781469661612
(cloth ; alk. paper) | ISBN 9781469661629
(paperback ; alk. paper) | ISBN 9781469663364 (ebook)
Subjects: LCSH: Canton Asylum for Insane Indians—
History. | Indians, Treatment of—North America. | Indians
of North America—United States—Biography. | Inmates
of institutions—United States—Biography. | Indians of
North America—Government relations—1869–1934.
Classification: LCC E93 .B95 2021 | DDC 970.004/97—dc23
LC record available at https://lccn.loc.gov/2020037060

Cover description for accessibility: The title, COMMITTED, written in
black, appears above the Jensen family quilt. The quilt's twelve squares
hold blue plates within larger circles of bright calico fabrics. Hand-
stitched names of family members surround each circle and are slightly
bumpy to the touch. This piecework could wrap around two people
and was made by Prairie Band Potawatomi healer O-Zoush-Quah,
who was institutionalized for decades, and her daughter, Pah-Kish-Ko-
Quah, ca. 1910–30 (photograph by Alexanderportraits.com, courtesy
of Jack Jensen). Near the bottom of the page the subtitle of the book,
REMEMBERING NATIVE KINSHIP IN AND BEYOND INSTITUTIONS,
appears in red. Beneath this is the author's name, SUSAN BURCH. The
quilt's border is repeated along the edges of the book cover.

Contents

Illustrations

Acknowledgments

Committed grew around life stories. Relatives of people detained at Canton Asylum shared memories, context, and abiding connections to their ancestors that fundamentally shaped my understanding of this cross-generational history. Some of the individuals who collaborated with me walked on before the project was completed. Often, other family members came forward to help this book take flight. I am immensely grateful to all of them. My deepest thanks to Faith O'Neil (Sisseton-Wahpeton Oyate) and Pete Alcaraz; the Jensen family (Prairie Band Potawatomi), Francis (Kitch-Kum-Me), Jack (Peatwatuck), Alison, Howard (Nash-Wa-Took), and Julie; Anne Gregory; Mary Garcia (Tohono O'odham); Pemina Yellow Bird (Mandan/Hidatsa/Arikara); Gary and Voncile Mitchell (Prairie Band Potawatomi); Lavanah Judah (Yankton Sioux); Cordelia Red Owl (Oglala Lakota), Irina Red Owl (Oglala Lakota), Lavina Red Owl (Oglala Lakota), and Rae Ann Red Owl (Oglala Lakota); Richard Iron Cloud (Oglala Lakota); Joe Rabon; Eddie Box Jr. (Southern Ute Indian Tribe); Kay Davis (Bois Forte Chippewa) and her daughters, Kathy Paugh, Kristi Foreman, Karen Davis, and Cheryl Botkin, and her granddaughter Jill Betancourt; Franklin James Longhat (Caddo Nation) and his sister Ina Louise Longhat (Fawn Richards, Caddo Nation); Frank Caldwell Jr. (Menominee Nation); Caroline Jean Kiger-StClair (Sisseton-Wahpeton Sioux Tribe) and her daughter Sheala Dunlap; Robin and Henry Yabah (Navajo Nation); Trevino Brings Plenty (Cheyenne River Sioux Tribe); Yvonne Stretches (Standing Rock Sioux Tribe); Maynard and Orsen Bernard (Sisseton-Wahpeton Oyate); Michael and Douglas Herman; Mary G. Vickmark; Diane Teeman; Edward Abrahams III; Manfred Hill; Donna Dexter; Pat Deegan; Kathryn Leslie; Steven Roth; Mildred Juel; and Bill and Marie Skelly. I also extend my heartfelt appreciation to the many people who are not explicitly named but whose presence is everywhere in this work.

Members of Tribal Historic Preservation Offices (THPO) advised me on ethical practices, exchanged ideas, and connected me to other community members, histories, and research projects. Special thanks to Dianne Desrosiers (Sisseton-Wahpeton Oyate), Tamara St. John (Sisseton-Wahpeton Oyate), and the Sisseton-Wahpeton Oyate THPO; to the colleagues at the Rosebud Sioux Tribe THPO, including Russell Eagle Bear (Sicangu Lakota Oyate), Ben Rhodd, and Peter Gibbs; David Grignon (Menominee Nation) and the Menominee Nation THPO; the Caddo Nation THPO and Robert Cast; Barnaby Lewis and the Gila River Indian Community THPO; the THPO of Tohono O'odham Nation; Bois Forte Band of Chippewa's THPO; and Ian Thompson and Choctaw Nation of Oklahoma's Historic Preservation Department.

Archivists and librarians located sources, offered valuable advice, and shared in the excitement of research. I want to extend my sincere appreciation to Tawa Ducheneaux (Cherokee Nation), Ellen White Thunder (Oglala Lakota), and Oglala Lakota College's special collections, Betty Veflin and the Sisseton Memorial Library (South Dakota), and to the S. Verna Fowler Academic Library at the College of Menominee Nation. I also benefited greatly from the help of archivist Meg Hacker and colleagues at National Archives and Records Administration–Fort Worth as well as from archivists Ken House (NARA–Seattle), Jake Ersland (NARA–Kansas City), Eric Bittner (NARA–Denver), James Huntoon (NARA–Riverside), and Rose Buchanan (NARA–DC). Staff at the Canton Public Library in South Dakota provided meeting spaces during visits as well as research assistance. I also thank Ken Stewart and the South Dakota State Archives, Linnea M. Anderson and colleagues at the University of Minnesota's Social Welfare History Archives, Curator Sam Herley and colleagues at the South Dakota Oral History Center (University of South Dakota), Lisa Peña and colleagues in Special Collections at the Mary Couts Burnett Library (Texas Christian University), Matt Messbarger at the Arizona State University's Distinctive Collections and Archives, and the Milwaukee Road Historical Association. St. Elizabeths Hospital associates Dr. Jorges Prandoni and Maureen Jais-Mick gave thoughtful tours of the grounds and museum, detailed broader institutional and cemetery history, and took great care in answering complex questions. Frances McMillen provided valuable insights about the architectural and lived history of St. Elizabeths as well.

Talented research assistants at Middlebury College and the Smithsonian National Museum of American History—Anna Mack, Dan Egol, Nicholas Aszling, Rachel Anderson, Patrick Schmidt, Aubree Minakami, HiMi Kanaumi, Cara Wattanodom, Mariana Bellante, and Napol Wills—have my high praise and deep gratitude. Carllee James, Alyssa Young, Amanda Senst, Levi Westerveld, Maddie Li, Thomas Lu, Katherine Randle, Sylvie Soulier, and Ben Meader greatly helped with locating, visualizing, and documenting historical sources. Katie Hill and Nicole Klungle lent their remarkable editing skills, for which I am very thankful.

I am fortunate beyond words to know Katherine Ott. She recognized the book that *Committed* could become, held me accountable to write it, and devoted abundant time and other resources to its development: hand-on-heart thanks. I am enormously grateful also to colleague-friends who read and gave insightful feedback on draft chapters, often multiple times. A gardenful of thanks to Alison Kafer, Kim Nielsen, Lisa Kahaleole Hall (Kanaka Maoli), David Chang, Jacki Rand (Choctaw Nation of Oklahoma), Ari Kelman, Alice Shepherd, Therí Pickens, Bobby Buchanan, Scott Riney, Greg Smithers, Peggy Nelson, Michael Rembis, Kim Drake, Lindsey Patterson, Mary E. Mendoza, Brenda Jo Brueggemann, Karlie Markendorf, Traci Voyles, David Gerber, Michael Stein, Kathy Morse, Susan Cahn, Jay Sibara, Steve Hoffman, Corbett O'Toole, Catharine Wright, Susan Pearson, Jacob Tropp, and Hannah Joyner. Many others patiently workshopped ideas with me, shedding light on historical contexts and themes and dreamscaping access features that shaped this project. Special thanks to Doug Kiel (Oneida Nation), Penny Richards, Tara Affolter, Jessica Cowing, Margaret Jacobs, Eunjung Kim, Audra Jennings, Ellen Samuels, Caroline Lieffers, Kevin Gotkin, Daniel Cobb, Juliann Anesi (Samoan, Pacific Islander), Holly Allen, Tavian Robinson, Jamie Axelrod, Sharon O'Brien, Bob Prasch, Falguni "Tina" Sheth, Ella Callow, Aly Patsavas, Liat Ben-Moshe, Natalie Eppelsheimer, Talila A. Lewis, Sandy Sufian, Regina Kunzel, Adria Imada, Barbara Ofosu-Somuah, Jay Dolmage, Sue Schweik, Ellery Foutch, Cathy Kudlick, Carrie Sandahl, Christian McMillen, Dane Verret, Elaine Gerber, Rachael Joo, Jiya Pandya, Sarah A. Whitt (Choctaw Nation of Oklahoma), Andrew Graybill, Dave Beck, Katherine M. B. Osburn, Karen Guttentag, Will Nash, Joyce "MoMo" Markendorf, and Matthew Gambino.

I would like to extend my deep appreciation to Napos (David Turney Sr., Menominee Nation), Jerome Kills Small (Oglala Lakota), Stella Iron Cloud (Oglala Lakota), LaDonna Brave Bull Allard (Standing Rock Sioux Tribe), and Dee BigFoot (Caddo Nation) for sharing tribal histories as well as insights and advice for this project. Special thanks to Wendy Carter, Helena Morris, and Stacey Dobek for their expertise in healing work. Gifted translators illuminated key sources. I thank Sisokaduta Joe Bendickson (Sisseton-Wahpeton Oyate) as well as Tammy DeCouteau (Sisseton-Wahpeton Oyate) and Our Treasured Elders members at the AAIA Native Language Program. Warm thanks also go to Omar Peterson, Father Charlie

Chan, Jerry and Linda Patchen, and Ellen Lofland for helping me better understand local histories and artifacts. Cory Myers and Abigail Dollins as well as the *Argus Leader* newspaper located and shared beautiful historic photographs.

Significant funding from organizations and institutions reduced many barriers to completing this book. I gratefully acknowledge the American Council of Learned Societies, the National Endowment for the Humanities, the National Archives Regional Residency Fellowship, and the Mellon Foundation. Middlebury College contributed valuable resources through the Digital Liberal Arts Grant (thank you, Anne Knowles, Alicia Peaker, Jason Mittell, and Mike Roy), the Faculty Professional Development Fund, Long-Term Professional Development Fund, Academic Enrichment Fund, and the Scholarly Publication Subvention Fund (with particular thanks to Jim Ralph, Amy Morsman, Sandra King, and Lynn Dunton). Franci Farnsworth from Middlebury's Grants and Sponsored Programs Office generously showered my numerous application drafts with astute feedback. Thank you.

I very much appreciate the Middlebury College colleagues and students whose enthusiasm for *Committed* sustained and propelled me across many years. The Disability Studies Reading Group at Middlebury literally and metaphorically nourished me: I offer my sincere thanks to its members. Intrepid library and academic technology staff at the college tutored me on software and found innovative ways to smooth the research path. An enthusiastic shout-out is due to Amy Frazier, Katrina Spencer, Bill Koulopoulos, Joe Antonioli, Dan Frostman, Janine McDonald, Rachel Manning, Michele McHugh, Heather Stafford, Todd Sturtevant, and Kimberly Marshall.

Colleagues at the University of North Carolina Press and Longleaf Services, including John Sherer, Mark Simpson-Vos, Jessica Newman, Cate Hodorowicz, Dominique Moore, Madge Duffey, Dino Battista, Mary Caviness, Erin Granville, Ellen Bush, Ihsan Taylor, and Kevin Brock, skillfully shepherded this manuscript from partial drafts to polished publication. I thank the anonymous readers for UNC Press for their constructive feedback as well. Series editors Jeani O'Brien (White Earth Ojibwe) and J. Kēhaulani Kauanui (Kanaka Maoli) asked brilliant questions, provided thoughtful advice, and offered unwavering support, for which I am very grateful.

"Book buddy" inadequately describes the many roles Eli Clare has held or the monumental amount of time he devoted to our collaboration. His contributions as writing mentor, sounding board, confidant, committed activist, and dear friend infuse every page. Thank you plus infinity.

Kinship is the heartbeat of this book. I am so deeply grateful for the people who are my people: thank you for the enormous and everyday ways you light my world. Ian M Sutherland lived this project with me for more than a decade. Thank you for being the Replica of My Multiplying Universe. Ti adoro.

A Note on Access

This book embodies a commitment to access, to conveying content with as few barriers as possible. Access is a practice, not a checklist. It is innovative, dynamic, and imperfect. To cultivate access:

- I intentionally use accessible language rather than technical terms to invite a wide range of readers.
- In cooperation with the publisher and designer, a sans serif typeface was chosen to maximize legibility.
- *Committed* is available in multiple formats: ebook, paper, and audiobook.
- The ebook is offered for free, in recognition that financial cost also creates barriers.
- Alt-text appears in the ebook version to convey transcriptions of photographed correspondence.
    - I also include plentiful visual descriptions of images in the captions and body of the book as a more inclusive option for access to the imagery across all formats.

The access practices in *Committed* hopefully reduce common obstacles to engaging with historical scholarship. At the same time, I recognize that access is an incomplete process, in general and in this book. I hope that this work ultimately serves as an appeal to others to cultivate more accessible histories and more accessible futures.

COMMITTED

Introduction: **Committed**

> *The story comes around, pushing at our brains, and soon*
> *we are trying to ravel back to the beginning, trying to put*
> *families into order and make sense of things. But we start*
> *with one person, and soon another and another follows,*
> *and still another, until we are lost in the connections.*
> —Louise Erdrich (Turtle Mountain Band of Chippewa
> Indians), *The Bingo Palace*

Saturday, May 29, 1915, began like most other days for Elizabeth and Jesse Faribault. Summer had started off cold and wet, but the land in South Dakota had thawed enough to put seed in the ground.[1] The Sisseton-Wahpeton Dakota couple prepared for the day: Jesse, heading to work their farmland with eldest son Solomon, left Elizabeth at their home with their two youngest children, Howard and Annie. But when Jesse returned with Solomon at the end of the day, Elizabeth was gone, and his daughter and son were there alone.

It is unclear how long it took Elizabeth's husband to discover that she had been forcibly removed from the Faribaults' home by representatives of the Bureau of Indian Affairs (BIA).[2] They had taken her to Canton, South Dakota, where the federal government operated a psychiatric institution specifically intended to contain Native Americans.[3]

Once Jesse learned that Elizabeth was incarcerated at the Indian Asylum, he immediately reached out to kin and others to seek her release. John Noble, a lawyer hired by the family months into her detention, surmised that the Sisseton woman had been institutionalized because of an altercation with a BIA agent earlier in May. As Noble explained to the commissioner of Indian Affairs, Elizabeth had appeared at the local agency office, which was about a mile from her home, "clad only in a 'camisole' and did some vulgar talking."[4] According to Jesse, Elizabeth "was only drunk" at the time. Noble challenged the justifications for taking the thirty-two-year-old mother from her home. "There were no known proceedings had to establish insanity in this case," the legal advocate argued, and Jesse, being away from the house at the time, was unable to prevent the wrongful intrusion into their home and life. Consequently, Faribault's lawyer reasoned, Elizabeth should be returned immediately to her family.[5]

BIA representatives at Sisseton described their confrontations in 1915 with Elizabeth Faribault this way: she was "violently insane" and ran "amuck near [the] agency" but resided "on patented land." According to a clerk, Faribault had "threaten[ed] to kill" and caused "great anxiety."[6] A telegram from headquarters in Washington, D.C., informed agency officials that medical examinations were required to declare a reservation Indian insane. A swift reply came from Sisseton on May 12: "Agency physician pronounces Elizabeth Faribault allotted Sisseton Indian insane. Wire authority to place her in government or other insane asylum at government expense."[7] That authority was granted the next day. Two weeks later, on May 29, an agency doctor and police officer went to the Faribault home and removed Elizabeth to the federal asylum in Canton. U.S. government reports generated months afterward suggested that the Dakota woman had "hallucinated" and was "delusional probably due to use of alcohol."[8]

No other records remain to explain what did or did not actually occur between May 8 and May 29.[9] Faribault's medical files over the next thirteen years show various diagnoses along with wide-ranging justifications for sustaining her institutionalization: Materially deteriorated. Incapable of looking after herself. Alcoholic. Chronically insane. Duplicitous. Eugenically unfit. Depressed and emotional. Abusive of Asylum privileges. Better off at the institution.

The story of what happened to Elizabeth Faribault and to her kin before, during, and after her internment reveals violent entanglements of settler colonialism, racism, ableism, and sexism. These forces continue to shape and distort histories of Native nations and families. While distinctive in many ways, the Faribault family's story is not unique. Their history, and those of other Indigenous people confined at the Indian Asylum and other federal psychiatric facilities, is inextricably tied to broader stories of Native self-determination, kinship, institutionalization, and remembering.[10] These stories constitute the heart of this book.

Messy and incomplete, the individual and family accounts that span the following chapters are not intended to coalesce into neat patterns. Their disorderliness is not without meaning or purpose, however. Following microhistories—the focused study of personal lives—enables us to understand better the consequences of settler colonialism, ableism, and institutionalization, among other broad transgenerational forces. People's lived stories also hold within them the potential to create, challenge, maintain, shape shift, and destroy. As Michi Saagiig Nishnaabeg scholar Leanne Betasamosake Simpson contends, stories provide resources for community and survival. Because of this, "storytelling is like air," she insists. "It's that important—especially as a tool of decolonization and transformation. Stories have spirit and power and come to us as small gifts of wisdom, but they only have power if the ones that hear those stories embody them and act."[11]

This book is called *Committed*, a title that embodies multiple meanings, all of which are found in this story. "Committed" entails dedication: Activists are committed to their causes; they are committed activists. It also can involve perpetration of crimes or misdeeds, as when someone commits an act of violence. In institutional contexts, confinement and loss of autonomy come to mind: Elizabeth Faribault and hundreds of others were committed to the Indian Asylum in South Dakota. And "committed" expresses the action of witnessing, transferring, or documenting, as when someone commits a story to memory.

Early in the research process for this book, I imagined that it would center on community histories within the Canton Asylum. A phone conversation with writer Pemina Yellow Bird (Mandan/Hidatsa/Arikara) lingers in my memory. We had been discussing the unequal power dynamics between those who built, worked for, and protected asylums and those who were held in them involuntarily. Pemina challenged my use of the term "inmate" in this context. I explained that the word "patient" seemed wholly inappropriate, given the violence of the Indian Asylum and my desire to work against the eclipsing influence of Western biomedical frameworks. "How about calling them *people*?" she asked. Silence echoed on the phone line as the distance between the terms "inmate" and "people" sunk in. I am thankful to Pemina and to many others for the ways they remind all of us that this is fundamentally a story of people. Their insight underscores a final meaning of "committed" that is tied to relationships—between people, the broader world around us, and to the ways we remember and respond to the connections we form with others.

———

When Elizabeth Faribault was forcibly removed to a place two hundred miles away from the Sisseton Reservation in 1915, she crossed a threshold into a distinctly institutional space—the Canton Asylum—and into a distinctly non-Native process: institutionalization. Tall wire fencing fortified the grounds. The Asylum's sweeping brick and concrete Main Building conveyed order and control under U.S. settler sovereignty.[12] From its opening in December 1902 until its forced closure in January 1934, the BIA-run Canton Asylum detained nearly four hundred people from more than fifty Indigenous nations. Canton confined children, adults, and elders, spouses and neighbors, cousins and classmates, healers and parents.

No medical records remain to describe Elizabeth's formal admission to Canton. Likely, she and her escorts were met at the Main Building by Asylum staff. It is possible that Dr. Harry R. Hummer, serving as both Asylum superintendent and sole physician, conducted a brief examination of the Dakota woman. Afterward she would have been led to a sex-segregated ward on the second floor, perhaps exchanging glances with other women and girls housed along the hall. During Faribault's confinement in this federal facility, she was forced to provide labor on behalf of the institution, including carework and other domestic service to Superintendent Hummer's family. Twice she escaped the Asylum grounds but was captured and returned. Faribault would spend the remainder of her life held in Canton's bounded geography.

Native Self-Determination and Settler Colonialism

As the Faribault family and many others experienced it, institutionalization at Canton violated their Native nation's as well as their individual family's self-determination.[13] Many Native American and Indigenous studies scholars have drawn our attention to ongoing processes that attack Indigenous autonomy. An offspring of imperialism, *settler colonialism* involves interlocking structures—political, economic, and cultural—that seek to transform colonized places into the settler's home. Fundamental to this systematic practice is the removal and supplanting of Indigenous peoples. As anthropologist Patrick Wolfe has explained, "Settler colonialism destroys to replace."[14] The creation of the Indian Asylum, and the disruption institutionalization and sustained confinement wrought in the Faribault family and hundreds of others, fit these broader patterns of settler colonialism.

Settler colonialism also entails the drive for profit and the extraction of resources. The economic gains that Canton Asylum provided to mostly non-Native staff members and local businesses embodies this typical settler practice.[15] Repeated thefts of Native land, of people, and of cultural artifacts crossed generations with cumulative effect.[16] These and other forms of violence fray national and kinship connections.

Settler colonialism directly involves contests over self-determination. In U.S. history, sovereignty is generally presumed to be self-evident: The United States is a sovereign nation. In contrast, Indigenous self-determination is denied in a variety of ways, including how Native North American history frequently is told. Military conquest, forced displacements, missionary efforts, and reservation policies are some of the more overt forms of settler attacks on Indigenous self-determination.[17] Both land and people bore its mark.[18] The U.S. government's Indian Asylum and the people whose lives intersected with it is a microcosm of these larger forces.[19]

Indigenous studies scholar Linda Tuhiwai Smith (Ngāti Awa and Ngāti Porou, Māori) and others have shown that settler colonial tactics also have more subtle expressions.[20] Some of the many ways settler colonialism saturates North American history and contemporary society include erasing American Indians from mainstream U.S. historical accounts and renaming places and communities to align with settler viewpoints and values.[21] So, too, are the imposing logics that primarily cast Native people as inherently dependent wards and settlers as primarily benevolent humanitarians.

Most archival sources about Canton Asylum and its confined members reflect battles over self-determination. For example, the majority of preserved historic documents—Asylum annual reports, medical files, BIA correspondence, and the like—were generated by U.S. government representatives and Western medical practitioners. The viewpoints expressed in these archival materials by superintendents, physicians, commissioners, and other authors underscore their position as well-intentioned and expert authorities over Indigenous people. This particular worldview similarly permeated most published and public historical depictions throughout the twentieth century. More recent books and scholarly articles, as well as mainstream U.S. newspaper accounts, increasingly acknowledge widespread abuse at the Indian Asylum. At the same time, these studies remained anchored to popular white settler frameworks, which individualize injustices, emphasize the exceptional, and overlook systemic inequities.[22] Of these accounts, the majority spotlight the story of an institution heralded in the mainstream press during its existence as "the first and only one of its kind." Such institutional biographies especially foreground administrative matters and the tenures of its two superintendents, former South Dakota member of Congress Oscar S. Gifford (1902–8) and Dr. Harry R. Hummer (1908–33).[23] The abundant evidence of physical and sexual assaults as well as disease and high mortality rates, among other troubling facets of life on the inside at Canton, similarly are portrayed as individual and exceptional—the failings of specific people in discrete circumstances.[24]

Self-Determination and Telling Histories

Attention to settler colonialism and Indigenous self-determination redirects historical interpretation. *Committed* resists a view of time and place dictated by a singular institution's material opening and closing. In other words, the story does not begin with the creation of Canton Asylum or follow the linear history of government policies or the rise of particular medical specialties and treatments. Rather, there are multiple origins and multiple centers to this story, all of which emerge long before the U.S. government broke ground to build the Indian Asylum. This book also extends past the final days of Canton Asylum's formal existence and into the twenty-first century, drawing attention to the larger issues and lived experiences that travel beyond individual brick-and-mortar structures.

The long reach of sovereignty battles shapes the production and consumption of history—what is preserved and passed down, how it is interpreted, and by whom. Usually, historians have little if any access to sources about institutionalized people. Remarkably, thousands of available documents related to Canton Asylum and to the people held there have been preserved in national and state archives across the United States. At the same time, their location, organization, and management obstruct tribal histories and sovereignties. Technically, all of the National Archives' holdings on Canton Asylum are publicly available. In actuality, barriers abound. Only visitors who can travel to the collection sites and navigate archival labyrinths can engage directly with these materials. Most often this means that comparatively privileged, non-Native researchers (like myself) have actual access. Other impediments permeate the collections. National Archives indexing labels reproduce settler dominance, privileging Western medical practices and practitioners over Indigenous ones. Most of the archival sources cited in this project are housed in the record group for the BIA and, specifically, are collected under the series title "Canton Asylum for Insane Indians."[25] The folders and boxes are organized by a pathologizing label: insane. Amid stacks of bureaucratic forms—bids for steam radiators, commitment requests by reservation superintendents, budget updates, and the like—are letters from American Indians seeking reunions with their kin and, occasionally, photographs of institutionalized people. This means that it is not possible to locate Elizabeth Faribault's handwritten letters by her name, family, or tribal affiliation. This is true of all the archived correspondence and testimonies by Canton's institutionalized people and their relatives. Dislocated from many of their intended recipients and separated literally and symbolically from relatives and tribes, these documents remain mostly unavailable to those for whom the materials are part of their family and Indigenous nation's history. The absence of common privacy measures for medical records and other details about institutionalized people similarly undercuts tribal self-determination. What and how much to reveal remains an ethical challenge for those with access to these sources and the intimate information they contain.[26]

Many terms used in *Committed* come directly from the American Indian people around whom this work has grown. For example, correspondence written by kin and the people confined at the Indian Asylum, including Elizabeth Faribault, consistently refer to the place that detained them as the "Indian Asylum," "Indian Insane Asylum," "Asylum," and "Canton Asylum." I've followed their lead in using these terms. The grammar, spelling, and other features of writing in texts created by any of the Native writers also intentionally have not been edited. This is in recognition of the ways the English language has been used to undermine Indigenous self-determination. As much as possible, contextual explanations and interpretations of these quoted materials will be included, recognizing that some of the distance between the authors and myself cannot be fully bridged.

When the U.S. government named its institution the Canton Asylum for Insane Indians, it followed a settler logic that grouped all Native people together as if "Indian" was a singular identity. In related ways, broad terms like "American Indian," "Native American," and "Indigenous people" are inherently limited. Every Native nation has distinctive characteristics, life worlds, and history, so a person's specific tribal affiliation, when known, will be noted in this account. The terms "American Indian," "Native American," and "Indigenous peoples" generally will be used in broader contexts. Each of these labels carry different legacies and valences and are not presumed to be interchangeable. Instead, all of these terms will be invoked as a way to reflect the varied preferences of the people whose family stories appear across the following chapters.

Sovereignty, as Native American studies scholar Amanda J. Cobb (Chickasaw Nation) has explained, also involves a living process and a story of peoplehood.[27] Affirmation of Native self-determination and the ability to flourish and continue into the future are central to experiencing sovereignty. Letters, affidavits, and other writings from people incarcerated at the Indian Asylum and from their relatives speak to the challenges settler interventions caused in the lives of Indigenous people. Richly varied responses, dynamic stories of adaptation, resistance, setbacks, and continuance, shine through these accounts, showing the endurance of Indigenous identities, relationships, and self-determination.

———

Hospital records created months after her entrance to the Indian Asylum report that Elizabeth Faribault was diagnosed with "Intoxication psychosis."[28]

Other pathological labels appear across her medical records, such as "dementia," "dementia praecox" (schizophrenia), "alcoholic deterioration," and "possibly trachoma" (an infectious eye disease) that made her "very greatly depressed and emotional."[29] BIA and Asylum representatives regularly invoked these terms as part of their rationale for keeping her separated from her relatives in Sisseton. Throughout the archival record, Faribault, and to some degree her family, were cast as a medicalized individual "case." In contrast, BIA and Indian Asylum officials presented themselves as experts. In many institutional accounts, people confined at Canton and those associated with them regularly appear as concerned but misguided individuals.

For Elizabeth Faribault and her kin, pathological diagnoses obscured the violent disturbance of family and community life caused by her sustained exile. In one letter written in 1922 to Commissioner Charles Burke, for example, the Sisseton woman emphatically states that Dr. Hummer had kept her unfairly at Canton. "I've been staying here in Asylum long enough." At home, she pointed out, she could tend to her mother and her children, care that benefited the whole family.[30] The details about Faribault's diagnosis, and her own assertion that being home with her family would best support their collective well-being, point to radically different understandings of health.

Medical Systems and Systems of Power

Asylum and BIA staff consistently judged Elizabeth Faribault and everyone else in the locked wards based on one system of medicine: Western (allopathic) biomedicine. At its core, this medical system centers on a concept of normalcy that is rooted in biology, evaluated according to function, and located in individual bodyminds.[31] Following this system's logic, diagnoses—understood as experts' objective judgments—are borne by individuals alone. Achieving and sustaining normalcy is a primary goal in this practice. Consequently, cure (or its closest approximation) drives Western medical treatments.[32] The power of this particular medical tradition in the twentieth and twenty-first centuries permeates not only the labels ascribed to each person committed to Canton Asylum but also how these adults, children, and elders were treated at the time and remembered since. Western biomedicine is a dominating force but not a universal truth.

As the Faribault family and other Indigenous people have always known, there are *many* types of medicine, including numerous, distinct Indigenous practices and knowledge systems used across time to the present day.[33]

Reflecting their individual Native nation's worldviews, these healing traditions vary widely, but many—including that of the Great Sioux Nation, to which Elizabeth Faribault belonged—emphasize holistic concepts of well-being anchored to relationships with other living beings, the collective environment, and spiritual realms.[34] As many have written, the particular Western biomedical concepts of "insane" or "mentally ill" do not have full equivalents historically among Native nations' systems of medicine and culture. Moreover, the practice of institutionalization runs counter to Indigenous values, relationships, and ways of being.[35] Acknowledging various forms of healing conventions and the communities from which they emerge also expands the borders of recognized experts. Over the generations, people who inhabit this story have carried knowledge about the modes, impact, and meanings of medicine in both Indigenous and settler senses of the term.

Recognizing multiple medical systems within a broader context of settler domination undermines the projected objectivity and commonsense logic of Western biomedical diagnoses and institutionalization. As Elizabeth Faribault and the many others detained at Canton experienced it, settler cultural values permeated medicalized judgments of them. The abundant examples varied in form and consequence. As just one illustration, Asylum officials and other settler medical professionals pathologized correspondence by Faribault and other Native people written in nonstandard English, justifying sustained confinement based on grammar and language. The mostly first- and second-generation Norwegian immigrant staff at Canton similarly described the Indigenous spoken communication they encountered as signs of disordered minds.[36] The differences between Western and Indigenous medical traditions and the many factors shaping judgments of peoples' bodyminds challenges us to grapple genuinely with texts generated by individuals whom the state literally deemed incompetent. When a wide range of sources is seen as valid, including those that are invalidated by pathologization, our understanding and telling of history changes.

Acknowledging multiple sovereignties and systems of medicine resists what American studies scholar Jessica Cowing calls "settler ableism."[37] Ableism is a system of power and privilege that hierarchically organizes people and societies based on particular cultural values of productivity, competitive achievement, efficiency, capacity, and progress.[38] Ableism appears in many forms, including social relations, institutions, and policies; its expressions include prejudices, discrimination, violence, and stereotyping.[39] By imposing settler forms of medicine and knowledge practices, settler ableism actively serves and reflects broader colonial principles and aspirations. Beliefs in superiority and practices of domination—inherent aspects of settler colonialism—regularly invoke ableist logics. Through the lenses of normality, fitness, and competency, settlers have judged Indigenous people and nations. Historically, settlers have interpreted Native people's unwillingness or inability to conform to colonial ideals, such as individuality, heterosexuality, and materialism, as indications of inherent deficiencies or defects.[40] Ultimately, settler ableism is a self-affirming mechanism; ableist rationales reinforce settler aspirations and further actions.[41]

Settler colonial understandings of diagnosis have long served as a tool to undermine Indigenous people. Medical specialists and social scientists historically have imposed settler values when judging concepts and experiences from other cultures, creating and enforcing pathologies in the process.[42] As Geoffrey Reaume and many other disability studies scholars have argued, psychiatric categories are themselves cultural creations and reflect distinct historical ideas rooted in racism and sexism.[43] Building on these insights, I intentionally use labels such as "Western biomedical diagnosis" rather than simply "medicine" in order to reflect particular interpretations, processes, and relationships. This book also resists settler colonialism's gravitational pull to "rationalize or normalize suffering and trauma."[44] Rather than using a lens of individual pathology, collective suffering is considered within contexts of multigenerational kinship, settler ableism, institutionalization, and Indigenous self-determination.[45]

The terms that have been imposed, claimed, lived, and contested reflect a disorderly past—and present. Many descendants of people institutionalized at Canton have shared wrenching confusion about their relatives: Were they whatever the BIA and Asylum superintendents said they were? Others flatly reject Western pathological labels but live with the cross-generational trauma and wounds of settler medical interventions.[46] Some actively claim their institutionalized kin, seeking paths of healing for themselves and their ancestors. I have also met people who, until recently, never knew they had family held at Canton: separation, isolation, and stigma, among other factors, contributed to the nearly full erasure of the person from their original homes and communities.

In the end, *Committed* does not and cannot answer whether anyone "was" or "was not" whatever the diagnoses in medical files and institutional reports suggest. Instead, I intend to reflect on how U.S.-imposed Western biomedical diagnoses, the diagnostic process, and the impact of these pathologized labels shaped many Native people's lived experiences and those of their kin.

———

In the fall of 1926, eleven years into her detainment, Elizabeth Faribault gave birth to a girl, whom she named Cora Winona. At the time of delivery, Superintendent Hummer explained the breach of Asylum policy to his supervisors as an indication of her mother's inherent defects. "Her statement to the effect that she would not have gotten into this condition if I had permitted her to return to her home and people is a fair index of the character of her mentality," he told the commissioner of Indian Affairs.[47] Despite demands from Elizabeth's mother, Mary Alexis (Sisseton-Wahpeton Dakota), that her kin be discharged, both her daughter and granddaughter remained at Canton.

We know little about the lives of mother and child over next two years. Brief notes suggest daily activities inside the Indian Asylum: Elizabeth dressing and feeding her daughter, brushing her hair. The elder Faribault also performed work not long after giving birth, cleaning the ward in addition to providing childcare. As Cora began walking, the pair sometimes spent time on the grounds, within the shadow of their locked dormitory. Conversations, likely in Dakota, threaded across their waking hours. At night the mother and daughter slept together in Elizabeth's single bed, pulling closer to one another in the cold winter months. Their patterned routine ended abruptly eighteen months later. In March 1928, a staff member discovered Elizabeth Faribault's lifeless body on the ward, the cause of her death clouded in uncertainty. Cora Winona, then a toddler, remained at Canton for two more years.

Kinship

Kinship's pivotal role in Native life and self-determination presents a different lens through which to understand diagnoses and institutionalizations in history. The combined measures of diagnoses and treatments (institutionalization) affected extended families and Native nations as well as the pathologized people themselves. Contingent and contextual, kin relations—in all of their manifestations—have always varied in the ways they are expressed and experienced. As with Cora Winona Faribault, people around whom this story grows had many mothers, fathers, aunts, uncles, and cousins as well as siblings and children. These kin relations did not and do not share connections or bonds exclusively through white codifications, such as genetic inheritance or institutionally recognized marriages. Kin networks also actively include ancestors.[48] *Committed* holds space for wide-ranging experiences of kin as a connection imbued with many meanings and obligations.[49]

As a foundational part of Indigenous identity, kinship has been targeted in settler colonial attacks on Native self-determination. BIA documents attest to this. Drawing on male dominance and heteronormative concepts of family, agency officials and Canton Asylum superintendents assigned specific roles to Indigenous people: references to mothers and daughters, siblings, and spouses appear regularly in medical records and officials' correspondence.[50] Invoking these settler concepts as a criteria by which they judged others, U.S. authorities regularly ascribed pathological labels to explain why Native people did not conform to their expectations. These perceived familial connections contributed at least in part to their institutionalizations. As just one example, sisters from the Southern Ute Indian Tribe referred to as Jane and Susan Burch (no relation to the author) came under BIA scrutiny in 1910, when Jane had a child outside of marriage who died in infancy and Susan gave birth shortly thereafter to a son described as disabled. Linking the sisters' perceived defectiveness to reproduction and their shared heredity, the Southern Ute Agency bureaucrat claimed that both women evidenced "insanity to some extent" and recommended that the siblings be forcibly committed to Canton.[51] The pathologization of entire kin networks meant that some relatives were removed to the Indian Asylum at the same time; commonly, additional family members were institutionalized in subsequent years.[52]

According to archival records, dozens of Indigenous nations had members stolen away to Canton, underscoring the compounded ramifications institutionalization had on kinship ties. For example, of the nearly four hundred people detained at the Indian Asylum, more than one hundred were members of the Great Sioux Nation, people who would be both immediate and extended relatives of Elizabeth and Cora Winona Faribault. Some, like George Leo Cleveland Marlow, came from the same reservation as Elizabeth Faribault. Their kin connections on the outside became more entwined during their shared incarceration; after divorcing Elizabeth in 1919, Jesse Faribault married Leo's sister, Mary Marlow.[53] Another Sisseton-Wahpeton member, Nellie Kampeska, likely had known and even socialized with Elizabeth's children before she was taken to Canton. On the inside, the two women claimed close bonds of kinship, providing care and support as well as other resources to sustain one another. Cora Winona Faribault was among the few infants to survive the Asylum, in large part because of kinship obligations. In the wake of Elizabeth's death, Lizzie Red Owl, a thirty-year-old Oglala Lakota woman, parented Cora, providing daily care and attempting to shield the little girl from institutional harms.

———

Seeking to understand people's complicated lived experiences and the broader historical environments surrounding them has required looking beyond standard research archives. Phone conversations, oral history interviews, and correspondence with descendants of those detained at Canton, as well as with tribal leaders and activists, have provided critical, authoritative knowledge in *Committed*. In particular, they vividly reveal the tensions between the long reach of institutionalizations and the tenacity of cross-generational kinship ties. Some people shared material artifacts with me, including beadwork, photographs, grave markers, piecework, clothing, and jewelry. These sources similarly hold stories unaccounted for in most archival documents—of artistry and childrearing, of empathy and symbols, of committed kinship and the touch and temperatures of everyday life. Family members' different types of storytelling additionally underscores a commitment among Native communities to sustain and innovate their traditions.[54] They also filled some of the historical absences with presence.

Over the years, some relatives of Canton's institutionalized people allowed me to visit their tribal lands, including those of Sisseton-Wahpeton Oyate (South Dakota); Prairie Band Potawatomi (Kansas); Standing Rock Sioux Tribe (North and South Dakota); Mandan, Hidatsa, and Arikara Nation (North Dakota); Rosebud Sioux Tribe (South Dakota); Menominee Nation (Wisconsin); Oglala Lakota Nation (South Dakota); and Bois Forte Band of Chippewa (Minnesota). These visits created different centers and spaces to this story. In homes and coffee shops, at tribal cultural centers and family cemeteries, and elsewhere, people whose family history intersects with Canton made clear the powerful connections between places and meanings of their stories. Relationships to land, community, and home, they explained, centrally shape Indigenous identities, belongings and exiles, self-determination and wellness, erasure and remembering.[55] I am indebted to many individuals with close personal ties to the people whose histories appear—often fragmented—in this work. Family members' memories, questions, and understandings of their incarcerated kin and the consequences of displacements on their lives have guided my understanding of this history.[56]

Although the names of people held at the Canton Asylum are available to the public in various sources, this work only includes actual names in the cases when Tribal Historic Preservation officers or relatives have granted me permission to use them. This decision was guided by ethical considerations and attention to the histories of conquest, genocide, oppression, and dislocation experienced by the people and communities described in this work, in addition to the ways that academic disciplines have contributed to this violence. Relatives of Elizabeth Alexis Faribault and others who figure centrally in this book wanted me to use their ancestors' names. Depending on what their kin remember about them, the names incorporated here might include Indigenous nicknames or formal ones, U.S.-English language glosses, U.S.-Christianized names, familial roles (like "grandmother" or "elder"), or a combination of one or more of these. Sometimes spellings of names, as with Elizabeth Alexis Faribault, vary in archival and family sources, including those written by relatives. Rather than enforce conformity, references will reflect these differences unless family members preferred a more consistent expression of names. Including qualifications such as "the person described in BIA documents as" also draws attention to the ways in which identities come from widely varied sources and carry different meanings in different contexts.

A "present absence" also circles around this cross-generational history.[57] Some of the people I have met through this project allowed me to see photographs of their relatives, including those forcibly taken to Canton. Amid scrapbooks and framed portraits on living-room walls, family pictures from the early twentieth century, often in black and white, lock eyes with the outside viewer. Others capture day-to-day moments: lifespans unfolding in living rooms, backyards, and pow-wows, some during birthdays and anniversaries, with smiles flashing or eyes glancing away. Most of these images, and some of the stories, intentionally are not included in the pages that follow. Similarly, actual names of some institutionalized people do not appear in the main text of this work. This is in deference to families' wishes and in recognition that not all knowledge is meant to be available to all people.

Engaging with kinship and historical storytelling ultimately presents opportunities for collective *survivance*—a process and practice, according to Anishinaabe literary critic-author Gerald Vizenor, rooted in resistance, transformation, and survival.[58] As Vizenor explains: "Survivance is an active sense of presence, the continuance of native stories, not a mere reaction, or a survivable name. Native survivance stories are active repudiations of dominance, tragedy and victimry."[59] Survivance invokes mixing—of lived histories and messy human understandings. Central to these stories are kin relations.[60] Mutual support, generosity and sharing, and a belief and practice of interdependence—defining qualities of many Indigenous nations—stem directly from kinship.[61] Affinity, relationship, and collective experience drive its meaning. Affirming interdependence and belonging, kin relations nourish survivance.[62]

———

Two years after the death of her mother, Cora Winona Faribault was transferred to the Good Shepherd Orphanage in Fort Defiance, Arizona. The four-year-old would come of age among many Native children (mostly from Diné Nation) and under the firm supervision of Christian missionaries.[63] Like many of her female peers, Cora Winona Faribault spent much of her youth in American Indian boarding schools and working in domestic trades, labor directly connected to educational policies and expectations. Faribault's time in school ended early when her pregnancy was discovered by administrators. The teenager spent the following year, 1945–46, as a "resident" in the Phoenix Florence Crittenton Home. Part of a national network established by Christian missionary-reformers, the Crittenton Homes provided shelter, vocational training, and maternity and child care primarily for unwed mothers and other so-called fallen women.[64]

According to relatives, Cora Winona initially attempted to keep her firstborn child, but after months of struggle trying to secure work, childcare, and housing, she returned to the Phoenix Home. An employee apparently counseled her to complete paperwork relinquishing her parental rights. For several years afterward, her son lived in foster care until, at age five, he was adopted by a white family in Scottsdale.[65] As with thousands of other Indigenous and non-Indigenous children separated from their birth families between World War II and the late 1960s, Cora Winona Faribault's eldest child had no contact with his birth mother or her other children.[66]

Institutionalization

As Elizabeth and Cora Winona Faribault lived it, locked wards of a psychiatric asylum, mission classrooms, reservations and allotments, and Crittenton's dormitories all shared the underlying feature of involuntary containment and were experienced as parts of broader institutional interventions to dismantle Native families.[67] Such institutions provided the built environment buttressed by policies and practices to eliminate and replace fundamental aspects of Indigenous life, including child rearing, education, and caregiving.[68] They also contributed to larger efforts to contain, unravel, and remake or erase communities and individuals through land, military, legal, and religious policies. In this way, institutionalization not only has an impact on those removed but also ripples through families, communities, and nations as well as across generations.[69]

Institutionalization—"the state of being placed or kept in a residential institution"—is an axis along which much of *Committed* travels.[70] The Faribaults' experiences of institutionalization, while profound, were unexceptional. Elizabeth and Cora Winona inhabited locked wards that confined nearly four hundred people before Canton was closed in 1934. These lived realities reflect another meaning of institutionalization: "the action of establishing something as a convention or norm in an organization or culture." For decades before, during, and after the Indian Asylum's existence, many other settler institutions specifically targeted Native people. Institutionalization is unexceptional in the broader history of settler colonialism as well. Confining many groups of people for many reasons has long been an established practice in the United States.[71]

Institutionalization takes numerous forms; one of them is incarceration. Involuntary confinement and intentionally limited agency and access commonly distinguish the material realities of incarceration from other kinds of institutionalization.[72] Despite rhetoric and even intentions of settler humanitarian medical care and concern, forced psychiatric confinement, like what the Faribaults and countless others have experienced, have always been—by design—carceral.[73] In detailing lives of people consigned to the locked wards in South Dakota and elsewhere, *Committed* links medicalized incarceration to other forms of confinement over the past two centuries. This account also places the Indian Asylum within broader histories of institutionalization, deliberately identifying commonalities between peoples' histories with settler-supported medical facilities and other kinds of institutions, including boarding schools, orphanages, and reservations.

The experiences of Elizabeth and Cora Winona Faribault attest that histories of institutionalized people often are histories of people experiencing *transinstitutionalization*—the process of moving individuals from one variety of institution to another—as part of sustained containment, surveillance, and slow erasure. This is a type of settler colonial removal. The process, practice, and lived histories of dislocations and confinements are dynamic, interlocking, and far reaching. Understanding institutionalization and transinstitutionalization as processes, practices, and experiences links human stories that might otherwise seem unrelated. This reality generates questions about struggle, adaptation, kinship, and remembering. It points us toward sources not affiliated with particular institutions, such as Canton Asylum.

Institutionalization and transinstitutionalization also hold another meaning directly relevant to this story: the damage caused by being institutionalized, typically for extended periods of time.[74] As some of the people incarcerated at the Indian Asylum detailed in letters and affidavits, life on the inside of Canton—like nearly all state-run psychiatric institutions—was filled with the crushing monotony of locked wards, stale air, overflowing toilets, and wails in the night.[75] Other institutionalized people's testimonies from this era describe an environment of isolation and vulnerability. Beatings and sexual assaults, tuberculosis epidemics, numerous deaths, and occasional births comprised interlocking patterns inherent in institutional life at the Indian Asylum. In his work on "total institutions," including asylums, prisons and jails, boarding schools, military barracks, and monasteries and nunneries, sociologist Erving Goffman drew attention to the material spaces marked by surveillance. Key features distinguished the phenomena of institutionalization: enforced isolation or sequestering, the loss of freedoms, and other human indignities.[76] Many scholars have since built on this insight, showing how psychiatric institutions are particularly important locations for studying the lived realities of removal because of their establishment as privatized spaces within public domains.[77] Their work and that of others often—and rightly—draw attention to the abuses common, even inherent, in such institutions. Some researchers have additionally detailed how displacement to multiple institutions over individual lifespans have cumulative, multigenerational impact.[78] *Committed* explores the overlaps of all these definitions of institutionalization.

———

For Faith O'Neil (Sisseton-Wahpeton Oyate)—Elizabeth Faribault's granddaughter and Cora Winona's daughter—kinship, institutionalization, and remembering reverberate across generations, regularly returning to the Indian Asylum. On May 17, 2015, O'Neil joined an annual honoring ritual initiated in the 1980s by Lakota journalist-activist Harold Iron Shield. She and other descendants, friends, and observers arrived in Canton from all over the United States. They came by trains, cars, and planes. Many came in small or large groups; others arrived alone. Most, if not all, claimed one another as kin.

Dozens of people gather on a summer day in 1997 for a ceremony near the fenced Canton Asylum cemetery. Most sit in a large circle conversing. A large stone marker inside the fence acknowledges many ancestors buried there. Harold Iron Shield began organizing honoring ceremonies at the cemetery in the 1980s. Since then, there have been many formal and informal gatherings on the former asylum grounds. Photograph by Frank Robertson. Courtesy of the Argus Leader.

The land on which they stood bore witness to the changes and continuities since the Canton Asylum was shut down in early 1934. The train depot had since closed, and the fencing around the Asylum grounds was removed. A historic marker identifies the former facility, invoking its non-Native colloquial name: Hiawatha Asylum for Insane Indians. The recreation area overlapping much of the original campus shares the term too: the Hiawatha Golf Club.

Slowly, the group made its way along lightly paved walkways toward the wooden- fenced area. Acquaintances and kin nodded to one another and welcomed newcomers. A plaque facing inside identified the Asylum cemetery. The registry of people listed reflects U.S. government interpretations: English, Christianized names or approximate English translations of Indigenous names.[79] According to the cemetery ledger, 121 known individuals have been buried in this cemetery; Elizabeth Faribault is not among those listed. An archaeological study from 2015 indicated that more people are

Faith O'Neil and Pete Alcaraz stand solemnly behind the Canton Asylum cemetery marker, 2015. O'Neil came to pay respects to her grandmother, Elizabeth Alexis Faribault, who was institutionalized at Canton from 1915 until her death in 1928. Courtesy of Faith O'Neil.

interred there than identified. Faribault's granddaughter Faith wondered aloud whether Elizabeth was nearby, present but unaccounted. She was both missing and missed.

For decades, Faith O'Neil has asked hard questions and sought their answers: How did her grandmother Elizabeth die? Where is she buried? What happened to her own mother, Cora Winona, during her childhood at Canton and afterward? In recent years, O'Neil has scoured archives, historical publications, and the Sisseton Reservation, but her questions remain unresolved. Joining others to commemorate this incarcerated community opened a river of stories—of grief, yearning, honoring, connection, hope, remembering, and survival. For O'Neil and many others, visits to Canton embody a story within many stories, stretching back to earlier moments in order to make meaning of the present.

Remembering

Remembering their ancestors is a regular practice of kinship for Elizabeth Faribaults' descendants, as it is for many people whose family history intersects with Canton Asylum. As part of a living story, remembering shifts and transforms: incomplete, disorderly, continuing, surviving. For Faith O'Neil, as for most descendants, remembering nourishes relations, sometimes creating new ties, stories, and futures. Ancestors past and emerging remember one another.

Remembering—a process of recalling the past and of repopulating it—activates this project too.[80] Reciprocity is an integral part of remembering. In admittedly much smaller ways, sharing knowledge and resources from my research hopefully bridges some of the damaging holes wrought by medicalized forced removals and sustained confinement. Extensive citations are intended as invitations and access points, ways to continue research and learning about the histories and themes *Committed* explores. Providing copies of archival materials and drafts of this work to people whose kin were detained at Canton and other federal psychiatric institutions reflects a commitment to accountability as well as reciprocity. This is an active effort to honor those who appear in this book as well as the many others whose stories converge, if less obviously, in its pages. But it is not a neutral act. As Faith O'Neil and others have made clear, original sources and scholarly works that draw on them contain features that can wound as well as comfort.[81] I am deeply grateful to the generosity of those who have collaborated with, supported, corrected, and educated me. This interdependent process in no way mitigates an author's accountability; I am responsible for all errors and missteps in this book.

In the end, *Committed* is not intended to provide a neutral or balanced account of history. As American Indian studies scholar K. Tsianina Lomawaima (Mvskoke/Creek Nation) contends, in the historical study of Native North America, "point and counterpoint are not evenly matched. We hope for a historical account whose quality is not measured solely by the cubic volume of archival boxes or linear feet of library shelves devoted to its sources. Finding the overlooked, recovering what has been suppressed, and recognizing the unexpected requires excavation, rehabilitation, and imagination. All history does."[82]

This particular practice of remembering is in some ways intentionally disorderly, an effort to "disrupt the systematic functioning or neat arrangement of" historical work.[83] My interest is less in the presumed veracity or truths of storytellings about particular institutions, individuals, or groups of people than it is in the many stories embedded within each. Exploring which stories have received more attention, and why, threads the chapters that follow.[84] Admittedly, much remains unknown about the everyday lives referenced in *Committed*. There are messy, illegible, still-overlooked, and yearned-for stories that are absently present, inviting future remembering.

Chapter 1: **Many Stories, Many Paths**

> *Our situation in the United States, as well as throughout the Western Hemisphere, is unique, for we are First Nations people, indigenous; we aren't so much a political minority as we are displaced persons.*
> —Paula Gunn Allen (Laguna Pueblo, Sioux, and Lebanese), *Off the Reservation*

> *Over the time we have been here, we have built cultural ways on and about this land. We have our own respected versions of how we came to be. These origin stories— that we emerged or fell from the sky or were brought forth—connect us to this land and establish our realities, our belief systems.*
> —Henrietta Mann (Northern Cheyenne)

In 2013, Bois Forte Chippewa historian Kay Davis traveled to Canton, South Dakota, to join in an honoring ceremony. Her destination was the former grounds of the Canton Asylum for Insane Indians. Davis brought with her a handmade map. The names of every Native nation and each of their individual members stolen away to the Indian Asylum filled the white spaces along the western and northern edges, creating a framework, archive, and collective story. Below the printed text appeared the common outlines of individual states. Colored strands stretched between the lists of affiliated Indigenous people and their reservations' geographic locations, transmitting the stories of people taken away and those to whom they belonged.

Focusing on the institutionalized people as members of Indigenous nations, Davis's map bore witness to the rippling, damaging impact of the Canton Asylum. At the same time, the collective names, strings, and homelands offered a counterstory, inverting settler boundaries and conquest with Indigenous centers and borders. Ancestors threaded in short and long lines to their kin, a tapestry stitched by trauma, defiance, and imagination. For Davis and others attending the ceremony, historic and contemporary threads held them to one another.[1]

Finding family members and their histories has united many people at the honoring ceremony. For Kay Davis, excavation and imagination became a practice in her adolescence. She was sixteen when her mother

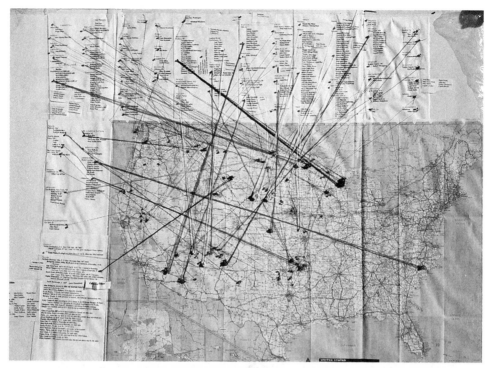

Bois Forte Chippewa Tribal Historian Kay Davis made this map sometime between 2010 and 2014 to emphasize kinship ties and Indigenous identities of the people stolen away to the federal institution in Canton, South Dakota. Names of Native nations and their members institutionalized at the Indian Asylum frame the left side and top. Pins and colored string connect the tribal information to geographic locations of reservations on a standard map of the continental United States. Photograph by Jill Betancourt. Courtesy of Kristi Foreman.

finally admitted what others had long asserted: that she was Native American, born in an Indian Hospital to a father who was an enrolled member of the Bois Forte Band of Chippewa and a mother who was non-Native. Seeking to better understand her own identity and those of her Indigenous community, Davis eventually took a job in the Bureau of Indian Affairs, specializing in genealogical work.[2] Searching for a more complete account of her Bois Forte Band's story ultimately drew her to the Canton Asylum. One of their members, Tom Floodwood, was forcibly taken to Canton on May 13, 1923. He died there four months later, on September 26.[3] Drawing on her genealogical expertise, Davis began writing short life stories for each known person confined at the Indian Asylum. In contrast to the U.S. government documents and most historical studies about the institution, Davis organized

*In this 2016 soft-focus portrait of Kay Davis, the eighty-year-old historian
looks thoughtfully at the camera, an art piece hanging on the wall behind her.
A commitment to family and Native self-determination propelled Davis's research
on people detained at Canton Asylum. Courtesy of Kristi Foreman.*

her biographical project by Native nations. "For me, it is the people who
went there and their Tribal affiliation," she explained.[4] Placing individuals
within their Indigenous communities and emphasizing their kin connections
to others, Kay Davis offered a different tale. The process, she pointed out,
intentionally countered some of the corrosive effect of settler conquest.[5] As
in her own experience, much of these ancestors' history has been lost to descendants, weakening the ties to American Indian community and identity.
Conducting genealogical research and sharing her findings has nourished
some of those roots. Davis's project embodies what Indigenous scholars,
artists, and activists call "re-storying": "retelling and imagining of stories that
restores and continues cultural memories."[6]

Reading Davis's threaded map evokes re-storying. Scanning from the outer edges and across the chart, people's histories of forced dislocations and a path to institutionalization emerge. Tracing from the various hubs outward, stories before and long after the Asylum's establishment rise up. The beginnings and ends of the strings emphasize peoples' relations to places, to homes, and to Indigenous worlds. Confinement and sustained exile pull at the threads, as do refusals by kin to fully let go. Uneven and incomplete, haunted and haunting questions swirl around what is remembered and imagined about the people incarcerated at Canton Asylum.

As the tribal historian's graphic representation illustrates, there are many centers to the lived stories of institutionalization at Canton. The constellation of pins, strands, Native names, and places contain beginnings of stories that continue to unfurl to this day. European colonial conquest in the Americas since the 1500s offers another center that includes Indigenous peoples' forced dislocations across the nineteenth century—brought about by war, hunger, profit, love, hope, epidemics, and genocide.[7] Christian missions, boarding schools, prisons, orphanages, and insane asylums punctuate this account. Broken treaties, wardship, and other attacks on Native self-determination pierce like barbed knots at every turn.

Sharing her map with others gathered at the site of the former Asylum, Davis invited them to grapple with the impact of the disparate stories and storytellers. The histories symbolically represented in the map and in white settler progress-centered accounts of Canton Asylum are uneven in detail and power, restlessly cohabiting a world of multiple centers, nations, and consequences. Questions posed between descendants, focused exchanges, and pondering silences underscored the ramifications of the stories: Which accounts are known in fragments or wide swaths, and which ones have been stolen, lost, or hidden? Where and from whom do the details come? Re-storying fills the hours spent between Davis and people whose kin are tied to Canton Asylum. Her map is an urgent call for more stories.

———

One white string in Kay Davis's creation arcs outward from the reservation in Sisseton, South Dakota.[8] According to descendants of Elizabeth Faribault, multiple removals simultaneously mark ruptures and starting points in their family history. As one relative explained, Elizabeth's parents were members of the Sisseton ("people of the marsh") and Wahpeton ("people of Lake Traverse") Band of Dakota Nation.[9] For generations, their home had been in what today is Minnesota. Born in 1882, Elizabeth was the firstborn child of Zihkanakoyake (also called Henry Alexis in U.S. documents) and Manzakoyakesuim (also known as Mary Alexis).[10] Like many Dakota people in the late nineteenth century, Zihkanakoyake and Manzakoyakesuim crossed Minnesota and South and North Dakota as part of an exodus forced by the U.S. government. Wars and treaties contributed to further splintering. Some of Elizabeth's extended Alexis family fled to Canada; those who returned had to relocate to reservations in South and North Dakota. Zihkanakoyake and Manzakoyakesuim were among those who were displaced to Spirit Lake. Later, Manzakyakesium moved with her children to Lake Traverse.[11]

Little is known about Elizabeth's early years. She clearly grew up among other Dakota people, absorbing daily lessons from elders and other kin. Her immediate relatives communicated exclusively in the Dakota language and appear to have held tightly to Sisseton-Wahpeton lifeways. Her family's aversion to Euro-American cultural assimilation was typical. The local U.S. Indian agent in the late 1870s, J. G. Hamilton, for example, had expressed alarm by how tenaciously women maintained Dakota culture and identity.[12] In this context, one can imagine some of the contours of daily life: helping and arguing with younger siblings; learning to cook, sew, garden; spending time with elders and with peers; listening to stories; yearning, struggling, belonging, and coming of age.[13] The children of Zihkanakoyake and Manzakoyakesuim almost certainly were known by Dakota names, which meant that Elizabeth had multiple names across her childhood and young adulthood. These ways of identifying Elizabeth and her siblings were never recorded or preserved by U.S. officials.[14]

At the turn of the twentieth century, seventeen-year-old Elizabeth was listed in U.S. rolls as the wife of Jesse Faribault, a member of a prominent Sisseton family. Like many relatives in his generation, Jesse spent most of his life on the Sisseton Reservation, often working as a farm laborer. Both Jesse and Elizabeth came of age at a time of considerable transformation among the Sisseton Band. Increasing land thefts by white settlers, unsuccessful military and political battles with the U.S. government, and the cumulative effect of disease, starvation, and displacement exacted heavy tolls on Dakota people.

The first reservation partitioned under the General Allotment Act of 1867, Lake Traverse (Sisseton)—where the Faribaults lived—was known for its resistance to U.S. assimilation.[15] Missionaries and educational reformers had campaigned since the 1870s to place American Indian children in schools away from their home communities as an intentional effort to eradicate Native cultures.[16] Defying the mounting pressure to submit to boarding schools, Sisseton relatives often kept children, especially girls, at home.[17]

Neither Jesse nor Elizabeth had attended boarding or day schools, although most of their younger siblings had. U.S. census rolls and anecdotal evidence suggest that the couple primarily spoke Dakota. Tied closely to their Sisseton community, the Faribaults would not have needed to learn much written or spoken English.[18]

In the first fifteen years of marriage, Elizabeth and Jesse had six children, two of whom died in infancy.[19] The couple lived in a three-bedroom home on the Sisseton Reservation. During the day, Elizabeth managed the house and mothered their young children. Meantime, Jesse worked their fields, described by one observer as "one of the nicest forty acres of wheat this part of the country and a nice garden, consisting of corn, potatoes, beans and other garden truck too many to mention."[20]

The Faribaults lived in a world where the battles between Sisseton members and the U.S. government could swiftly shift from national to personal, distant to everyday, quiet to loud. In the 1880s, the U.S. government began criminalizing features of American Indian cultures.[21] By 1913, the United States, through its Indian agent at Sisseton, abolished the tribal government.[22] The BIA superintendent there, Eugene D. Mossman, sought to limit dancing, communalism, and other distinctive qualities of Dakota life.[23] Tensions had long simmered between BIA agents and Sisseton members. Contests over authority, citizenship, and land sometimes erupted into open conflict. For example, in 1914, representatives of the Sisseton-Wahpeton Bands went to Washington, D.C., to challenge U.S. theft of their land and treaty violations.[24]

Archival documents detail that Elizabeth Faribault also directly challenged BIA representatives, engaging in yelling matches and disrupting their work on the reservation. The clerk in charge asserted that Faribault's pattern of behavior indicated mental disorder; the only solution, he insisted, was to remove her to a government medical facility. Describing the larger battles over sovereignty between American Indians and white settlers in the twentieth century as "a quieter kind" than the bloody wars decades earlier, Ojibwe anthropologist and novelist David Treuer identified new weapons in the U.S. arsenal: "Instead of guns the combatants carried petitions; instead of scalps, people held aloft legal briefs."[25] One should add pathological diagnoses and treatments to this inventory.

When reservation and school doctors, Asylum superintendents, and rank-and-file BIA agents claimed that Elizabeth Faribault and others were insane and needed to be institutionalized, their knowledge, actions, and interactions drew upon Western medicine's imperial framework.[26] As Indigenous studies scholar Sean Kicummah Teuton (Cherokee Nation) has explained, "Since early settler colonial history . . . European thinkers were swiftly led to target non-Europeans and especially communally defined tribal peoples as innately intellectually inferior. Rather abruptly race became inextricably tied to mental deficiency."[27] In this context, diagnosis and pathology authorized the underlying settler ableist beliefs in hierarchies of peoples and societies based on productivity, ambition, capacity, and competency.[28] Across Europe, North America, and other continents, colonizers applied ableist ideas of Native people as deficient as they built governments and military outposts, pursued missionary work and schools, and refined medical techniques and erected hospitals.[29] This transatlantic system of political-medical power surrounded and trapped Elizabeth Faribault as it did many others.

The Sisseton woman and her kin understood that the reach of Western medicine stretched beyond singular diagnoses. The Faribault family's campaigns for her return drew on politicians, local white neighbors, missionaries, and others whose cultural standing might counter Canton's administrator and the broader federal asylum system that employed him. In one appeal to the commissioner of Indian Affairs in 1922, Elizabeth asserted that she wanted to be reunited with her family, but Dr. Harry Hummer, the Asylum's superintendent, blocked the way.[30] The letter, like her advocates' other efforts, implicitly underscored the reality of settler approaches to medicine inside Canton and similar institutions: the power of superintendents was left virtually unchecked. Hummer's responses—like those of all asylum superintendents—illustrated this power. The growing number of petitions, in the doctor's estimation, served as evidence of inherent defects in Faribault as well as in her advocates. He insisted that she should not be discharged. His opinion prevailed in each of the numerous petitions for Elizabeth's release. This was typical of psychiatric institutions across the United States; in virtually every instance when superintendents suggested a person remain or be allowed to leave, their recommendation held sway.[31] This was always true for Elizabeth Faribault and H. R. Hummer.[32] And it was true across the history of Canton Asylum: the BIA commissioners overwhelmingly followed the Asylum superintendents' lead.

———

For the Faribault family, as with many others whose members were institutionalized at Canton, settler applications of Western medicine were an incursion into their lives. Broad categories such as "mental illness" or "insanity," as well as an ever-expanding array of specific pathologies and diagnoses, had no full cultural equivalent in any of the American Indian communities directly touched by the Canton Asylum. "Native peoples generally do not have a notion of 'insane' or 'mentally ill' in our cultures," writer Pemina Yellow Bird has explained. "Indeed, I have been unable to locate a Native nation whose Indigenous language has a word for that condition."[33] Recognizing and adapting to this dissonance, kin sometimes challenged or dismissed such diagnoses, as when Jesse Faribault insisted that his wife was "only drunk" at the time she argued with the BIA agent.

Explicitly and implicitly, Faribault's family drew on an understanding of well-being rather than a settler notion of normalcy. Although tribal systems of medicine and spirituality vary widely, common qualities of well-being are shared by many Native nations, including Dakota people: harmony between body, mind, and spirit as well as between people and the broader natural and supernatural worlds. Describing the connections among these factors for American Indian peoples, scholar and poet Paula Gunn Allen includes "active respect for these Natural Powers" and mythologies based "on a ritual comprehension of universal orderliness and balance; and on the belief that a person's every action, thought, relationship, and feeling contributes to the greater good of the Universe or its suffering. Human beings are required to live in such a way that balance is maintained and furthered, and disorder (also perceived as disease) is kept within bounds."[34]

For the Alexis and Faribault families, as with other people institutionalized at the Indian Asylum and their kin, displacement to Canton, South Dakota, was a violation of home and homeland—and therefore well-being. In this context, the story of Western medical interventions includes pathological diagnoses but concentrates primarily on their associated treatment: institutionalization. Across the archive, letters from relatives consistently opposed medicalized forced removals, citing their negative impact on whole families and communities inside and outside the Asylum. Institutionalization eviscerated Native ways of being, separating individuals from their families and communities and restricting access to the physical and spiritual worlds that nourished them. "I am having a hard time last three years with children and also she want to come back now," a distraught Jesse Faribault explained to Commissioner Sells in 1918. "She like to see her children and also the children want to have they mother come back."[35] Also writing to the BIA, Elizabeth's mother, Mary Alexis, explained, "I have a daughter name Elizabeth Fairbault who was sent to Canton Insane Institution, Canton, S.D." She added, "I am a woman of 66 years and I need her at home to help me out, so if you please help me get her back as soon as possible."[36] Her daughter agreed. In one of her own written petitions to BIA commissioners, Elizabeth lamented, "I've often wished I was home and taking care of my mother and also my children."[37]

Many other families of Canton detainees expressed similar frustration and despair over their forced separation. Wellness required ending pathologized dislocation and returning members to their rightful place—physically among their people and physically and metaphysically to an Indigenous world. When Jesse Faribault, Mary Alexis, and Elizabeth Faribault made direct connections between their loved one's well-being and their own, they insisted on an understanding of medicine anchored to Native self-determination and kinship. Their advocacy efforts, like those of many families directly disrupted by incarceration at Canton Asylum, were not merely for the individual institutionalized but on behalf of the family, broader kin community, and tribes as well.

In these accounts, spouses, parents, siblings, and adult children of institutionalized people insisted that *they* knew their kin best and that their relatives should be sent home.[38] For years, Jesse repeatedly insisted that Elizabeth could manage and be supported well by her kin, noting that a reunion with her children "would help her" and underscoring the urgent action needed: his wife's immediate return to them.[39] In a similar 1926 petition on Elizabeth's behalf, her mother described a second visit with her daughter, asserting that Elizabeth had "acted and talked all right" and should be brought back to the family.[40] Other relatives of incarcerated people also assured U.S. officials that they could and should take care of their kin.

———

On Kay Davis's map, a black thread and pin anchor to the reservation in Oklahoma where Caddo people had been removed to in the nineteenth century. One Caddo Nation member from Anadarko, Amelia Moss, was born in 1917, the second child of Ruby Moss (Yun-nin). As a toddler, Amelia, along with her mother and brother, lived with her maternal grandmother, Nin-Hoon, and grandfather, Tom Reynolds.[41] According to the agency physician on the reservation, by 1922, the child commonly experienced seizures. He added, "She does not talk, is destructive, bites and fights."[42] In one report to the Department of Interior, Dr. W. C. Barton also suggested that five-year-old Amelia had attempted to run away, requiring others to supervise her. Such reports included no family observations or explanations of how they interpreted their young kin. The doctor concluded that Amelia needed to be placed in an institution where "proper care can be given her if there is such a place available."[43] In his own exchange with other BIA officials, reservation superintendent J. A. Buntin described the little girl as "an imbecile, subject to epileptic spasms," while also conceding that she "cannot be classed as insane."[44] He sought guidance from Washington officials, wondering aloud whether a federal psychiatric institution should be considered appropriate under the circumstances. Canton's administrator smoothed the waters. "This institution is for the care of insane Indians," Superintendent Hummer wrote Buntin. "Our broadest definition of insanity is that it is a mal-adjustment. Certainly, an imbecile is mal-adjusted, ergo, insane." Dismissing concerns about the sweeping pathological interpretation, Hummer quickly turned to the opportunity his definition afforded. "Without quibbling over words or terms, I have a vacancy here for a female patient and shall be glad to relieve you of the burden of caring for this child, if you wish it."[45] Buntin quickly accepted the offer. On May 31, 1922, the Indian Asylum matron removed the Caddo girl to Canton.[46]

Over the next decade, reservation and Asylum representatives continued to debate where Amelia Moss should be institutionalized.[47] BIA officials, and possibly family members, proposed that she be relocated closer to her home at the state-operated Oklahoma Institute for the Feeble Minded in Enid. Diagnostic claims and related institutional expectations circled in an eddy of bureaucratic inertia; reports and correspondence filled folders over the next several decades. Both quiet and conspicuous was the underlying assumption by federal representatives that Moss would not leave the locked wards. According to hospital records, she remained incarcerated in a psychiatric facility for the remainder of her days.[48]

Shadows cover most of Amelia Moss's life within institutional walls. Among the few government sources referencing her, none describe how she looked, what she may have liked, or meaningful events or relationships she may have experienced. Canton staff described her as "a mute." Other institutional reports note that she "mumbles to herself," probably in Caddo. Still other behaviors drew ire from Asylum employees. According to one, Amelia "made a habit of eating various foreign bodies, wood, paper, etc."[49] Almost certainly, this required physical interventions that staff resented. Amelia resented it too. She was known for biting and kicking, sometimes effectively holding staff members at bay. Her fierce resistance often thwarted medical examinations throughout the years she was detained.

Knowledge of Amelia Moss's experiences generally remain beyond the historian's reach as well. As younger generations in the Caddo member's family recognize, she and others locked inside Canton still had lives and stories.

The walls, policies, and beliefs that made incarceration possible winnow down the moments and stories that were preserved. Relatives of Amelia Moss now know of her primarily through fragmented, uneven, and contradictory archival and oral accounts. Searches for more information have mostly yielded echoing questions.[50] Institutional barriers have collectively limited who is able to remember these people, to re-story their histories.

––––––––––

As a response to institutional barriers, Davis's map is an act of refusal.[51] Conspicuously unmarked on her paper-and-thread rendering is Canton Asylum itself. For the Bois Forte Chippewa researcher, prominent historical accounts of the Indian Asylum have for too long eclipsed Native people's lived experiences. That settler story follows a familiar plot, a linear tale of exceptionalism, pioneers, and progress. It begins like this: In 1897, Peter Couchman, an Indian agent at South Dakota's Cheyenne River Reservation, proposed the creation of an Indian asylum to a receptive member of the state's congressional delegation, Senator Richard R. Pettigrew. In his petition to Congress, Pettigrew, chairman of the Senate Committee on Indian Affairs, insisted that the federal government must "rescue . . . the demented Indian" from uncaring and incapable Indigenous kin and tribes. "While these conditions exist," the senator continued, "there is little hope that insanity can be cured or its victims made comfortable."[52] Pettigrew reminded his colleagues that a unique federal jurisdiction applied to Native Americans as "wards" of the U.S. government, and thus medically managed and federally supervised care was the only option.

The proposal for the U.S. Government Asylum for Insane Indians in Canton, South Dakota, initially faced opposition from multiple quarters. The superintendent of St. Elizabeths Hospital—the original federal psychiatric institution—derided the Republican senator's proposal, describing it as a "pet project" intended solely to bring revenue to Pettigrew's home state while unnecessarily increasing the federal government's costs to oversee Native people.[53] Others, however, saw opportunity in Pettigrew's idea, which would expand the reach of the Indian Service and the field of psychiatry. Former congressman and mayor of Canton Oscar Gifford supported the cause, as did the local residents of Canton. Ultimately, the Indian Asylum advocates prevailed.[54] In what was obvious at the time and since, the appointment of Gifford as the first superintendent reflected the Asylum's political and economic underpinnings.[55] Gifford selected the location of Canton (where he had practiced law) and oversaw the construction of the Asylum.[56] In December

1902, the proponents' dream was realized in brick and mortar as Canton Asylum for Insane Indians began to fill its wards. The townspeople of Canton celebrated the news. As one local newspaper explained, "The asylum will make our city famous as the location of the only institution of its character in the whole world."[57]

This story of opportunity drew many staff members and their families to the South Dakota town. Primarily a tale of settler immigration fueled by economic pressure and aspiration, more than two million Scandinavians came to the United States across the nineteenth and early twentieth centuries.[58] Many understood themselves to be pioneers who would "tame" the American frontier. As author Kay Melchisedech Olson explains, "It was an emigration of rural folk with a strong family composition" closely bonded through "traditions, mores, and religious as well as secular values" rooted in their lives in Scandinavia.[59] Historian Odd Lovoll adds that "footloose and land-hungry Norwegian peasants . . . wished to re-establish the conservative way of life they were accustomed to in rural Norway, but with a greatly improved social and economic status."[60] In 1868 alone, twenty-three families arrived in Lincoln County, Dakota Territory, via a wagon train.[61] By the 1880s, those who settled the area began referring to Canton as "the gate city of Dakota."[62] Within decades, nearly 80 percent of first- and second-generation Norwegian Americans, roughly one million people, claimed the upper Midwest region as their home.[63] In Canton and elsewhere, strong connections to Norway sustained the sense of a cohesive community. The Lutheran Church, Norwegian newspapers and festivals, as well as Norwegian cultural organizations proliferated during the late nineteenth century and into the early twentieth century. Educational institutions also reflected the proud ethnic identity of Canton. For example, in 1884, the town celebrated the opening of Augustana Academy, a Norwegian-Lutheran-heritage school.[64] For some Scandinavian Americans, the Canton Asylum provided economic opportunity near the place they claimed as their new home.

The local townspeople nicknamed the institution at the core of their economy the "Hiawatha Asylum," which they had inscribed in iron above the seven-foot-high gateway and fence. The name alludes to Hiawatha, the Mohawk statesman who is credited with facilitating the creation of the Iroquois Confederacy. In white American literary and historical representations, Hiawatha embodied a tamed (and doomed) hero. Fusing multiple Indigenous stories, Henry Wadsworth Longfellow's 1855 epic poem, *The Song of Hiawatha*, for example, imagines an eponymous hero skilled in medicine and art, hunting and farming, and writing and peacemaking.[65] To many white settlers,

Hiawatha also symbolized American Indians as a "vanishing race."[66] By the early twentieth century, this message was reinforced across virtually every popular cultural form—films, magazines, music, literature, and art.[67] In this particular folktale of Canton, the violent sovereignty battles between white settlers and Indigenous nations disappear, vanishing with the figure of Hiawatha himself as pioneers replaced Native people and began a new history.[68]

Contrasting sharply with a brightly lit future of the Canton Asylum, Superintendent Gifford detailed the plight of American Indians shortly after the institution opened. In a 1904 article entitled "Gain in Indian Insanity," he offered a tale of progress evidenced by the expanding facility and an expanding field of psychiatry. It was "difficult to find Indians who are insane. At first we could not find more than a half dozen in the entire United States," Gifford explained. "But we are beginning to hear from them now from the remotest districts."[69] Reflecting on the Asylum's first year and its promising years to come, he assured the reporter that there was "no doubt that all the 50 rooms will be taken up within another year."[70] As he viewed it, Native Americans' "brooding over troubles and disappointment" expressed itself in various ways, but that "most of these manifestations would have been improbable or impossible in the former wild life of the Indians."[71] Echoing the sentiments of early nineteenth-century race scientist Charles Caldwell, Gifford and his assistant superintendent, Dr. John F. Turner, claimed that it was "natural" for Native people to "brood" since they "cannot have" opportunities for Indigenous lifeways, including hunting, free movement, and practicing customs like dances. According to these experts, Indigenous "victims of misfortunes" suffered primarily from "domestic difficulties" that "have caused the insanity, specifically 'worrying over family affairs.'"[72] In this common account, Native people were biologically tied to an inevitable path of erasure. Their mental incompetence would increase along the way, and white people would take care of their wards as a reflection of their benevolent superiority. Optimistically, Gifford noted, "additions will be necessary," and "it is believed that the ratio of insanity will undoubtedly continue to grow."[73] The growing institutionalized population, from Gifford's vantage point, was a positive indication, reflecting the great humanitarianism of white people taking care of the "Indian problem" and the "problem Indians." This ideology continued into the next administration of the Indian Asylum. Across his tenure, Superintendent Hummer made clear that he sought to enlarge the facility so that it could achieve its "entire function" by "caring for *all* of the insane Indians in the United States." His correspondence with many reservation superintendents served as public awareness and recruitment initiatives, providing evidence that other BIA administrators wanted and needed the Asylum to hold more people.[74]

During the Asylum's formal existence, the account that staff, superintendents, BIA officials, and newspapers across the United States primarily told was one of progress.[75] Pictures showcased the three-storied Main Building, its brick walls rising around the stone foundation and dormers.[76] Other changes to the campus materially conveyed orderliness and advancement: a laundry was added in 1909 and enlarged in 1918; the superintendent's house was built in 1915; and a dairy barn followed in the next year. In 1917, the two-story Hospital Building was erected, its brick-and-concrete facade intended to "harmonize in appearance" with the other structures on the campus.[77] Amplifying the humanitarian-medical story, observers claimed that the addition was needed because of the "advanced age" of Canton's institutionalized population "and the inevitable encroachment of physical ailments among them." Advocates added, "The sick will be provided with the best that science means and experience can contribute."[78] Initially envisaged to hold fifty people, the Asylum from 1917 onward typically reported twice as many inhabitants—nearly one hundred institutionalized individuals. By the time the Indian Asylum closed in January 1934, nearly four hundred people from dozens of Native nations had been confined in its locked wards.

This version of history casts its white characters as exceptional, including original advocate Senator Pettigrew and Superintendents Gifford and Hummer. Local townspeople—the supporting cast—oversaw the Asylum's day-to-day operations, often enduring cruel treatment at the hands of the temperamental Hummer. In this narrative, Canton Asylum appears as noble but mismanaged. Across the twentieth and twenty-first centuries, historical encyclopedias, exhibits, and most popular and scholarly publications have echoed this interpretation.[79]

———

Near the very center of Davis's map, red pins and string mark what today is known as the Prairie Band Potawatomi Nation Reservation. This is one beginning place of Seh-Tuk and his family. The fourth child of Wam-Te-Go-She-Quah and Me-Shan (also known as Mitchell), Seh-Tuk was born sometime between 1892 and 1895 on the Kansas reservation designated for Prairie Band Potawatomi people.[80] He appears in U.S. government documents with many other names: Willie Mitchell, John S. Mitchell, and William John S. Mitchell. It is unknown whether Seh-Tuk attended school like some of his siblings or what his earliest years were like. Anecdotal evidence suggests that the teenager may have encountered strong medicine, perhaps peyote, and that it profoundly affected him.[81] In October 1921, physicians C. W. Reynolds and R. Robson examined the tall, slender man. No details remain about the exchange between them, only the doctors' conclusion that the young Potawatomi member was "of unsound mind."[82] They recommended that he be removed to Canton Asylum.

Virtually all that is known about Seh-Tuk during the rest of his life comes from Asylum staff members. Apparently, he was among the many incarcerated people who provided unpaid labor for Canton, cleaning the floors and the stairway to the yard with a polishing machine.[83] Employees and administrators encouraged this kind of work, but Seh-Tuk's efforts afforded him only minimal benefits. Hospital workers wrote in his medical files that he still required supervision "because he wants to go home and tries to run away."[84] Details of his efforts to escape the Asylum remain elusive.

During Seh-Tuk's twelve years of detention at Canton, his family sought different ways to bridge the distance. After months without news of his son, Me-Shan petitioned the BIA in March 1930, seeking to compel Canton Asylum officials to provide detailed monthly updates.[85] Each year, Me-Shan also traveled three hundred miles from Kansas to Canton to visit Seh-Tuk, using his own meager funds to support the trips.[86] Likely, the father and son were able to connect in person during the summer of 1933, just months before the Asylum closed and Seh-Tuk was relocated to another federal psychiatric facility, St. Elizabeths Hospital in Washington, D.C. It appears that the yearly reunions for Me-Shan and Seh-Tuk ended with this transfer east.

Over the next seventeen years, Seh-Tuk would be repeatedly shuttled between various federal institutions. In 1942, he was among a group of twenty American Indian men formerly detained at Canton who were transferred out of St. Elizabeths.[87] An executive decree directed them to be held during World War II in a federal prison-hospital in Fort Worth, Texas, colloquially known as the Narcotic Farm. For unknown reasons, he and the other Native men were moved in 1944 to the other Narcotic Farm in Lexington, Kentucky. Six years later, in 1950, Seh-Tuk was transferred back to St. Elizabeths. According to hospital records, the Potawatomi man was discharged from the Washington facility in 1961.[88] It appears that he died not long after, in 1962. Seh-Tuk was buried among his people in the Mitchell family cemetery in Mayetta, Kansas.

In the account framed by Canton Asylum staff at the time and reiterated by most historians since, Seh-Tuk's story essentially ends in 1933, exiting with the haze of a train barreling eastward to Washington, D.C. But individually and collectively, the institutionalization of Seh-Tuk and others embodies a more complicated story of displacement.

Like Asylum archival materials about Seh-Tuk, most historical accounts of people involuntarily removed commonly end at or shortly after their subjects cross the threshold from "original place" to "removed space."[89] This includes Native people, institutionalized people, and people who have lived at the overlaps of both communities. There are practical reasons for this approach. For example, the phenomena of institutionalization reinforces the impression of finite dislocations and experiences. Through settler's Western biomedical framework, pathological problems and treatments were located within individual people. As just one illustration, according to the government doctors who examined Seh-Tuk, he had an unsound mind and required sustained institutionalization. Communication differences and limited access to sources by and about institutionalized people present significant barriers to outsiders. Defining removal as essentially fixed (beginning with intervention and ending with transfer to new location), however, obscures some of the messy, human realities. Many Native Americans have been involuntarily removed—from ancestral lands and other places.[90] Numerous institutionalized people across the range of Native and non-Native identities also have been involuntarily dislocated—to prisons, psychiatric facilities, boarding schools, reformatories, and the like.[91] Seh-Tuk's lived experiences of forced dislocations echo and rebound, inhabiting shifting places in a multitude of displacement stories.

The experiences of Seh-Tuk, Elizabeth Faribault, Amelia Moss, and other institutionalized people attest that histories of removals are more complicated than typically assumed. They do not have an easily defined beginning and ending. Across the brick-and-mortar life of Canton Asylum, many, if not all, of the people detained in the locked wards had immediate prior experiences of institutional dislocations. Their stories hold different centers, unfold in different directions, are cut short or bent back, double over, shape shift, fan outward, and cascade into the present day.

For Gary Mitchell, the late Prairie Band Potawatomi tribal historian, recollections of his grand-uncle Seh-Tuk carried power. His family's stories have traveled across multiple removals, interlocking experiences of loss, healing, reckoning, and continuance. In Mitchell's storytelling, Seh-Tuk's life and the Prairie Band Potawatomi's history remained intimately bound to wide-ranging locations of displacement from homelands, reservations, and boarding schools to prisons, other asylums, and elsewhere.[92] They intersected with particular ways to honor the dead, desires for privacy, and practices of well-being. Reflecting on his family's and his tribe's past, Gary Mitchell returned to the importance of re-storying. "It's best to tell it: tell all the things that happened," he explained, so that damaging histories will not be repeated. "That's why it needs to be told."[93]

––––––

Hundreds of miles away, Kay Davis lingered at the grave site of fellow Bois Forte Chippewa Tribe member Tom Floodwood, hoping to close the distance that years, politics, and geography had placed between them. During the honoring ceremony at the Canton Asylum cemetery that Davis attended, organizer Lavanah Judah (Yankton Sioux) recounted that a number of her kin had been returned to family members after their deaths, some were interred at Canton, and a few remained achingly missing.[94] Other relatives of people confined at Canton exchanged addresses and family histories, re-storying on the land their ancestors had forcibly inhabited decades earlier.

The labels holding space for these stories similarly vary: for people, places, and experiences. Each carries the seeds of its storyteller, refracted through time and spaces: Grandmother. Insane. Sister. Indian. Uncle. Dakota. Ward. Unknown. Political prisoner. Child. Potawatomi. Mother. Caddo. Many more names are known but sheltered, yearned for and inaccessible, imposed and contested.

A place that marked their lives also holds many stories. Like stratigraphy, the layers contain speckled elements of culture and power: Indian Asylum. Warehouse. Canton. Cemetery. Home. Not home. Yankton Dakota ancestral land.[95]

For Kay Davis, Lavanah Judah, and others directly and indirectly tied to those detained at the Indian Asylum, stories circle around one another. Across generations, contradicting and echoing, all the accounts carry meaning. Some point to the tribal lands marked by Davis's map pins and to stories of each known member dislocated to the Canton Asylum, others to more cloudy locations and people. Stories like these—fragmented, detailed, settler, and Native—hold numerous forms of power, including the potential to erase whole communities from regional and national narratives, to justify conquest and colonialism. To survive.[96]

Chapter 2: **Erase and Replace**

As was common on the Menominee Reservation in Wisconsin in the early twentieth century, three generations of the Bear family lived together. Elders Rose and Mose (Little) Bear spent much of their days with two grandchildren, seven-year-old Madeleine and two-year-old Luke. The youngsters' mother, Agnes, and her spouse, George Caldwell, had likely grown up together and been married since Agnes was sixteen and George was twenty. Agnes's siblings and their immediate families lived and worked nearby. Extended and intergenerational Menominee families interacted with one another daily, often sharing homes and other resources.[1]

In their diagnosis of Agnes Bear Caldwell in 1917, BIA officials read ordinary features of Menominee kinship through a Western biomedical lens. An adult mother, her children, and her spouse living with her parents—in the observers' estimation—indicated trouble. That Agnes had "always been dependent upon . . . her parents" especially concerned the white agents. They described the woman as "filthy in her habits and utterly incapable of being . . . independent of her mother."[2] Implicitly, they pathologized Caldwell's extended family. The elderly parents, according to this settler ableist framework, had failed to raise an independently capable daughter and were themselves decreasingly capable of managing her or her young children.[3] The agency physician considered Agnes's spouse, George, as similarly incompetent, describing him as "worthless and contributes very little if any thing to support of the family."[4] The configuration and day-to-day life of the Bear-Caldwell household, in other words, medically justified her institutionalization. In November 1917, she was taken, along with several other Menominee people, to Canton.

The medicalized form of family segregation and containment that Agnes Caldwell and her kin experienced fits into a pattern of other settler interventions. Intensifying during the latter half of the nineteenth century and the early twentieth century, settler advocacy of boarding schools, adoption, and fostering into white families emphasized logics of Native peoples' perceived inherent dependency and incapacities. According to Mark Rifkin, a gender and Indigenous studies scholar, settler policies propelled "processes through which a particular configuration of *home* and *family* is naturalized and administratively implemented."[5] This process discredited and sought to erase Indigenous kinship customs, including multiple generations living together, elders' central role in childrearing, and interdependent caregiving. As evidenced across a vast array of archived government correspondence, BIA officials and medical specialists regularly judged Indigenous extended-family relationships and home life as unhealthy and abnormal, using these presumed defects to buttress interventions into family life.[6]

The BIA's narrow focus on Agnes Caldwell and her immediate household members obscured the larger conflicts between U.S. government agents and Menominee Nation members over self-determination, family, and home. Referring to the Native people on the reservation as "my family of 1700 children of every age and temperament," field matron Mrs. H. P. Marble reported in 1916 that "home life was the crucible of Indian civilization and as such was a legitimate field for government investigation." Her own investigations of Menominee homes found them wanting. According to Marble, most mothers were "not willfully neglectful of their child's welfare, but through mistaken idea of kindness often permit[ted] the child to follow its own inclinations, as to food, habits, etc." This problem could be corrected when the mother was "impressed with the extent of her own responsibility." Without such changes, the field matron warned, there would be no "material progress toward intelligent citizenship."[7] As the twentieth century began, many other assimilationist advocates, including social reformers, missionaries, and bureaucrats, similarly judged Native women's progress according to white settler ideals of family and household.[8] Often, nonconformity to this model was read as a biomedical deficit, as when Keshena Agency physician W. R. Bebout diagnosed Agnes Bear Caldwell as defective because he believed she was incapable of being "taught to live right."[9]

The overarching process of institutionalization that this Menominee family and many others experienced pursued fundamental settler colonial goals: erasing Indigenous cultures and families and replacing them with white settler models. Within an ableist framework, defectiveness always has to be eliminated. Pathological judgments that the Bear-Caldwell family members were permanently defective justified administrators' choice to isolate them—and hundreds of others—from their Indigenous homes and communities. Simultaneously, this process affirmed that federal-medical oversight in the form of Canton Asylum was necessary.[10]

In Agnes Bear Caldwell's life story, the process of erasure often targeted home as well as family. Eugenic judgments of flawed families and households interlace across generations: her parent Rose was viewed as unfit because she maintained Menominee customs and instilled these ways of being in her daughter. Caldwell also was found deficient for failing to cultivate settler values and behaviors in her own children. BIA representatives and others invoked the prospect of new generations of nonconforming people across Indigenous nations to justify their removal and containment, pulling many of their members into the Canton Asylum. Among those ensnared were sisters from the Southern Ute Indian Tribe.

———

The women referred to as Jane and Susan Burch, the eldest daughters of Steve and Ruth Bent Burch, came of age as focused attacks on Southern Ute Indian Tribe families and self-determination intensified.[11] According to U.S. government documents from 1900, the parents had held out against some assimilationist efforts, residing in a wickee-up (teepee) and speaking only Shoshoni. Federal pressures mounted, and within a decade, the younger Burch children had been taken to boarding schools. In contrast, Susan and Jane remained on the reservation and near their parents. For them and for many other Southern Ute people, family was the center around which daily life moved. Often together, the sisters had helped tend to their younger siblings, shared the work of gathering and preparing meals, listened to elders' stories, and started their own families.[12]

In 1910, BIA representatives honed their attention on the elder Burch siblings. In letters to the commissioner, Agent Charles Werner emphasized that Jane had born a child out of wedlock and that the baby had died within the month. The child's father, the agent continued, was "a partly demented unallotted Ute from Navajo Springs, who wandered over here some time ago returned again to Navajo Springs, Agency."[13] Jane's status agitated the agent: she had "good" allotted land "valued at $1500" but was, in his estimation, irresponsible. As an unmarried mother, she challenged mainstream white cultural norms. Her child's death and her sexual relations with a man judged "partly demented and unallotted" were viewed as evidence of incompetence and as a threat to broader settler society.

Kinship ties undergirded Werner's concern. Jane's sister Susan was married to James Allen, whom the agent described as "a well meaning Ute." In the same letter to the commissioner, he explained that Susan, too, had valuable land (worth $2,000). She also recently had given birth. Werner characterized her son as "born disfigured; the upper lip is cleft and the nose is turned to one side." He added, "The mother is unable to care for this child."[14] Despite the assets conveyed by being married, and to a "well-meaning" husband, Susan, according to Werner, should be removed from the reservation. Specifically pairing Jane and Susan, the BIA representative asserted that they evidenced "insanity to some extent." Their offspring further cemented his judgment: "I did not realize the consequences of letting these two women remain at large until those children were born." He closed his letter with a plea: "Could not they be removed to the Canton Insane Asylum?"[15] Over the next two years, Agent Werner sought to institutionalize the sisters. In 1912, his request was granted. Jane and Susan Burch were forcibly dislocated to Canton that fall.[16] At the time she was stolen from her family, Susan was in the second trimester of another pregnancy.[17]

Five months after their incarceration began, on March 9, 1913, Susan Burch gave birth to a daughter. Superintendent Hummer offered a bleak assessment in his report to the BIA commissioner: "The baby is premature by a month or six weeks and its prospect of living are not particularly bright at this time."[18] A month later, the Southern Ute mother was noticeably ill, coughing, congested, and dealing with fever and headaches. Her infant, according to Asylum reports, was "doing as well as can be expected."[19]

Federal documents offer few other details about Burch's baby daughter during this time. Correspondence from Ute Agency superintendent Stephen Abbott to the commissioner in May 1913 suggest that there had been concerted efforts by the extended Burch family to unite the child with her father, James Allen. The superintendent rigorously fought this: "I regard it is absolutely impossible to provide for the child of Susan Burch here at Southern Ute," he began. The earlier assessment of Allen was now eclipsed by a new label—incapable. "It would be almost the same as murder to let the helpless father have the child," Abbott contended, offering an alternate option: "It seems that the only possible solution is to put the child in a charitable institution. The Office probably has had such cases before." His conclusion cast Canton and unnamed "charitable institutions" as more appropriate settings than Allen's home or those of other relatives. "While I realize the burden that the child is at the Insane Asylum, I believe almost any other place would be better for the child than this isolated and new country."[20] Ultimately, Superintendent Abbott lost his campaign. The infant was brought to Colorado that summer, where her grandparents and other family members raised her.[21] The daughter of Susan Burch and James Allen grew up surrounded by Jane's two surviving sons and other kin.[22]

As they welcomed the child home, the Burch family continued to seek a reunion with the two institutionalized sisters. Canton's superintendent and the BIA fervently resisted their efforts, insisting that their release would be inhumane.[23] The administrators prevailed, and both Burch women spent their remaining days in the locked wards. Susan died within a few months of her daughter's discharge. The BIA returned her body to Colorado for burial. Jane died four years later and was buried in an unmarked grave in the Asylum cemetery.[24]

As with the Burches, U.S. authorities consistently targeted families with their medicalized interventions of containment and elimination. Part of the government's rationale to place Susan and Jane at Canton was that they came from a family with presumed inherent mental defects.[25] This viewpoint, anchored to eugenics and Western medicine, emphasized biology as the determining factor in people's behavior and in their fundamental worth.[26] The hereditary relationship between the sisters drew settler authorities' attention. Medical interventions, including sustained containment of multiple generations of the Burch family, BIA agents and physicians believed, were necessary measures for the health and well-being of U.S. society.[27]

The collective removal of Susan and Jane Burch was unexceptional. BIA officials frequently ordered Native relatives to be institutionalized at the same time or sometimes within one or two years of a family member's initial incarceration. References to multiple sets of institutionalized parents, siblings, and spouses appear frequently in reports and medical files and in officials' correspondence. These recognized kinship connections appear to have contributed at least in part to many peoples' placement and retention at the institution.

Unlike a growing number of state facilities in the twentieth century, administrators at the federal Canton Asylum did not surgically sterilize their incarcerated wards.[28] Sharing the standard eugenic belief that unfit people should not procreate, however, Superintendents Gifford and Hummer spotlighted their responsible management of the facility and its close supervision by staff. As at all asylums, the employees managing the Indian Asylum tacitly surveilled and disciplined people on the inside to ensure and enforce a strict prohibition on sexual reproduction. Women of all ages, including Susan and Jane Burch, were segregated physically from the men.[29] Following a eugenic logic of biological elimination within this particular institutional setting, no new marriages were sanctioned.[30] Also by design, the Indian Asylum was intended to hold the Burch sisters, and many others, indefinitely. For the Southern Ute siblings and nearly half of the others in the locked wards, confinement at Canton typically lasted until death.[31]

The various rationales to detain—and continue detaining—Susan and Jane Burch reflect overlapping concerns about Native kinship and especially future generations of families.[32] Repeatedly, government representatives referred to Susan and Jane collectively, their status as sisters compounding the justifications for removing each of them. Emphasizing their shared experience of pregnancies and loss of infants, agents projected the eugenic idea that the Burch sisters both carried and transmitted hereditary flaws. In this judgment, Susan's and Jane's children became evidence of their mothers' inherent defectiveness and social threat. Jane's relationships outside of marriage, understood by Superintendent Werner as a moral failing, also tainted Susan, even as a married spouse. The prospect of growing generations in this family motivated Werner's medicalized intervention. As he explained to Superintendent Hummer in 1912, Susan was "about to become a mother for the third time," and he believed that "it [was] deplorable that such conditions should exist."[33] Pregnancy—previous, current, and future—was among the reasons why the Burch sisters had to be removed to the Indian Asylum.

The larger project of elimination hung over the birth of Susan's daughter on the inside of the institution. None of the staff at Canton or at the Colorado Agency expected the baby to survive. When she did, the Colorado agent advocated that she stay at the Indian Asylum or be transferred to an orphanage or similar institution, not sent to her family. That the child ultimately was discharged from Canton was unusual, but her family's fight to salvage their home, as well as the damage wrought by removals and deaths on the inside, were common. A presumption that institutionalized people and their relatives on the outside could not sustain settler forms of families permeates BIA and Indian Asylum records. This viewpoint encouraged agents and others to remove adults like the Burch sisters. Many younger people, including little children, also were ensnared in this practice. Amelia Moss was one of them.

In 1922, the Kiowa Agency superintendent in Oklahoma began petitioning for five-year-old Amelia Moss's institutionalization. Initial requests specifically presented Amelia's mother, Ruby Moss, as seeking appropriate care for her disabled daughter "in a government institution." No evidence remains from the parent, child, or other family members to corroborate this. According to the agency physician, the little Caddo girl had a pattern of biting and fighting with others; she also attempted to run away, which, he claimed, required others to regularly supervise her. Suggesting that Ruby Moss could not adequately parent her daughter, Dr. W. C. Barton recommended that Amelia be institutionalized so that "proper care can be given her."[34] Asylum superintendent Hummer responded favorably to the request, presenting Canton as a suitable solution. J. A. Buntin, the Kiowa Agency superintendent, quickly accepted his offer.[35]

The anticipated presence of Amelia Moss and other children, however, were conspicuously absent from Canton Asylum plans. Historically in the United States, architects and advocates of psychiatric institutions assumed that only adults would inhabit the locked wards.[36] Across the nineteenth and early twentieth centuries, settler society viewed most children as innocents, legally dependent, and temporarily incompetent, but having the potential to become fully engaged citizens. Rhetoric like "danger to self and to others" rarely attached to most young people in white settler imaginations. The Canton Asylum (and similar places designed to contain people believed to have disordered minds, violent tendencies, uncontrollable habits, or deviant desires) emphasized symmetry and order, control and protection.[37] The material contents carried the same cultural DNA. Dining halls were lined with linear tables and benches, while unadorned bathrooms and showers offered limited privacy or freedom of movement. Seclusion rooms with tiny—if any—windows were built within dormitories distinguished by rows of iron bedsteads. Conspicuously absent from Canton's architectural designs were birthing rooms, nurseries, children's playrooms, or classrooms—standard settler architectural features for babies and youth.[38]

In Amelia Moss's Caddo Nation community, and in many other Native and non-Native cultures, children were understood to be the living embodiment of the past, present, and future. Dee BigFoot, a Caddo psychologist, has described it this way: "Children were gifts. When a child was born . . . however a child came, that would be accepted. Family and extended family took care of them."[39] Then and now, children are the hope of their people. Uprooting and institutionalizing Amelia and dozens of other children sent a message that American Indians were irredeemable within a settler nation. In the early twentieth century, pathologizing young girls and boys, in particular, galvanized the white American belief that Native people were destined to vanish. The sustained detention enforced this settler worldview and materially pursued its realization.

––––––

Across the many years of Elizabeth Faribault's detention, Superintendent Hummer offered widely varied justifications for keeping the Sisseton woman at Canton. "Personally I feel that danger would attend her release that she is incapable of looking after herself, let alone looking after her mother," the doctor informed Assistant Commissioner E. B. Merritt. He later claimed that Faribault had recently sustained an infection in her right eye ("possibly trachoma"), which made her "very greatly depressed and emotional" about the possibility of "total blindness." Discharge from Canton, Hummer suggested, could harm her whole family by exposing them to a contagious disease as well as having to care indefinitely for a mentally unstable person.[40] On another occasion, he assured the BIA that Elizabeth had "practically no chance for ultimate recovery and this is about as good a home as she could possibly find." Longstanding battles with the extended Faribault family over her institutionalization also became a justification: "On many occasions," Hummer reminded the commissioner, Faribault and her relatives had written to them both, and every time the "results has always been to keep her here."[41] Inferring that these repeated efforts lacked credibility and perhaps even reflected inherent deviance within the family, Hummer concluded his critique of Faribault by recommending her continued detention. The federal office—following its usual practice—upheld the doctor's advice to keep Elizabeth Faribault at Canton.[42]

Facing mounting challenges from Elizabeth's husband, the Asylum superintendent pivoted, now offering a diagnostic assessment of Jesse Faribault. "The husband impressed me as being either very ignorant, or possibly imbecilic," Hummer opined to the BIA in 1918, raising doubts that Elizabeth would be "properly taken care of at home."[43] Extending eugenic reasoning, the Asylum administrator warned that the couple also might produce more children. "In all probability the offspring from such a union would be defective and the entire number become charges upon your Office," he told the commissioner. Hummer and the BIA concluded that *Elizabeth* must remain incarcerated because of *Jesse's* presumed defectiveness as a father and husband.

These officials often argued that people already institutionalized must remain confined because their kin on the outside were defective. Superintendent Hummer had offered nearly identical responses when Agnes Caldwell's family sought her release. Referring to one note written by George Caldwell in October 1919, the Canton administrator suggested to the BIA that Agnes's spouse likely "was not mentally alert," thus his wife should remain at the Asylum. Hummer pointedly added, "Another potent argument against her discharge is that she is well within the child-bearing age and any offspring *must* be defective."[44] Although the Menominee woman "wants to go home and care for her family," the doctor insisted that she was "mentally unable to . . . and the great danger of increasing the number of defective offspring should outweigh her wishes."[45] Institutionalization, Hummer argued, was best for all the individuals held at Canton, their families on the outside, the federal government, and settler society at large.[46]

When BIA agents and Canton administrators repeatedly asserted that Amelia Moss, Agnes Caldwell, Elizabeth Faribault, and Susan Burch's baby were "burdensome" to their kin and communities, they reaffirmed a familiar story of settler interventions in Native peoples' lives. Indigenous families were depicted as too overwhelmed, incapable, and often unwilling to correctly care for especially vulnerable members.[47] Following this settler worldview, the BIA justified committing Caldwell in order to "relieve" her family "of the burden of the care" they believed she required.[48] Cast as objective observations, phrases like "nuisance," "a considerable burden," or "menace" appear regularly in diagnostic processes for many individuals, including those of a four-year-old Menominee boy and a sixty-three-year-old Menominee man.[49] Officials believed that federally managed asylum settings would alleviate the burdens created by such individuals. BIA commissioners regularly complied with physicians' and reservation superintendents' recommendations in these instances.[50]

Western medical professionals and BIA employees also consistently claimed that Native individuals were "better off" at Canton Asylum, an opinion anchored to the belief that they themselves modeled benevolence, expertise, and cultural superiority.[51] "She is well taken care of here," Dr. Hummer wrote to Faribault's relatives, fending off discharge requests.[52] To Caldwell's family he regularly insisted, "She has a splendid home here in every respect."[53] Superintendent Gifford had offered nearly identical claims to petitioners and bureaucrats during his tenure at Canton as well.[54] Following this cultural logic, their settler institutions similarly represented a better option to Indigenous homes. Even as the Burch relatives on the outside sought their baby's return, the Ute Agency superintendent told the BIA commissioner that keeping the child in virtually any institution would be preferable to her living in her father's Colorado home.[55]

Inherent in administrators' position was the belief that the institutional family (staff) and the institutional home (the asylum) were better than Indigenous ones. In his diagnostic assessments of Faribault, Caldwell, the Burch sisters, and many others, Harry Hummer presented himself as head of the institutional nuclear family and household, resembling what historian Cathleen Cahill has described as "federal fathers" and a "surrogate family" to Native people.[56] In the context of the Canton Asylum, this paternal oversight emphasized active, sustained containment. Both Superintendents Gifford and Hummer discouraged relatives from visiting, and other forms of contact, such as letters and packages, were closely scrutinized by administrators. Canton and BIA representatives implicitly expected the institutional family and home to replace Indigenous ones. They regularly made fundamental decisions that would have otherwise involved Native kin, from prohibiting marriages to arranging the funeral services when people were buried in the Asylum cemetery.

At the same time, upkeep for Canton relied largely on coerced labor of its institutionalized population. Across the campus, Native people routinely cleaned, cooked, farmed, sewed, and tended to others—among many other tasks that sustained the Indian Asylum. The maintenance of the superintendent's quarters and caregiving to the extended Hummer family, in particular, expanded in the early 1920s. It appears that Agnes Caldwell worked for a time in the Hummer family's bungalow, although the details of her experiences there were never recorded.[57] As his own parents aged, Superintendent Hummer assigned Elizabeth Faribault to work in the cottage. Demands on her increased after Georgiana Murphy Hummer, the psychiatrist's sixty-six-year-old mother, died. Faribault likely was expected to provide care and support for the grieving family, including Hummer's widowed father and children, in addition to cleaning and laundry work.

In their various correspondence from this time, Agnes Caldwell and Elizabeth Faribault repeatedly pleaded to be discharged. For Faribault, "working for the doctar's folks" and the daily interactions with the Hummers inside their home contributed to her own suffering. As the Dakota woman explained to the BIA commissioner, she longed to be back at Sisseton, taking care of her aging parent and her children.[58] Caldwell echoed this sentiment in her own letters, lamenting, "I . . . need to go home."[59] The institutionalized women and their families drew attention to what gender and sexuality studies scholar Sau-ling C. Wong has called "diverted mothering," contexts in which "time and energy available for mothering are diverted from those who, by kinship or communal ties, are their more rightful recipients."[60] Tending to their *own* parents and children, not Hummer's, was a familial obligation Caldwell, Faribault, and many others expected to meet. They did not want others to replace them at home, and they did not want Hummer's home to replace theirs. "I don't see why he couldn't let me go home," Elizabeth Faribault complained in a letter to the BIA. She asked Commissioner Burke to intercede: "kindly help me out some way" with Hummer, and "look after this."[61] But continuing the practice of deferring to Asylum administrators, Burke declined her repeated requests. The greater isolation of the cottage

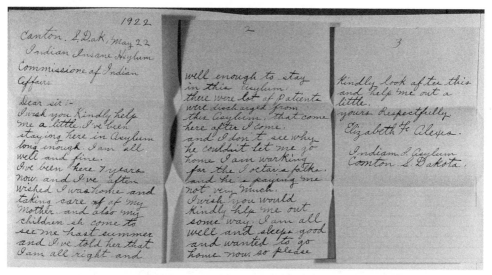

In this 1922 three-page handwritten letter, Elizabeth Fe Alexis (Faribault) sought
assistance from the BIA commissioner for her release. "I've often wished I was home
and taking care of my mother and also my children," she explained. Instead, she
was forced to take care of Superintendent Hummer's family, "and he is paying me
not very much." Coerced labor, including domestic work like Faribault provided,
was common at Canton Asylum and other institutions. Photograph by Susan
Burch and used with permission from Elizabeth Faribault's granddaughters and the
concurrence of the Sisseton-Wahpeton Oyate Tribal Historic Preservation Office.

and the particular demands on Faribault and Caldwell magnified the complicated circumstances they each faced in the 1920s.

As family correspondence described illness sweeping through her house
and community in early 1920, Caldwell's insistences for a discharge intensified. Noting that her mother and husband could no longer provide full
care for other family members, she pleaded with federal authorities to be
allowed to look after her siblings, parents, and children. "We all want to
see are children," she told the BIA commissioner, "We all want to see are
folks."[62] Death took her daughter first. The grieving mother wrote again to
the commissioner: "I was sad to hear the my little girl die . . . at the Hospital. . . . Yes if I was there . . . I would took good care of her I will. Never. See
her again." Caldwell believed her absence contributed to the loss. "I was all
good hands to my girl. I know my little want me to come home that why she
got sick and now she die and I will never see her. Again."[63] Within weeks,
her son also died, followed by her father later that year.[64] In the wake of this

pointed heartache, Caldwell focused her energies into renewed petitions for her release to tend to her elderly mother, but she remained in Canton.

Elizabeth Faribault, like many others inhabiting the close confines of the locked wards, would have been aware of Caldwell's poignant circumstances. Much of their worlds were intimately familiar. Assigned the same tasks, they both inhabited remote locations on the campus: the basement laundry and the superintendent's bungalow. The distinctive power of places weighed heavily on the women. Walls and miles separated them from their spouses, parents, and siblings. The ache of missing sons and daughters lodged into their memories, bones, and heartbeats. Their sustained absences from home and assigned work for Hummer's family pulsed loudly.

The kind of domestic service Agnes Caldwell and Elizabeth Faribault provided the Hummer family was readily found at similar institutions, and Canton's superintendent was accustomed to female servants cleaning, doing laundry, and providing other household support. During the early years of Hummer's tenure, the family had relied on Asylum staff—always female—to tend to their quarters. Archival records show that between 1912 and 1915, Clara Christopher, Ione Landis, and several other kitchen and dining staff members at various times had been expected daily to clean the superintendent's residence. Some of the women claimed that they were threatened with dismissal if they did not comply.[65] None received additional compensation for their labor. Hummer asserted that the work was appropriate and did not interfere with their other duties. Unpaid and underpaid domestic work was common. Women in settler contexts often were expected to attend to housework—their own and that of more affluent families. This support directly reinforced the broader familial structure upon which Canton Asylum was based, enabling the head of household— the superintendent—to focus his time and energy on management, employment, and civic engagement.[66]

Institution, family, and household sustained one another in other ways. Upon her arrival to Canton, Norena Hummer, the superintendent's wife, was made matron, a position she held for two years until pressure from the BIA over accusations of negligence forced her resignation.[67] By 1910, the couple increasingly sought greater physical distance from the locked wards and campaigned for a separate cottage on the Asylum grounds.[68] Congress approved the request several years later, and a Craftsman-style bungalow was constructed.[69] The Canton administrator subsequently brought his elderly parents, Levi and Georgiana Hummer, to live with his family in the new home. Levi, then in his seventies, was added to the Asylum payroll as a gardener. When sons Francis and Harry Junior were teenagers, they also earned incomes at Canton. The younger Hummer men continued to hold the position of laborer when they returned home from college during summers.[70]

The Hummer household became a flashpoint of conflicts during the superintendent's tempestuous administration. An array of accusations thread across Hummer's tenure: harassment, inappropriate touching, verbal abuse, and extramarital affairs. One of the employees, Ione Landis, provided a detailed account of sexual harassment and an assault that occurred in 1914. According to Landis, Hummer ordered her to work in his private quarters after he propositioned her during a drive.[71] She claimed that Norena Hummer intentionally humiliated and menaced her while she cleaned the bungalow. Within a year, Landis was dismissed from service by Dr. Hummer.[72] Commissioner Cato Sells gently chided Hummer afterward, writing: "It is suggested that you keep a more careful watch on your conduct and especially control your temper so that this Office may not be subjected to the necessity of investigating charges of that character. You must be aware of the fact that, while charges of immorality may not be proven, the fact that such charges are made should indicate to you the necessity for an extremely careful watch on your conduct in relation to the female employees of the institution." Seeking to eliminate problems for the superintendent, himself, and the BIA, Commissioner Sells counseled Hummer, "Your actions should be so carefully under the control of a well-balanced judgment that such charges, if made, would naturally fall of their own weight."[73]

Over the nearly twenty-five years of Hummer's tenure, BIA administrators repeatedly reprimanded him for his conduct as superintendent. Ultimately, the supervisory gestures themselves fell of their own weight: most of the systems and structures that undergirded Canton Asylum, including unpaid and underpaid domestic service for the Hummer household, remained unchanged. The BIA eventually insisted that government staff should not be required to provide private assistance. The Hummers then used incarcerated Native people—Agnes Caldwell and Elizabeth Faribault—to fill this role. The BIA tacitly endorsed this.[74]

At the same time Elizabeth and Agnes tended to the superintendent's home and family, correspondence from their relatives rippled with distress, frustration, questions between the lines. The attempted erasure of their own families wrought by institutionalization was shared by Caldwell and Faribault kin within and outside of the Indian Asylum. Nested in this process was the Hummer household and the expectations placed specifically on Agnes and Elizabeth to maintain it. But home, these women and others detained at Canton insisted, was with their own families, far beyond the institution's walls. They wanted to be with them there.

On a mild winter evening in January 1920, Elizabeth Faribault escaped from Canton. Having permission to walk the Asylum grounds, the Sisseton-Wahpeton woman probably had spent time beforehand exploring the perimeter of the campus, gazing at the open expanse beyond the gates. Upon leaving the grounds, she headed east as the stars rose in the night sky. Staff informed Superintendent Hummer the next morning, and a search began. His report to the commissioner fused a diagnostic process with a resolution to the new context. Assuring him that Faribault's condition had been "fairly comfortable" before she "left without permission," Hummer then offered a different treatment: if the Dakota woman reached her home, and if her family wanted to "keep her," he would recommend that Faribault be "discharged" from the institution that she had already left.[75] The commissioner supported this plan.[76] We can only wonder what Elizabeth thought about as she ran, walked, hid, slept, woke, and distanced herself from the Indian Insane Asylum during the next three days.[77] Her descendants understand Faribault's act as resistance, escaping from the Asylum and institutionalization and returning to her home and family.

After covering twenty miles, apparently all on foot, Faribault was apprehended. Superintendent Hummer personally drove to Alvord, Iowa, to retrieve her. It is unknown whether Jesse Faribault or her children ever knew that Elizabeth had escaped or stayed at large for days. In a subsequent report to the BIA, Hummer now invoked her failed escape as justification for keeping her institutionalized, concluding, "It is much better for Elizabeth that she remain here."[78] Faribault vigorously disagreed. In her own letters to the BIA then and for years after, she argued again that she should be with her family in Sisseton.[79] Ultimately, a return to her family was not to be.

Chapter 3: **Generations**

In a posed black-and-white photograph, probably taken in a studio in Holton, Kansas, during the early 1900s, the family of O-Zoush-Quah (Prairie Band Potawatomi) and Nash-Wa-Took (Prairie Band Potawatomi) stands solemnly in a semicircle.[1] Flanking the couple are their four daughters; their young son sits on a small stool in front. Intricately beaded and sewn patterns of flowers, leafy plants, and geometric shapes wrap around the males' pants, while sashes outline their waists and crisscross their chests. The daughters' draping skirts serve as a palette for beautiful ribboned patterns along the bottom. Long strands of beads drape around their necks. O-Zoush-Quah's sash emphasizes dark, intersecting diagonals interspersed with diamond-shaped designs. Wide shawls, also awash in a delicate display of sewn artistry, cover the shoulders and fronts of the mother and daughters, their hands held underneath.[2]

The decision to visually document their immediate family together and O-Zoush-Quah dressed in her finery directly challenged the efforts pressing in on their household. The BIA already had insisted that the two older daughters attend the United States Indian Industrial Training School in Lawrence, Kansas.[3] Shack-To-Quah and Ta-Com-Sa-Quah (or Nettie and Anna, as they increasingly were called by agency officials and subsequent generations of the family) bridged their physical distance from home by writing letters. Kin in Mayetta, Kansas, probably translated the English correspondence for O-Zoush-Quah since she (and many of her generation) communicated exclusively in Potawatomi. More separations further fractured the family.

Within a few years of the family portrait, in 1908, the BIA removed O-Zoush-Quah from her home and placed her in the Indian Asylum. For decades after, the Potawatomi healer's kin, like so many families, regularly and unsuccessfully sought their loved one's return. Daughter Nettie Hale Tork regularly petitioned the BIA on behalf of her mother, asking, "How long she compelled to stay?" Pointedly, she added that she felt "no pleasure . . . to think of her being up there," noting that the short monthly reports on her mother left her doubtful that O-Zoush-Quah was receiving adequate care.[4] Nettie asserted familial authority, cautioning staff to limit beadworking and instead to offer her mother some quilting pieces to sew as a more comforting activity.

*Formal photographic portrait of Potawatomi healer O-Zoush-Quah
(center left) with her husband, four of their daughters, and their son in regalia
she made for them, ca. 1900. Courtesy of Francis and Jack Jensen.*

Ways for O-Zoush-Quah to pass the time until their reunion was a pressing concern of Nettie, who realized that her mother knew "enough to want to come home."[5] Younger sister Anna's impending graduation from the Indian Industrial Training School in May 1909 added urgency: "I would like very much to take mother to see sis graduate," Nettie told the superintendent. In closing, she appealed to Dr. Hummer's generosity: "Trusting and praying she will be home soon."[6]

Over the many years of O-Zoush-Quah's detention, her Potawatomi family directly linked her well-being with their own. Nettie and her sisters understood institutionalization as the main cause of unwellness for the family, insisting that their mother be reunited with her home and kin on the outside.[7] Their claims, as with many others from inside and outside of Canton, refuted the BIA's oppressive view of American Indian homes and families as inherently inferior. "I can manage her better than anyone," Tork informed Canton staff overseeing her mother.[8] Consistently, O-Zoush-Quah's children affirmed that all their relatives belonged with them and not under the management of the Asylum's superintendent or in a federal institution. Repeatedly in words and actions, incarcerated members demonstrated that they, too, would never forget their Indigenous homes or their relatives waiting for them there.

Outside the Indian Asylum, O-Zoush-Quah's younger children matured into adulthood. Many started families of their own. Their kinship adapted and continued, sometimes on paths increasingly distant from isolated members, sometimes circling back and intersecting with shifting memories, spaces, and presence.[9] Threading across the years was the family's insistence that O-Zoush-Quah was not forgotten. Her spouse and children kept framed photographs of her on their living room walls, wore her beaded clothes, and held on to a family Bible with inscriptions documenting her place in the family.[10] The Potawatomi woman's perspective of this story exists beyond her descendants' reach, but her present absence remains palpable to them. Through family stories, dreams, fragmented correspondence, and institutional reports, the distance between them exhales and narrows. In this incomplete space of remembrance, they imagine outward from the homestead, federal asylum, and archives—hands moving across threads, colored beads growing into flowers, eyes looking out to them, then and now.[11]

Enforced dislocation and its wake of trauma eroded O-Zoush-Quah's family ties. Various scholars have described this broad phenomenon as "doing time on the outside": the material and relational harms inflicted by incarceration on generations of kin and communities far beyond brick-and-mortar prisons.[12] O-Zoush-Quah's family had no idea how long she would be detained. They resented the pathological labels attached to the medicine woman and the authority others claimed in the name of her care. O-Zoush-Quah and her kin also shared frustration and hurt caused by their inability to protect one another from institutionalization's reach. Those in kinship with O-Zoush-Quah or any of the other hundreds of people detained at Canton experienced displacements to the Asylum in both direct and indirect ways.[13]

During O-Zoush-Quah's confinement, and for decades after, her family members—like many others separated by the Indian Asylum—struggled, adapted, hoped for, lost, and claimed one another.[14] The combined measures of Western biomedical diagnoses and institutionalization affected extended families and Indigenous nations as well as pathologically labeled Native individuals.[15] Institutionalization was a corrosive force, fraying family obligations, including cross-generational caregiving and child rearing, that closely knit Native communities.[16]

———

In 1926, almost exactly five years after Elizabeth Faribault's unsuccessful escape from the Asylum, her mother set out on another arduous trip from Sisseton, South Dakota, to Canton. Mary Alexis probably camped on the Asylum grounds upon her arrival there, as was commonplace when Native relatives came to see their loved ones. Remaining documents do not confirm whether she knew or even suspected that her daughter was pregnant. Their meeting would have left little doubt: Elizabeth was near the end of her third trimester. No staff reports or letters detail their conversation. It is unknown whether Elizabeth Faribault had told her mother the circumstances of her pregnancy. We are left to imagine the questions that hovered between them, spoken or unspoken—about the baby; about Elizabeth; about their daily lives, their future. Both Mary and Elizabeth experienced the piercing inability to protect their children. The destructive force of institutionalization weighed heavily on the family.

Mary Alexis's visit to the Indian Asylum challenged institutionalization's process of erasure. Meeting with kin on the inside was more exceptional than common. While families with loved ones incarcerated at Canton widely shared experiences of anguish and of desire for reunion, most relatives never met with their kin on the Asylum grounds. Some, like Elizabeth's spouse, Jesse, visited soon after their relatives were taken but were met with scorn and paternalism by the superintendent.[17] Few people returned for subsequent visits. Other barriers limited the opportunities for Elizabeth Faribault's family to physically cross through Canton's walls. The cost of travel and time directly decreased their frequency. Arranging trips to the Asylum also required translators for many extended family members, as was the case with Mary Alexis, who did not speak English. Additional obstacles, including the superintendent's close policing of correspondence, intensified family members' separation from one another.

A few weeks after Mary Alexis returned home, the Sisseton Agency received a monthly report about Elizabeth Faribault. Staff forwarded it to her mother. On the small slip of paper, dated October 1, 1926, Dr. Hummer had left the mimeographed description of Elizabeth's diagnosis as "unchanged" but had added "in bed." In the "remarks" section, he maintained the same refrain as previous updates: she was generally clean, seldom sick, and assisted with work at the bungalow (the superintendent's family cottage on the Asylum grounds). In the right margin, he wrote simply, "had a daughter."[18] A few days earlier, in the afternoon of September 28, Elizabeth had given birth to a girl, whom she named Cora Winona. In the following days, Asylum correspondence to the BIA claimed that both mother and child were "doing fairly well."[19]

Faribault's family understood the situation in starkly different terms. Mary Alexis recognized Elizabeth's extended exile and unplanned pregnancy as a violation of her daughter and their family.[20] Outraged by her daughter's circumstances, she turned to relative and friend Rose D. Renville, a school-teacher from a prominent Sisseton family that had long served as mediators between their nation and white settlers.[21] Renville offered Alexis English-language skills as well as her political connections to aid Mary, Elizabeth, and Cora Winona. Recognizing white male power as a valuable commodity in this advocacy effort, Renville dictated a message to Royal Johnson, a South Dakota Republican congressman and former state attorney general.[22] A flurry of letters ensued. Pointing to stories of mistreatment at the Indian Asylum and Cora's birth as proof that Superintendent Hummer was untrustworthy, Elizabeth Faribault's Sisseton kin demanded an intervention. Congressman Johnson complied, asking the BIA to investigate and report back to him.[23] In written exchanges, her advocates explained that the birth of Elizabeth's child made Mary "desire her release more than ever."[24] Drawing attention to the violation—of Elizabeth, her family, and her Sisseton community—the letter continued, emphasizing that Mary did not feel that "her daughter has been treated right and is very anxious that something be done for her . . . release."[25] According to a related institutional report from the time, Elizabeth Faribault held Harry Hummer directly accountable for her condition, blaming the superintendent for not allowing her to be with her family at home.[26]

Deflecting attention from himself, Hummer presented Elizabeth as the true source of her own predicament: "Carrying out a policy of making this institution as nearly homelike as circumstances would permit," he explained to the BIA, "this woman has had restricted parole privileges of the institution grounds for many years." But this "privilege she abused . . . giving birth to a child." The superintendent alleged that another institutionalized person, Willie Dayea (Diné Nation), was Cora Winona's biological father.[27] Modeling BIA responsibility, he assured the commissioner, "Of course, [Faribault's] privileges were withdrawn after that date and have not been restored." His focus on the institutionalized woman intensified. "Elizabeth Fairbault is, at present, materially deteriorated (demented) and, in my opinion, it is decidedly for her best interests to remain in this institution."[28] The BIA accepted Hummer's medical assessment and his recommendations, declining also to investigate the circumstances leading to Cora Winona's birth. Elizabeth and her infant daughter remained in the locked wards.

In the context of the Indian Asylum, Elizabeth Faribault's pregnancy in 1926 was both remarkable and familiar. Official Asylum correspondence and population rosters between 1903 and 1933 suggest that at least six other incarcerated women became pregnant while at Canton.[29] The actual number of pregnancies and births of live children remains unknown. Government records suggest that at least several miscarriages also occurred. It is probable that the actual numbers were greater. For many reasons, these kinds of details rarely appear in existing sources. Few institutional updates directly addressed childbirths that occurred during a given year. References to infants appeared primarily in annual reports alongside statistics on illnesses and deaths, embedding them firmly but marginally within the Asylum. Sadly, we have no direct testimony from Elizabeth Faribault or other people who gave birth while institutionalized at Canton. Their silence permeates this chapter of the story.

Kinship also permeates this account, surfacing amid constrained institutional records. Across many years, Mary Alexis insisted that her daughter belonged with their family in Sisseton.[30] Elizabeth Faribault's own actions—attempted escapes, writing petitions, and verbally denouncing those who institutionalized her—also affirmed kinship in the face of corrosive forces. For these women and their kin, family, home, and institution tangled across generations.

Elizabeth's daughter, Cora Winona Faribault, spent her first few years in Canton's locked wards. She was one of only two infants born inside the Asylum who made it out and who survived to adulthood. Conspicuously, Canton enrollment lists and other medical reports frequently referred to institutionalized infants generically. Little Cora, for example, appeared merely as "Baby Fairbault."[31] Elizabeth made a noticeably different claim, however, calling her daughter Cora Winona.[32] According to historian of Dakota culture Collette Hyman, "personal names reflected and reinforced core values and beliefs, cultural identity, and social organization."[33] The name "Winona" commonly denoted a first-born daughter.[34] Elizabeth had given birth to six other children before Cora Winona, including daughter Annie, who was born in 1904. Siblings Annie, Solomon, and Howard were still living when their mother was institutionalized in 1915. Did the new baby, whose conception likely came from an act of violence, tie Elizabeth more fully to the Asylum? Calling her Winona, the firstborn daughter, suggests a life severed from Sisseton. At the same time, this name holds glimmers of hope, claims of belonging. The presence of Cora Winona and other children born and living on the inside of Canton also disrupted institutionalization's process of elimination, a tender and complicated understory of kinship's continuation.

What happened to Elizabeth and Cora Winona was uncommon but not singular. Their lived experience of family spanning the inside and outside of Canton Asylum was shared by many others, including extended kin from the Sisseton-Wahpeton Dakota Band.

———

By the time Elizabeth Faribault entered the Indian Asylum in 1915, fellow Sisseton-Wahpeton member George Leo Cleveland Marlow had been detained there for nearly a decade. The age peers who had grown up in close proximity on the Sisseton Reservation likely would have remembered one another, shared news of their families back home, and recognized the rolling hills, lakes, farmsteads, and clapboard houses of each other's memories. Over Faribault's and Marlow's shared detention, other Sisseton-Wahpeton people were confined to the Asylum as well.[35] Between 1902 and 1934—Canton's formal existence—more than one-fourth of the nearly four hundred institutionalized people were members of the Great Sioux Nation.[36] Elizabeth Faribault and the other 105 Lakota, Dakota, and Nakota people would find familiar faces, hear their Indigenous languages spoken by others, and be recognized while on the inside.[37] Other people confined at Canton had similar experiences. More often than not, numerous members of the same Native nations concurrently inhabited the Asylum wards.

Thin documentation inversely casts thick shadows over most relationships within the Indian Asylum, making it impossible to conclude with any certainty the actual lived connections between people. In this cloudy context, passing references to instances of caregiving, to advice sought and given, and to bilingual individuals interpreting and translating for others embody meaningful experiences of relationships that shaped everyday life.[38] While their individual life stories varied, many if not all of the Native men, women, and children likely knew at least one other person as kin or recognized familial connections among them. This, of course, does not mean that every incarcerated person could or did adhere to their nation's cultural norms for expressing or understanding kinship. Indigenous people's active kin connections, in all their known, unknown, and imagined forms, defy the institutional forces that rendered them invisible and that BIA representatives and others actively sought to erase.[39]

For Elizabeth Faribault, the fundamental tenet of Dakota life—being a good relative—anchored her to people outside Canton and held her close to others on the inside.[40] This was evident with her kin, Nellie Kampeska. In 1917, Kampeska, a Sisseton-Wahpeton Dakota student at the Pipestone Indian Boarding School, was transferred to Canton Asylum. After the intake process was completed, staff placed her in the women's wing on the second floor. Gazing at the others living in the locked ward, the young woman may have wondered how she would navigate this new and imposing environment. It would not have taken her long to find a familiar face. Tall and striking, Elizabeth Faribault had known Kampeska's family back on the Sisseton Reservation. Perhaps she previously had even spent time with the younger woman, who was an age peer of Elizabeth's older children, Solomon and Annie.

Circumstances imposed physical proximity between Faribault and Kampeska, but kinship imbued the experience with meaning. In her own written accounts, Kampeska referenced regular visits to "Elizabeth's room."[41] Some evenings they would sit in the parlor, listening to music or to the conversations around them. Both had parole privileges, allowing them to walk the grounds together. The two also conversed easily with one another in spoken English and Dakota. The latter language probably served them well when they sought to convey private information around the watchful white staff. Hours spent in the company of someone who cared and understood, who listened, commiserated, and advised, gave some respite from the stagnating days of institutionalized life.

Nellie Kampeska and Elizabeth Faribault claimed one another in ways that had sustained families generations before them. In Dakota Nation, as with many other Indigenous communities, inter- and intratribal adoptions have been (and still are) significantly valued. Adopted kin fortified communities.[42] In the wake of deaths, for example, a family might adopt someone who had been a close friend of the relative who had passed on. The adopted member would keep their original kin connections, names, and living arrangements but gain new kinship obligations and rights to the mourning family members.[43] Like most of their daily experiences, the names Kampeska and Faribault might have called one another were never recorded. Mother. Sister. Auntie. Cousin. Friend. How the Dakota women identified their relationship exists outside institutional sources, but the deep connections they shared repeatedly emerges.

Kampeska generously shared valuable knowledge of written English and of "white cultural ways" that Faribault (who had never attended school and could not read or write in English) certainly appreciated. In 1918, Kampeska helped Faribault write the plea that inspired numerous neighbors and allies back at Sisseton to support her cause. It must have taken many hours for Kampeska to show her how to write out carefully crafted messages. The teenager would have repeated her signature phrases to Faribault, emphasizing to BIA recipients that she would "kindly like to go home" and that she needed them to "please kindly help."[44] The lettering she learned in the boarding school became templates for Elizabeth Faribault, who drew upon these phrases, approximating Kampeska's clean cursive in letters written years after their shared detention.[45]

Kinship and English literacy combined to resist the forces of institutionalization. With Kampeska's assistance, Faribault began writing numerous letters to relatives back in Sisseton, exchanging written updates with her husband and mother and orchestrating an extensive campaign to achieve her release. A subsequent petition signed by more than fifty people demanding her discharge prompted more forceful responses from Canton representatives. At the time, Superintendent Hummer contended that the signatories had been duped by Faribault's written plea. The Dakota woman, he charged, was "unable to write such a letter." "In fact," he countered, "the letter was written by another patient for Mrs. Fairbault." Pointedly, he named Kampeska as the duplicitous author.[46]

Nellie Kampeska also seems to have shared with Elizabeth Faribault other forms of resistance, including strategies for escape. On January 20, 1919, the teenager broke out of the locked wards, heading east and south from the Asylum grounds. Two days later, she was captured about twenty miles away, in Rock Valley, Iowa. On the day she reentered the Indian Asylum, Kampeska struck back, penning a detailed affidavit that threatened to expose at least six workers there for harassment, moral delinquency, and dishonesty.[47] Superintendent Hummer released her shortly thereafter, placing the defiant young woman on a train to Ortley, South Dakota.[48] The superintendent's decision may have helped avert scandal of his employees' misdeeds. It also separated the two Dakota kin.

It is unknown whether the women wrote to one another after Kampeska left Canton. Even if they had tried to send letters, it is unlikely that Hummer—who read all outgoing and incoming mail—would have allowed their transmission. Kampeska's imprint on Faribault's life clearly extended past their shared time on the inside, however. Prior to the teen's arrival,

Faribault was described by Canton employees as "quiet and causing no trouble." After Kampeska returned home, however, Faribault made repeated attempts to escape. Her first breakout mirrored Kampeska's: she bolted on January 13, 1920, heading east but then turning north. Perhaps she had learned from her Dakota kin that escape efforts during the wintertime were more likely to succeed because of the seasonal influx of tourists to Canton, which, since 1912, boasted the largest Nordic ski jump in the state. By the 1920s, thousands of visitors flocked to the area to watch and to participate in regional competitions. No sources remain that help us understand Elizabeth Faribault's experience during her three-day flight, as the space between her and Canton grew like the snow drifts around her. The anguished outcome received a brief mention in the Asylum record: on January 16, Faribault was apprehended in an Iowa town twenty miles from the Indian Asylum. Hummer personally drove to retrieve her, a task typically undertaken by attendants.[49]

Faribault's second known attempt to flee Canton Asylum was made possible by kinship as well. During the summer of 1921, her mother, Mary Alexis, first visited her daughter at Canton.[50] No Asylum reports log this visit, but shortly afterward both women directly disputed Elizabeth's institutionalization. Alexis dictated a letter to Superintendent Hummer, pleading for her daughter's release. Days later, on September 24, Faribault jumped through a screened sun porch to the ground, bolting away from the Asylum campus.[51] She traveled due north toward the Sisseton Agency, following a path similar to the one her mother had taken just days earlier. The Dakota woman arrived at Flandreau Agency—seventy-one miles from Canton—three days later. The local superintendent, identifying Faribault as an "outsider," contacted Hummer. In replays of May 1915 and January 1920, a sheriff arrived at the family home, where Elizabeth had sought refuge, apprehended the defiant woman, and waited for the doctor to arrive. Hummer reported to the BIA the following day, "Barring the fact that her feet are blistered from the three days of walking, she seems not particularly worse for her escapade."[52] For the Alexis-Faribault family, heartbreak and indignation trace across this memory. Returning to paper and Nellie Kampeska's tutelage, Elizabeth Faribault tried again to bridge the distance.

Elizabeth Alexis Faribault began her seventh year of incarceration, 1922, with a letter to David Mazakute, the adult son of a prominent Dakota leader. "My Dear friend Hello," she began. Drawing on her writing lessons from Kampeska, Faribault, in halting English, informed Mazakute that she "will write" or "tell you every thing" and that she hoped that he "gets the picture."

The letter suggests that the two had corresponded previously, although no other copies of their exchanges remain in the archives. Into her nonstandard English, Faribault inserted Dakota. Previously, speaking in Dakota had enabled her and Kampeska to exchange information without staff understanding or intervening. Writing in Dakota circumvented Hummer's authority at the same time it reaffirmed Faribault's kin connections beyond the Asylum. She cautioned Mazakute that "mis de iwahasni" ("I do not laugh/this is not funny") and alluded to barriers, departures, losses, and hopes. Fears of being erased from memory during her lifetime punctuate the letter: "nobody even thought of me or remembered me," she lamented.[53] Repeatedly calling him "koda," she claimed the right as kin to be with her tribe.[54] As a form of kinship, "koda" entails obligations and interdependence.[55] Invoking the cultural ritual of shaking hands, she exhorted Mazakute to remember her to others on the outside, also offering to him her own extended hand of friendship. Affirming, perhaps asserting, her existence within her broader tribal community, Elizabeth Alexis Faribault emphatically reiterated and closed her note with the phrase "he miye"—"it is me."[56]

It appears that this letter never reached its intended recipient but remained in Dr. Hummer's files. Six months after Faribault wrote it, Hummer still had the letter. After additional communication written by Faribault, her family, and other advocates intensified their demands for her release, the superintendent sent Mazakute's letter to BIA Commissioner Burke in June 1922 as an "index of her mentality."[57] Hummer discounted Faribault's written correspondence as an incoherent rant, evidence of mental disorder.

In leveraging insanity, Hummer used frameworks of settler ableism to deny Faribault's agency. Pathologizing Indigenous language and relations, the superintendent dismissed the Dakota woman's self-determination, even her full personhood. Fracturing generations of Indigenous kinship was one of the outcomes of all of these denials.

Compounded losses pool into Faribault's letter. Her memories hover between the lines: attempted escapes from Canton and long drives back to the Asylum with Dr. Hummer, hours cleaning the superintendent's cottage and tending to his family, Mary Alexis's visit and the news that husband Jesse had divorced her, Nellie Kampeska's face, her own children back in Sisseton—the life and community beyond the locked wards. Symbolically and literally, violence and theft wither the edges of her correspondence. The harms Faribault referenced—barriers, departures, abandonment, unremembering—continued for years to constrain her life on the inside. Her letter to Mazakute was likewise diverted, detained. It appears now amid hundreds of crumbling

BIA files held in National Archives boxes labeled "Canton Asylum." No subsequent communication by Elizabeth Alexis Faribault remain in the record, although other correspondence suggests she may have continued to write.

Faribault's piercing fear of being forgotten was not an abstract concern. Her sustained absence from home and life on the outside unwove swaths of her family tapestry. This embodied loss was shared, though unevenly so. Imagining Faribault and other Native people imprisoned at Canton Asylum, author Pemina Yellow Bird has written, "They must have longed for a familiar face, their own food, their own homes, their own tongues, trying to hang onto what they loved—their culture that told them who they were, who they belonged to."[58] In this fractured history, Faribault's closing words to Mazakute—he miye (it is me)—whispers, clamors.

———

There are more questions than answers about what happened to Elizabeth Faribault at the end of her life. Early on Friday March 2, 1928, an employee had observed her rise and begin her daily routine, briefly leaving and then returning to her room to tend to her daughter, Cora Winona, who shared her bed. It remains unclear whether Faribault spoke to attendant Katie Knox that chilly morning while the staff member monitored the locked ward, but Knox claimed that she did not express any complaints or appear unwell. Several hours later, Knox circled back past Faribault's room and found the forty-six-year-old Dakota woman's lifeless body. Acknowledging no prior illnesses, Superintendent Hummer informed the BIA that Elizabeth Faribault must have succumbed to "heart failure."[59]

Archived sources from the Asylum to the Sisseton Reservation superintendent imply that Faribault's body may have been returned to northeast South Dakota. However, her descendants have never been able to locate their relative. Granddaughter Faith O'Neil insists that Elizabeth Faribault never left Canton. It is more likely, O'Neil contends, that she is among the unaccounted-for people buried in the Asylum cemetery. She wonders about the circumstances of her grandmother's death, whether overt violence or quieter forms—heartbreak, resignation—brought about her end.[60] What is known without question in this complex, cloudy situation is that O'Neil's mother, Cora Winona Faribault, remained at Canton for years after her own mother's death.[61] For the Alexis-Faribault family, ruptures, trauma, and reclamations reverberate across generations. Faith O'Neil vigorously remembers Elizabeth Faribault, assuaging her grandmother's anxiety of being lost, forgotten. She keeps near her bedstead a copy of Faribault's letter to Mazakute and other correspondence. Photographs of family members surround them. But O'Neil cannot as yet close the full distance between her family's past and current lives. So she lingers—like so many other descendants of institutionalized people—waiting and searching at the edges of history.

Little is known about the early years of O'Neil's mother, Cora Winona Faribault. Oblique references in the medical file suggests that Elizabeth Faribault had bathed, dressed, and tended to her daughter daily. Witnessing children like Cora Winona clearly motivated some of the other nearby adults to offer what parental protection and support they could. In this way, young people's presence especially fortified kinship connections with others around them. Extended networks of relations, common in many Indigenous communities, had always proliferated within the institution (and despite it). Since earliest times, recognized relationships based on affinities, not merely heredity, played a central role in organizing and sustaining many Native nations.[62] "Even now," anthropologist Jay Miller has explained, "members of the First Nations of the Americas uphold the axiom that everything comes down not to a matter of money but to a matter of kinship. Who is connected to whom, from mortals to immortals, defines these tribal universes as much today as it has always done in the past."[63] U.S. settler society is strongly built around relationships anchored in marriage and heredity. While kinship in many Native American nations shares these characteristics, their meanings can vary widely. For instance, the role of "mother" is not limited merely to an individual's biological status but includes patterns of relationships and obligations as well.[64] Individuals have multiple mothers who are equally understood as such.

One of the women who additionally mothered Cora Winona was Lizzie Red Owl (Oglala Lakota).[65] As a young girl, Red Owl had been sent to the Carlisle Indian Industrial School, where she was assigned domestic service work for a local white family. She had grieved the separation from her parents at the time, a sense of loss repeated during her eleven-year detention at the Indian Asylum.[66] Institutionalized at Canton in 1922, Lizzie Red Owl had known Cora Winona since her birth. Raised with the common understanding that "being good family" was a daily practice, she regularly looked after the little girl. During evenings when the Asylum screened films, the child often accompanied Red Owl. In one 1929 report, for example, a staff member noted, "Winona has never cried at the movies yet nor fussed either, she always sits quietly on Lizzie's lap and bothers no one."[67] Medical files also mention Lizzie Red Owl escorting the child to the toilet and tidying the bathroom area and ward afterward—work that Red Owl felt reflected her maturity and reliability.[68]

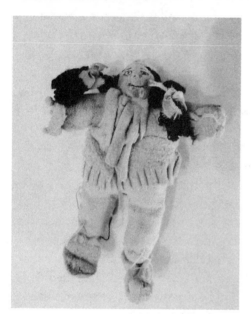

Lizzie Red Owl made these three fabric dolls during her detention at Canton Asylum, ca. 1920s. Red ribbons adorn the sleeves, shirt front, and hair of one doll, while fringed deerskin and tiny beaded necklaces distinguish another. The third doll, made with textured linen, yarn, deerskin, and yellow ribbons, smiles with outstretched arms. Photographed by Susan Burch and used with permission from relatives of Lizzie Red Owl.

Other references suggest that Elizabeth Faribault, Lizzie Red Owl, and perhaps others had instilled in Cora Winona Siouan language and cultural ways of being. For example, Canton's superintendent described the three-year-old's speech as "backward talking."[69] Shortly thereafter, Hummer admitted that the child was developing in a typical manner. His pattern of disparaging peoples' written and spoken forms of Dakota raises the possibility that the little girl may have been overheard communicating in her mothers' language.

The strict confines of the Indian Asylum narrowed opportunities for Indigenous forms of childrearing, but oblique references in archival sources suggest imaginative ways Red Owl and others navigated these barriers. Craftwork became one such outlet. During her incarceration at Canton, Lizzie Red Owl was known for making beautiful dolls. Dressed in fringed shirts and moccasins, they were meticulously constructed. Long braided hair tied with ribbons adorned some of her creations.[70] Tiny strands of clear and colorful beaded necklaces encircled their necks. On at least one creation, Red Owl painted designs on the moccasins and vest that matched the doll's red undershirt. Arms outstretched, her dolls would fit comfortably in a child's hands. Lizzie Red Owl would have played with similar dolls during her own childhood, having learned the craft of dollmaking from her kin.[71] A local Canton girl whom Red Owl had befriended, Clarice Juel Mikkelson, received several dolls from her.[72] Likely, the woman from Pine Ridge also made some for Cora Winona.

Donated by Clarice Juel Mikkelson decades later, four of Lizzie Red Owl's dolls currently sit inside an enclosed glass case in the Canton Public Library. Faith O'Neil, Cora Winona's daughter, stopped by the library on the centennial anniversary of her grandmother Elizabeth Faribault's removal to the Indian Asylum. Her visit to see her family's material archive countered institutionalization's denial of kinship. The presence of Elizabeth and Cora Winona Faribault's descendant affirmed that kinship ultimately, if incompletely, survived Canton Asylum. Taking the dolls into her cupped hands, Faith O'Neil thanked Lizzie Red Owl for being kin.

Chapter 4: **Familiar**

On November 6, 1917, Menominee members Peter Clafflin, Seymour Wauketch, Agnes Caldwell, Susan Wishecoby, and Christine Amour sat close to one another under the watchful gaze of their BIA escorts as the train they rode gathered speed. Earlier on that gray and overcast day, the agency representatives had shown up at their homes on the Menominee Reservation in Wisconsin, authorized to transport the five men and women to the Indian Asylum in South Dakota.[1] Sources about what happened in the wake of this dislocation remain uneven and fragmented.

Following typical procedures, staff separated the group at the Canton Asylum. Likely, Caldwell, Wishecoby, and Amour were assigned to the first-floor dormitory rooms in the newly opened Hospital Building; empty beds in the second-floor men's wards would have awaited Clafflin and Wauketch.[2] Later, administrators transferred Amour to the Main Building. Eventually, Caldwell also would be moved there. It appears that the men rarely left the hospital wing. Across their decades on the inside, these individuals regularly would hear the clicking sounds of keys locking them into rooms and hallways, look through barred windows to the world outside, and inhale air saturated by years and lives inside the brick-and-mortar walls around them.

The experiences of these Menominee men and women also fit broader patterns. Each person institutionalized at Canton daily encountered its foundational form: involuntary containment and surveillance.[3] By design, detention penetrated every level of the institution.[4] Padlocked wards, secured windows, walls, and fences held people within its grounds. On a routine basis, straightjackets, shackles, and iron beds, as well as ward attendants, subdued numerous individuals.[5] From the moment Caldwell, Wishecoby, Amour, Clafflin, Wauketch, and others on their wards arose, a small fleet of employees oversaw them: bathing and toileting, eating and working, wailing and waiting, averting gazes and staring back. At night, watchmen and other staff patrolled the buildings. Institutional confinement and surveillance touched every moment of every day. Involuntary servitude, a worn and recognizable routine within Canton, buttressed the process and experience of institutionalization.

———

Early into her detention, Elizabeth Faribault was assigned to work details. Initially, she assisted the matron in the laundry.[6] After stripping soiled bed-sheets and gathering clothes, towels, and other linens from the wards, the Sisseton woman would spend hours in the basement of the Main Building, loading washers and folding sheets, dampness and the fused smell of detergent and coal residue clinging to her own clothing. Her performance in this role likely contributed to the superintendent's decision to increase Faribault's workload in the 1920s.[7] As Superintendent Hummer's parents moved to Canton to be with their son and family, the administrator sought additional domestic service at his home from institutionalized women. Faribault was among those selected. Her predecessors had described a daily regimen of picking up discarded clothing, scrubbing the bathrooms, making the beds, and sweeping the wood floors. Verbal attacks and intimidation by members of the Hummer family sometimes accompanied this work.[8] Faribault resented the assignment, arguing with Commissioner Burke in 1922 that she should be discharged from the Asylum.[9] Her grievances went unheeded. Faribault labored in the superintendent's cottage for four more years, up until she gave birth to her daughter, Cora Winona.[10] Less than eight weeks later, Faribault was recorded as working again. A monthly update noted that she "assists with work on [the] ward."[11] The tasks would have been familiar—hours of removing dirty linens from the dorm rooms, cleaning bathrooms, and mopping floors.

Elsewhere on the grounds, Willie Dayea also had compulsory work. The Diné man from Lupton, Arizona, apparently plowed the surrounding fields during the warmer seasons. In addition to driving the tractor, he may have overseen others doing harvesting work. Asylum employees apparently trusted the young man as a laborer, describing him as "a good worker and needs no supervision."[12] During Dayea's thirteen-year incarceration, the Asylum significantly expanded its acreage, which created additional demands for farm hands.[13] References to his "fine work" and "good natured" demeanor suggest that his efforts notably helped the staff and the institution.[14] It was taxing, ongoing labor. In 1925 alone, for example, Dayea and other institutionalized men, along with paid employees, enabled the Asylum to cultivate ten acres of potatoes, ten acres of oats, and twenty-five acres each of corn and alfalfa, in addition to pasturing hogs and cows.[15] When indoors, Dayea contributed to Asylum workings as well, sometimes assisting with menial tasks. On a daily basis, he would have observed other institutionalized people similarly working on behalf of Canton, bathing and feeding especially frail members, preparing the meals he and others ate, washing dishes, and mopping the floors.

Elizabeth Faribault and Willie Dayea were among many institutionalized people who regularly labored on behalf of the Indian Asylum. According to the superintendent, "a very large percentage" (often 25–30 percent) of the people detained at Canton were assigned work details.[16] The federal asylum mirrored many other carceral institutions in this practice. Long before the Indian Asylum was established, medical professionals had considered labor a critical form of therapy and administration.[17] In this context, it is unsurprising that more than seventy-five of the nearly four hundred people confined at the Indian Asylum had direct references to their labor as part of the medical assessments: "assists farmer," "polishes floors," "cleans wards," "general housework," "assists in kitchen," "helps with untidy patients," "a good worker."[18] Canton's superintendent understood assigned work as an effective way to keep his charges busy and manageable.[19] Like other institutional administrators, he cast involuntary labor as a sign of efficiency, economy, and scientific management. Asylum reports to BIA officials claimed that the people detained at Canton had annually produced hundreds of fabric items, including clothing, dining linens, towels, and bedding. The vast quantities of vegetables grown, herds milked, and living areas cleaned by those from the locked wards materially reduced Asylum expenses.[20] For Faribault, Dayea, and numerous other institutionalized people, laboring was a required and often unpaid part of their daily lives.[21]

Some assigned tasks amplified vulnerability, particularly when the work occurred in unsanitary or physically isolated spaces. For Elizabeth Faribault and countless other people, precarious jobs were customary, damaging, and unending. Incarcerated indefinitely, Willie Dayea and many others were motivated to serve the institution as a way to survive. According to archival sources, "good workers" like Dayea typically received additional food rations, time away from the padlocked dormitories, access to more people and spaces, comparatively less surveillance, and sometimes comparatively greater status and influence.[22] Although coerced labor marked people's lives in varied ways, everyone detained in the locked wards shared experiences of persistent harm.

―――――

As her descendants tell it, thirty-six-year-old Emma Gregory (Cowetas and Wind Clan of the Creek Nation) was forcibly removed from her mother's home in Kellyville on Creek Nation land to the Canton Asylum in 1905.[23] Most likely, Gregory spent her first four years primarily in one of the large and crowded dormitory rooms filled with rows of iron bedsteads and other women.[24] Mundane, hourless time pulled on her, as it did every confined person at the Indian Asylum. According to institutional reports, this mother of three "held her own" and was "unchanged" for several years. When she challenged staff, Gregory was labeled "combative." At other times, she was described as "a frail little woman weighing only 76 pounds and easily managed."[25] The nighttime sounds of coughing and fevered thrashing of roommates would be as commonplace to Emma Gregory as the sight of soot dust from the heaters that layered on her clothing and sheets. One might imagine many reasons for the "periods of depression and excitement" staff claimed Gregory experienced during her detention.[26]

In May 1909, staff locked Emma Gregory in an isolation room on the women's ward. Superintendent Hummer believed that she had contracted pulmonary tuberculosis.[27] Public health campaigns at the time emphasized hygienic measures to reduce the spread of tuberculosis, but Canton's practices and the environmental conditions surrounding Emma Gregory and many others magnified the likely transmission of this and other infectious diseases.[28] Although standard tests for tuberculosis had been developed years earlier, medical staff at Canton had never administered them.[29] While Gregory was removed to solitary confinement, another institutionalized woman in the last stages of pulmonary tuberculosis was housed with others who had not yet acquired the contagion.[30] Two staff physicians, John Turner and L. M. Hardin, disagreed with Dr. Hummer's diagnosis of Gregory, claiming that she had not shown common tubercular symptoms.[31] No subsequent explanations or challenges accompany Hummer's decision to keep the woman in the dark isolation room. The result was both devastating and familiar for Gregory, as it was for other incarcerated people.[32] Eleven months later the Creek woman was still locked in the "single room without a ray of sunshine."[33] When she tried to escape its confines, staff blocked her, relocking the door.[34] Down the hallway, others would have heard her pounding and yelling. More often than not, Gregory's acts of adaptation, struggle, and resistance—and those of everyone around her—went unrecorded. Later, a medical inspector opined to the BIA that "a mistake in judgement was made" by denying Gregory time outdoors in the warmth and sunshine.[35] As was usual, Washington did not intervene. Extended solitary confinement for three years would have undermined the petite woman's health and well-being even if the forty-five-year-old had not contracted a serious lung infection.[36] As her great-great-granddaughter views it, institutionally induced exposure to tuberculosis and the traumatic effects of isolation served as a punishment alongside other government practices of Indigenous erasure that Emma Gregory suffered.[37]

"The atmosphere awfully bad," James Herman, a member of Rosebud Sioux Tribe, wrote during 1914, his second year of confinement.[38] For the Lakota father of seven, the fundamental act of inhaling air inside the Canton Asylum was an experience of deterioration. Herman detailed many instances of attendants refusing to flush the toilets, prompting him to intervene. "I have gotten up on the cold floor & gone in & flushed them because the smell was non endurable."[39] Like everyone else in the locked wards, he also would have been regularly accosted by the distinct smell of formaldehyde and molasses—used to catch flies—that wafted down the corridors.[40] Poor ventilation and coal soot from radiators floated in the stale air and coated the linens in his dormitory, while the steam heaters cooked molecules of sweat, food stains, tobacco smoke, and human breath.[41] The fifty-three-year-old's account resembled others in detailing the dehumanizing effects of their circumstances—indefinite detention and separation from loved ones, inadequate food, dirty clothing and filthy rooms, people left unclothed, and others handcuffed for weeks and months.

As James Herman intimately knew, the implicit violence of daily life at Canton Asylum sometimes erupted into overt violence. Over his years of detention, he witnessed multiple accounts of physical abuses: employees tossing men from beds, extinguishing all the lights so people could not locate bathrooms, and knowingly leaving incapacitated individuals overnight in beds filthy with their own urine and feces.[42] Some men understood attendants denying them access to toilets at night as an expression of domination over all the Indigenous adults and children detained at Canton.[43] According to Herman, staff members regularly menaced men on his ward. The Sicangu Lakota man from Rosebud detailed how Martin Van Winkle and others on night duty randomly woke individuals up, screaming and shaking them, or forced other incarcerated people to beat elderly men with broomsticks.[44] Following such incidents, the male attendants would slip back to their quarters, laughing at their prank. On one occasion, Herman witnessed a friend who had become sick in the evening and was laid down on another man's bed. His hallmate "hollered & cried all night keeping the other patients awake on account of his anguish and pains."[45] Attendants argued with one another about how to respond to the man's agony, but they provided little intervention. In the morning, a shot of medicine was administered, but, according

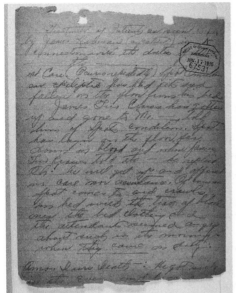

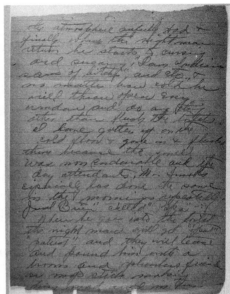

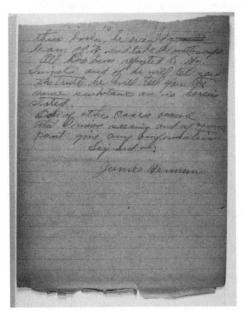

Sections from James Herman's ten-page handwritten statement detailing repeated incidents of staff abuse at Canton Asylum, ca. 1915. Photographed by Susan Burch and used with permission from Michael Herman and Douglas Herman and the concurrence of the Rosebud Sioux Tribe Tribal Historic Preservation Office.

to Herman and several staff members, it was too late. James Herman and others watched, powerless, as the man died before their eyes.[46]

Herman's wrenching account was unique only in that it was preserved and transported beyond the Asylum walls.[47] Overt violence and the threat of violence permeated life within Canton.[48] Medical files and Asylum reports to the BIA provide a fragmented mosaic of attacks. Filtered through staff reports, acts of intimidation—like shoving or charging at someone—usually escaped notice or may have seemed, comparatively speaking, insignificant or expected by institutionalized people. Incidents of staff mistreatment, like the harassment Herman referenced, appear regularly but marginally in institutional sources. Altercations that involved lasting physical damage or death appear as a well-worn path across the archives.[49] James Herman and many people in the locked wards understood that assaults could erupt at any time, from many directions and from many people—including those detained nearby or those hired to oversee them. Targeted harassment repeatedly escalated into more aggressive violations. A population and location repeatedly singled out were the women locked in the Main Building.

Nellie Kampeska and Christine Amour shared the double bedroom on the second floor of the Main Building in the women's ward. Located next to the stairway and with windows facing the yard, the room was especially accessible to predators. In early 1919, engineer Chad Endicott was observed verbally harassing and exposing himself to Kampeska while she was in the bedroom. It appears that Amour was present and directly harassed as well. According to Kampeska, the man had been entering the women's ward for months, approaching her in the sewing room and bathroom, offering candy, alcohol, cigarettes, and promises to help her escape if she would have sex with him. Endicott sought out additional secluded places to corner the Sisseton teenager, including the basement, hedged areas on the grounds, and bathrooms.[50] Threats followed in the wake of her refusals.[51] Another employee, Walter Shephard, also regularly tried to coerce her into sexual relations, following similar strategies to Endicott.[52] After her unsuccessful attempt to escape the Asylum, Nellie Kampeska penned a long affidavit attesting to the men's actions as well as to other staff members' complicity. A few months after Kampeska's July 1919 discharge from the Indian Asylum, night watchmen Louis Hewling and William Juel began entering the second-story women's ward. Using the keys issued to them, the men regularly unlocked and entered the double bedroom, sexually assaulting Christine Amour and her new roommate, Agnes Caldwell.[53]

Sexualized violence permeated life on the inside of Canton Asylum for Kampeska, Amour, Caldwell, and others.[54] Scant documentation remains to shed light on what happened to the women who were directly targeted, often by staff members. It is likely that many of the institutionalized people recognized that sexual assaults generally were suppressed, downplayed, or actively ignored by BIA administrators, as well as by Canton's staff and superintendents. Responding to Nellie Kampeska's testimony, for example, Dr. Hummer informed Washington that she was an unreliable source. Describing the nineteen-year-old as a "pathological liar" and possible "nymphomaniac," he implied that she had fabricated or invited Endicott's attacks.[55] He similarly blamed Agnes Caldwell for the assaults against her by Juel and Hewling, asserting that she was "over-sexed."[56] Consistently, the harassing employees were encouraged to quit their jobs. Across the Asylum's archival record, sources confirming employees' voluntary departures sit alongside letters referencing their sexual exploitation of institutionalized people.[57] The BIA regularly affirmed resignations over structural or systemic changes. "In view of the fact that all of the employees indicated . . . have left the institution," Assistant Commissioner E. B. Merritt wrote to Superintendent Hummer in 1919, "it is doubtful that anything further should be done."[58] No charges were brought against Endicott, Hewling, Juel, or any other staff member accused of violating people confined at the Indian Asylum.[59]

In this context, it is not unexpected that we have no direct testimony from Agnes Caldwell from this time period, despite her prolific correspondence in prior years. Neither are there written accounts from Christine Amour or most other survivors of sexual violence. Many factors, including fear of retribution and language barriers, discouraged people from lodging complaints, and there is every reason to believe that many more such abuses occurred at the Indian Asylum than were reported. We know little about most of the people Canton detained during their time on the inside, a particular kind of patterned violence, unfurling, incremental, and buried.[60]

Agnes Caldwell, Elizabeth Faribault, James Herman, Nellie Kampeska, and others in the locked wards came to recognize that institutionalization's persistent harms would not change. Dozens of individuals, including Herman, Kampeska, and Faribault, broke out, fleeing toward their homes.[61] Like the majority of escapees, they were captured. Many also testified in letters to loved ones, formal petitions, and other declarations that challenged white administrators' fraudulent claims that Canton and its staff were safe and nurturing.[62] Kampeska, Faribault, Herman, Caldwell, and numerous incarcerated people sought redress for wrongs against themselves and others on the inside. By so doing, they insisted on the humanity and dignity of the people similarly detained around them.[63] Institutionalized peoples' accounts repeatedly tell of malnourished and undernourished people; of people writhing in physical pain as employees watched; of anguish, terror, and the harm of solitary confinement; of sexual violence and abductions; and of tuberculosis coiling children and adults. In a context of persistent harm, it is unsurprising that death was deeply familiar too.

———

In March 1912, after three years in solitary confinement, Emma Gregory died.[64] According to Asylum medical reports, the forty-five-year-old's untimely death was the result of pulmonary tuberculosis. It is unknown whether or when her brother and guardian, James Self, was notified.[65] She was buried in an unmarked grave in the southeast section of the Asylum cemetery, next to a Diné woman whose cause of death similarly was listed as pulmonary tuberculosis.[66] Long rows on either side of the women held dozens of people who had perished on the inside of Canton before Gregory—and would hold many dozens more who met similar ends after her.[67]

Emma Gregory's Asylum medical files and those of other individuals obscure a collective truth of institutionalization: death hemmed its daily edges. A practical reality that at least some people would not outlive their confinement motivated the creation of the cemetery where Gregory was buried.[68] News of the Creek woman's passing closely resembled that of others across the historical record of Canton. Crosshatching stories of individual deaths, perfunctory notifications to the BIA, and annual mortality statistics closely followed the Indian Asylum's opening in 1902 and continued unabated until its closure in 1934. In total, nearly half of the people forcibly removed to the Asylum—at least 189 individuals—died there.[69] Emma Gregory was among the 123 people listed as buried in Canton's graveyard.[70] More recent archaeological research suggests that at least six more individuals, as yet unidentified, are also interred there.[71]

As with Emma Gregory, staff doctors primarily attributed deaths to tuberculosis.[72] Superintendent Hummer, who subscribed to the popular and erroneous settler belief that American Indians were inherently susceptible to contagious diseases, interpreted Canton's high mortality statistics as the result of the "scourge of the human race, and more especially of the Indian race." To him, the predictable outcome was rooted in racial pathology: "The result is that these patients must inevitably succumb."[73] Various medical observers at Canton and public health officials across the United States at the time offered a different interpretation, emphasizing that conditions in carceral institutions fueled the bacteria's deadly reach.[74] Mortality rates inside and immediately outside the Asylum reflected stark environmental differences. Fewer than 3 percent of townspeople in Canton, South Dakota, died from tuberculosis at the same time the contagious disease was the listed cause for one-third of the fatalities inside the Indian Asylum. Like Gregory, most of the individuals who died at Canton were young. The average age of death at the Indian Asylum was forty-two years old. The typical age when nonincarcerated people in the town of Canton died in this era was sixty-four years old.[75] In short, institutionalization itself was lethal.

Only faint details convey how people detained at Canton Asylum experienced death and dying—their own or those around them. The frequent loss of life directly and indirectly touched everyone there, albeit in uneven ways. For sisters Susan and Jane Burch, death and kinship intersected their daily lives. Regular staff updates describe a grief-stricken Jane crying frequently and pounding her arms on her head. The goiter on her neck, which slowly restricted her ability to breathe, concerned both sisters. Months into their shared detention, Susan began to experience irregular fevers and headaches. Her coughs resembled those of others who had contracted pulmonary and intestinal tuberculosis.[76] She, too, was often found sobbing, sometimes unable to leave her bed. Mostly confined indoors, the Burch women spent their days in each other's close company. Feeding one another became its own ritual. "Takes care of her sister" appears in both women's medical files. So do details of their decline. Less than a year into their detention, the Southern Ute women each had withered to less than ninety pounds. One was described as "thin and pale. Losing weight. . . . Seldom complains." The younger sister died first, in August 1913. She was returned to Colorado for burial.[77] The elder sister survived another three years. No other details about the thirty-five-year-old's life or death are available, except that on March 1, 1916, she was buried in the Asylum cemetery, in the same row as Emma Gregory.[78]

———

Continued institutionalization threaded across the Burch sisters' story, as it did all of the people confined at Canton. At the individual and collective level, lived time on the inside unfolded across months, years, and generations. For many of its confined members, medicalized institutionalization also extended past the Indian Asylum's gates.[79] A web of other federal and state facilities ensnared these Native elders, children, and adults.

For O-Zoush-Quah and George Leo Cleveland Marlow, the autumn of 1933 began unremarkably. Both spent most of their days surrounded by other detained people in relentless hours of hallways, enclosed porches, dining halls, and dormitories. In early September, the elderly O-Zoush-Quah met briefly with Dr. Samuel Silk, a psychiatrist from St. Elizabeths Hospital in Washington, D.C., who had come to inspect the Asylum for a second time.[80]

Standard interview questions were posed. Could she tell him about her family and home, how long she had been committed at Canton, and why? Twenty-five years had passed since her forced dislocation from her home on the Potawatomi Reservation in Kansas to the Indian Asylum. Language barriers and hovering staff, among many compounding factors, would have constricted the exchange between the Potawatomi healer and the visiting doctor. Consulting O-Zoush-Quah's fragmented medical files would have yielded letters from her daughters repeatedly seeking her release. In one exchange prompted by her kin in 1930, the BIA superintendent at the Haskell Institute advocated that O-Zoush-Quah be transferred to a facility in Topeka, Kansas, so that her family could visit with her. Nearby in the folder would have been Superintendent Hummer's recommendation (with BIA endorsement) against the transfer.[81] Vague descriptions from staff reports—"does beadwork" and "needs supervision of some sort"—may have prompted additional questions for the woman. Dark eyes perhaps flashed back at the examiner. Silk's schedule filled with other interviews, the St. Elizabeths representative concluded his meeting with O-Zoush-Quah and moved on.

George Leo Marlow was among the others Samuel Silk interviewed. To the stock questions, the Sisseton man likely offered few details about his family, whom he had not seen or communicated with directly for almost three decades. The lanky forty-eight-year-old usually gave brief answers to staffs' inquiries, his head often turning back and forth as he spoke.[82] Marlow's medical file provided little insight into the man's life. Ward attendants had described him as quiet and usually compliant. After Silk finished his brief assessment, Marlow returned to his daily regime: sitting by himself, sometimes watching and sometimes disregarding the others nearby, and looking at walls stained a yellowish hue from lives and years trapped inside.

O-Zoush-Quah and George Leo Marlow were among the many unnamed people Silk referenced in his subsequent report to the BIA. "Some of them never had any schooling, can neither read nor write," the doctor noted by way of contrasting white settler society's cultural norms with Indigenous ones. The inspector recommended that upward of half of Canton's detained population could be discharged. He concluded that the others, to use the parlance of O-Zoush-Quah's medical file, "needed supervision of some sort" in an institution. Joining colleagues from the federal psychiatric hospital in Washington, D.C., and an array of U.S. government agencies, Silk recommended that the people be relocated to St. Elizabeths Hospital. It is doubtful that O-Zoush-Quah, George Leo Marlow, or any of the others confined at

Canton Asylum were apprised of Silk's report or the plans to bring about their collective dislocation to Washington.

———

In the 1930s, shifting economic, political, and cultural factors motivated national leaders and BIA representatives to reconsider maintaining the Indian Asylum. As the Great Depression unfolded and New Deal politicians claimed ascendency, consolidation of federal power gained momentum. President Franklin Roosevelt's new appointee to the Office of Indian Affairs, John Collier, increasingly asserted that the Indian Asylum belonged to the "horse and buggy era," connecting images of a bygone past to its western location. "The physical plant is condemned as being hopelessly archaic, and the administration is condemned as sensationally inefficient," the new commissioner proclaimed shortly after Silk had returned from his inspection.[83] Contrasting itself with Canton Asylum, St. Elizabeths Hospital administrators and staff in Washington argued that their institution modeled efficiency and modern medical practices. The contests between the two federal psychiatric facilities underscored broad and familiar settler ableist practices. Invoking rhetoric of medical progress and competent institutional management, Samuel Silk, St. Elizabeths, and the BIA bolstered their authority and status. Responsible government and good medical practice, the logic went, necessitated in this instance the closing of one institution—Canton Asylum—to maintain and strengthen the broader medical system, which included St. Elizabeths Hospital.[84] Undergirding this process, settler ableism served to make continued institutionalization of diagnosed people seem essential and unquestionable.

News that the Indian Asylum might be shuttered prompted a former engineer there, Norman Ewing (Sioux), to contact the BIA. Telegramming Commissioner Collier in October 1933, Ewing asserted that he had "first hand knowledge from observation most brutal practices under Hummer." Years prior, Ewing—the only Native employee at Canton at the time—had sought to expose the inhumane conditions at the Asylum, conveying James Herman's written affidavit to U.S. government officials and adding his own testimony in person to BIA leadership in 1915.[85] Administrators had responded by reassigning Ewing to a post at Fort Peck, Montana.[86] Ewing nevertheless offered to assist the emerging effort to close the Asylum: "Can testify or send you copy of record abuses observed while employed there if same of value to administration."[87] Commissioner Collier and Interior Secretary Harold Ickes released Ewing's testimony alongside details from earlier Asylum reports that described conditions as "sickening" and spotlighting transparently in-humane treatment, such as a child chained to a steam pipe.[88]

Not surprisingly, Superintendent Hummer and many of Canton's towns-people opposed the unfavorable depictions and plans. Insisting that pre-tentious easterners were meddling in matters they did not understand or that officials were exceeding federal jurisdictions, they insisted that Asylum staff were dedicated and effective caregivers to otherwise helpless Native Americans. Although visits from relatives of institutionalized people had been discouraged, the Asylum's closer proximity to many reservations was invoked as benefiting members of Indigenous nations within and outside of South Dakota. Legal brawls ensued over the next several months, as local representatives clashed with Washington about the future of the Indian Asy-lum.[89] Ultimately, the federal government dismissed Dr. Hummer, replacing him temporarily with a physician and superintendent of the Pipestone Indian School in Minnesota who was directed to oversee Canton's closing and to transfer the majority of the people held there to St. Elizabeths.[90] Modern medical understandings and social and scientific efficiency, federal officials proclaimed, had promoted deeper insight, enhanced trustworthiness, and promised real solutions to the persistent threat of mental illness. The BIA returned seventeen people deemed not to have "sufficient mental derange-ment" to their homes.[91] Celebrating what he claimed was true democracy, Commissioner Collier cast the decision to close Canton Asylum and relocate most of its institutionalized population by the end of 1933 as an indication of a "New Deal" for American Indians.[92] The Washington Post described the seventy-one American Indians being sent to St. Elizabeths as being "freed."[93]

O-Zoush-Quah, George Leo Marlow, and the many Native people around them, however, experienced a very different story, one both familiar and un-settling. News of the Indian Asylum's closing glossed over the reality that institutionalization would continue for many people held in its locked wards. Some may not have been aware or understood that they were being trans-ported to another psychiatric facility hundreds of miles away, but these real-ities became swiftly apparent. The locked quarters where they had lived for years hummed with activity on Wednesday, December 20, 1933. Attendants ordered individuals to pack their belongings and assist others in anticipation of the transfer. As evening approached, staff from St. Elizabeths Hospital escorted the Prairie Band Potawatomi woman and the Sisseton-Wahpeton man, along with sixty-seven others, out of the buildings. The group traveled the two miles to the train depot on foot, flanked by local onlookers.[94] Some of the Native people, a young observer later recalled, expressed anguish and disorientation as the serpentine line approached the seven Pullman cars awaiting them.[95] At least one individual who resisted walking was carried onto the train.[96] Women wrapped in blankets, bars on train windows, and fragmented exchanges with those being removed jumbled together in subsequent accounts of the night. Later, as the train hurtled eastward, people spent hours grouped together in isolated carriages under the guarded supervision of hospital staff—continued institutionalization in mobile form. We know nothing about the Indigenous group's conversations, questions, or imaginings that filled the two days before they arrived in Washington and were consigned to the locked wards of another federal psychiatric hospital.[97]

Chapter 5: **Continuance**

> *If I had to discuss the ideas and name them, I would call them continuance—the remembrance of times, places, and people; the knowing of those times, places, and people through imaginative acts; and finally, the going on, the telling of the stories.*
> —Amanda J. Cobb (Chickasaw Nation), *Listening to Our Grandmothers' Stories*

As the railcar pulled into Washington's Union Station in December 1933, representatives from St. Elizabeths Hospital likely met O-Zoush-Quah, George Leo Marlow, and the sixty-seven other former detainees from Canton Asylum, escorting the travelers onward to the facility in the southwest region of the District of Columbia.[1] Since its opening in 1855, St. Elizabeths had served as a central hub in federal psychiatric institutionalization and research.[2] Crossing the fenced threshold, the group entered what would have seemed like a small city. The Government Hospital included nearly one thousand acres and incarcerated upward of five thousand people in its expansive constellation of buildings.[3]

During her intake, O-Zoush-Quah stared blankly at hospital staff.[4] Her responses to their line of questions confounded the interviewers. She mumbled, perhaps in Potawatomi, which employees described as "unintelligible."[5] Personnel recorded that the woman before them disclosed hearing "voices talking to her but will not give any ideas as to what they say."[6] Frustration surfaced. When asked "how are you?" O-Zoush-Quah responded pointedly, "Old, no good, can't get out."[7]

Eight decades later, O-Zoush-Quah's grandson Francis Jensen (Kitch-Kum-Me) sat in his living room in Holton, Kansas, looking at family portraits adorning the walls. Born in 1923 in the house that had belonged to O-Zoush-Quah, he had grown up on the Potawatomi Reservation.[8] Studying a painted photograph on the wall near him, Jensen described his grandmother as "a pretty lady with her dark hair parted slightly to the right and brushed neatly behind her ears. The picture, her deep brown eyes look at me winsomely and the suggestion of a smile curves her lips." Her dress also stood out to him. "A white brooch trimmed with silver holds the high collar of her white blouse. A long narrow scarf embroidered with beads and a geometric design encircles her neck."[9] O-Zoush-Quah's descendant, like others of his generation, came of age under her sepia likeness. In his mind's eye, Jensen had continued to hold

Francis Jensen smiles gently, sitting in his living room in Holton, Kansas, 2014. Family photos, including a framed oval portrait of his grandmother O-Zoush-Quah, hang on a nearby wall. Photograph taken by Susan Burch and used with permission of Francis Jensen and Jack Jensen.

her in a moment of beauty, in a time when she was among her people. Meeting the framed gaze of his grandmother, the ninety-one-year-old man pondered in a soft voice "what Grandmother had done to be sent away."[10]

Throughout her lengthy incarceration and since, O-Zoush-Quah and her family viscerally understood that institutionalization was never finite or discreet. The elder Potawatomi's rebuttal to staff's questions—"Old, no good, can't get out"—and Jensen's trailing question about why the U.S. government had taken her away carry remnants of the harmful, cross-generational effects of extended time in institutions. For this family and countless others, the forces that enabled Canton Asylum's creation in 1902 extended far past its closure in 1933. O-Zoush-Quah and her relatives continued to bear the consequences of institutionalization during her transfer to St. Elizabeths Hospital and detention there for many years after. The slow violence of her incarcerations wove into the worlds of subsequent generations as well.

"I wonder what her life was like," Jensen mused while looking at her portrait. The retired barber knew that his grandmother was medicine, someone from whom others had sought blessings and healing. Physically uprooted from her Indigenous world and deprived of virtually all vestiges of Potawatomi lifeways, O-Zoush-Quah experienced daily harm in the name of Western medical care. Perhaps Jensen's mind flew to specific incidents obliquely recorded in her hospital file and to the physical marks left on her body—slight lacerations, bruises, and other discolorations.[11] Describing her as "excited most of the time" and "very cross amongst other people," hospital attendants had viewed her struggles through a pathological lens and imposed amplified isolation in response.[12] During November and December 1941, staff forcibly secluded the octogenarian for an average of fifteen hours almost every day.[13] In stark contrast, family members viewed O-Zoush-Quah's documented attempts to take a nurse's keys, the yelling and running around the rooms, the arguing and tearing her clothing, and her continuing to speak Potawatomi as legible acts of refusal.[14] From an imposed distance, Jensen recounted, her kin sought to support her. When staff wanted to bob the healer's long hair, for example, her daughters refused to grant consent.[15] They continued to petition hospital administrators, demanding her return to them.[16] O-Zoush-Quah's children held on to her eagle feather bundle, to her quilt pieces, and to their memories of her. Some held on to one another, raising Francis Jensen and O-Zoush-Quah's other grandchildren among their extended family.

When news arrived from St. Elizabeths that O-Zoush-Quah had died, her family made plans for her return to the Potawatomi Reservation. According to one relative, she was laid to rest in July 1943 at the "family burial ground in a wooded area about an eighth of a mile from her home."[17] Like many of her extended family, O-Zoush-Quah had followed the Drum Religion, and the community honored the Potawatomi healer with a vigil. "The Drum service lasted all night and until the late afternoon of the next day," Francis Jensen later recalled. O-Zoush-Quah's grandson remembered the "hypnotic drumbeats" that echoed across the area, vibrating across his body even as he drifted into sleep.[18] In Jensen's world, his ancestor remained both absent and present, surfacing partly and poignantly in memories, photographs, and healing feathers that he received and passed on to the next generation. For O-Zoush-Quah's kin as for many others, inheritances—imposed, dislocated, and claimed—lace together across place, time, and people. For the family of George Leo Cleveland Marlow, the multitude of institutions spanning decades and thousands of miles came close to severing kin connections.

———

Sifting through boxes of family photographs and mimeographed letters, Joe Rabon described the accounts of his great-granduncle George Leo Marlow as a silhouette rather than a portrait, the edges of the person shaded by an endless maze of institutions. "It has been like listening to a river of other languages around you, yearning to know what they mean but not understanding it," he explained.[19] Following the imagined river, interlocking memories across time and places, Rabon sketched the contours of Marlow's early years: a childhood in the 1890s among his Sisseton-Wahpeton kin in Dakota Territory, a fall down stairs that damaged his bodymind, a family adapting and struggling.[20] No records remain that detail the BIA's removal of Marlow from his family, but by 1905, the nineteen-year-old was listed at Canton Asylum. He remained in its locked wards until the institution was shuttered in December 1933. Rabon never learned how his ancestor experienced the Indian Asylum's closing, but for him, it was bittersweet: "After surviving the wretchedness of Canton," he pointed out, "Leo was transferred to St. Elizabeth's Hospital in Washington, D.C." In Rabon's account, other institutional corridors shaped subsequent chapters in Marlow's story, including campuses of federal prison-hospitals in Texas and Kentucky. In their wake, St. Elizabeths loomed again. Reflecting on the expanse of places and the decades the federal government detained his ancestor, Rabon shook his head. It was simultaneously unbelievable and predictable. "You can't make this up," he quipped.[21]

With an aged photograph of the family homestead on the Sisseton Reservation nearby, Rabon reread Marlow's 1933 St. Elizabeths admissions file. "I live in the little white house with the bay window," George Leo Marlow apparently told the doctor.[22] According to the report, he then broke into laughter. Personnel did not know why. Rabon chuckled with recognition, imagining Marlow both teasing and refusing to go along with the interview. His great-granduncle had answered confidently that the hospital was located in Washington, D.C. A *big* White House was only a few miles away. Rabon's wide smile narrowed as he absorbed the remaining medical notes describing Marlow's "tense" and "unchanging" facial expressions. His moment of "inappropriate laughter" had ended with imposed and claimed silence. George Leo Cleveland Marlow did not—or would not—say more about his relatives to St. Elizabeths's inquiring staff members.

As Joe Rabon saw it, repeated themes call loudly in Marlow's biography. Forced dislocation, disruption, and confinement underscored the erosion of self-determination for Marlow, his family, and their tribe—to remain, to leave, to return. A photocopied letter in Rabon's hand, dated May 30, 1942, informed Marlow's family that he had been transferred from St. Elizabeths to an even larger federal enclave four miles outside of Fort Worth, Texas.[23] Marlow's siblings likely had no idea that other Native families had received similar notices. According to a report at the time, mobilization for World War II had "caused a let-up in the normal intake of patients at the federal Narcotic Farm at Fort Worth, enabling the government to send insane Indians that are from St. Elizabeths Hospital."[24] Marlow was moved with at least nineteen others who had inhabited the locked wards with him in South Dakota and Washington, D.C.[25] Years later, Joe Rabon wondered what his ancestor would have shared about the experience.

To George Leo Marlow, who had spent nearly four decades institutionalized, the Texas facility may have seemed both familiar and strange when compared to Canton Asylum and St. Elizabeths. Five main buildings, including dormitories and dining rooms, as well as a quadrangle yard defined the closed-off area.[26] According to one Fort Worth staff member in the 1950s, the Public Service Hospital was "almost campus-like in appearance."[27] At the same time, its carceral mission dictated everyday life for Marlow and the other people detained there. Inside the yellow brick dormitories with red tile roofs, the fifty-seven-year-old man from South Dakota would have looked through barred windows made to resemble Spanish wrought iron.[28]

Joe Rabon recoiled at the almost certain likelihood that his great-granduncle underwent additional admissions procedures. This would have included a physical examination and the beginnings of new medical files. Narco–Fort Worth's regimented life echoed Canton and St. Elizabeths: hours were set for waking up, bathing, eating, exercise, medical tests and treatments, and sleep. The institution's signature focus on drug use heightened surveillance of people detained there. Labor undergirded the hours.[29] At once a common and exceptional member of this imposed community, Marlow may have been treated differently when it came to vocational expectations.[30] Recorded as unable or unwilling to provide labor, George Leo Marlow probably spent the next two years in the more confined spaces of dorm rooms and sitting areas while younger, able-bodied members of his group assisted with the animals and crops on the farm or worked in the industrial shops and kitchen. Rabon wondered how Marlow felt in early 1944, when he and other Native men were transferred from Fort Worth to the other federal Narcotic Farm in Lexington, Kentucky.[31] Perhaps the disruption was welcomed—changing scenes accompanied by the smell of outdoor air, the Texas campus shrinking into the distance. Arriving in Lexington, Marlow would pass through a stone archway and iron gates, entering another vast complex with "miles of corridors" and "acres of floor space."[32] Nearly 1,300 institutionalized men and women were held at the facility at the time he was escorted to his locked room, inspected for contraband, and given a supervised shower. The explicit prison underpinnings of Narco-Lexington filled the spaces between the mortar and up the towering walls.[33] Unlike others whose sentences to the Narcotic Farms were finite, Marlow and his aging American Indian hallmates were not expected to leave the bounded federal system. Their number dwindled over time in the wake of death rather than discharge.[34]

After six years inside this fortified compound, George Leo Marlow and other surviving members were transferred to St. Elizabeths again.[35] Almost certainly, the Sisseton man would have undergone yet another formal admissions process and asked nearly identical questions to the previous intake at the Government Hospital. No remaining conversations are recorded in the historical archive—silence echoes on silence. "It was here," Rabon explained, holding the hospital campus in his mind's eye, that "Leo spent the remainder of his life."[36] According to St. Elizabeths records, Marlow died unexpectedly at the Washington facility on February 22, 1961.[37] He was seventy-six years old. Many barriers, including limited resources, Rabon surmised, likely contributed to the family's decision to bury Marlow in Washington rather than in South Dakota.[38] Smiling wryly, he suggested that his ancestors chose the historic Congressional Cemetery as a quiet act of dissent—placing their kin beyond the reach of St. Elizabeths's campus and its own sprawling cemeteries.[39]

A century after the BIA removed his great-granduncle to Canton, Rabon returned to the Asylum grounds. For him, attending annual honoring ceremonies at Canton's cemetery became a way to extend his family's connection to Marlow. Looking around at others whose ancestors also were detained at the Indian Asylum, Joe Rabon shared remembrances and questions about their entangled histories. Drawn to Bois Forte Chippewa historian Kay Davis, he scanned her handmade map, its slender strings connecting every tribal nation with members incarcerated at the Indian Asylum. Fingers swept down from Sisseton's pinpoint, tracing George Leo Marlow's forced dislocation southward to Canton. In Rabon's imagined atlas, additional threads extended his family's story to Washington, Fort Worth, Lexington, and around to Washington again. Davis and Rabon registered the constellation of centers—prescribed, contested, and claimed—in shared knowing looks.

————

A few hundred feet away and eight decades earlier, four-year-old Cora Winona Faribault had walked down the steps of Canton's Main Building and entered employee Clara Christopher's automobile.[40] Having rarely (if ever) left the confines of the Asylum grounds before, the young girl might have wondered about the worlds that passed by her window in the summer of 1930 as they headed to the southwest. Neither Faribault nor Christopher left behind records of the two-day trip that spanned 1,200 miles, leaving question marks trailing after likely landmarks: the box-shaped Tséhootsooí (Bonito Canyon), strewn with Arizona cypress and oak trees; the south-flowing Be'ek'i[d] Halchííd'ęę'nlíní (Black Creek); and the majestic sandstone of Tségháhoodzání (Window Rock). With few stops along the way, the two drove into the ancestral lands of Faribault's alleged father, Willie Dayea, who remained institutionalized at Canton Asylum. Eventually, the car rumbled down a dirt road leading to a stone chapel. Having arrived at Arizona's Fort Defiance Agency, Christopher delivered the little girl to representatives from another institution created to contain Native people: Good Shepherd Mission Orphanage.[41]

By the time she reached her seventeenth birthday, Cora Winona Faribault would be sheltered and confined by several more institutions, including a Navajo Methodist boarding school, white households where she was consigned to domestic service, a Navajo reservation, and a home for unwed mothers. While locations and expressed missions of each place varied, comparatively little changed in Faribault's closely scripted world.[42] The mostly non-Native adults scrutinized her, judging the extent to which she met (or failed to meet) their expectations—what she wore, how she spoke and with whom, where she went, and how she behaved.

By institutional design, domestic chores threaded across Faribault's young life at the mission orphanage and schools: tidying up beds and shared bathrooms, washing clothing items, and running errands for white staff members.[43] Like Lizzie Red Owl and a generation of other Native girls before her, she was assigned work through the "outing system," an assimilationist program that placed adolescent American Indians in white settler households and farms to provide manual labor.[44] Faribault spent the summer of 1943 working in a private home in Iron Springs, Arizona.[45] Echoing the compulsory service that her mothers, Elizabeth Faribault and Lizzie Red Owl, earlier had rendered at Canton Asylum, she performed cleaning and laundering tasks for each of the institutions that housed her.[46]

Later generations of the Faribault family would wonder about the cumulative damage of institutional life on their ancestors.[47] The relocation from Canton to the Arizona orphanage, as just one notable experience, clearly had terrified Cora Winona. Orphanage employee Ruth Harmon later recalled the small child's early experiences: "The bundle of nerves she was, like a little, frightened animal." The new environment seemed filled with potential threats. "The slightest noise would send her scurrying to some hidden corner." Harmon and others would "spend hours searching for her, and all the time she would be within hearing."[48] Growing up inside multiple institutions compounded Faribault's sense of alienation. She had limited exposure to cross-generational Indigenous family life, to its lived obligations, expectations, and relations.[49]

As she grew into young adulthood, Cora Winona Faribault struggled to find out to whom she belonged and what her family story had been. Although she received regular allotment funds as a recognized member from an enrolled Sisseton-Wahpeton Oyate family, she knew little about her Dakota kin and had to rely primarily on BIA representatives for details. Cora Winona sought clarity about her parentage. Confessing to a BIA agent, "I never really knew my mother's name," she had the impression that it may have been Rose. More confidently but inaccurately, she asserted that her birth year was 1925 (it was 1926). Filling out her ambiguous origin, the teenager "guessed," perhaps optimistically but erroneously, that she had been born at the Sisseton Hospital.[50] Kinship questions reverberated across the Faribault family. Cora Winona's older brother Solomon initially was skeptical of the news that his mother had given birth during her detention at Canton. He, too, was compelled to seek authentication from the BIA and Asylum officials. For many years after, Cora Winona and Solomon only knew of one another through federal agency sources.

In their own ways, Cora and Solomon Faribault worked to close the gaps that institutionalization had laid open. Engaging BIA representatives at Sisseton, the seventeen-year-old probed around the edges of her known kin. Initially, she asked whether field agent Diamond Roach knew her brother. Later, she asked whether Roach "had heard from my Brother or seen him around yet."[51] Over time, the younger Faribault urged the agent to pass messages to Solomon, inviting him to contact her directly.[52] Solomon apparently sought greater connection to his sister as well. At one point, Elizabeth Faribault's oldest child had suggested to Roach that Cora move to Sisseton after completing school, a choice the Indian Service representative considered "a mistake." The field agent discouraged Cora Winona from pursuing this option because he believed she was "not acquainted with this part of the country and with the Indian people of this reservation."[53] Roach counseled her to "stay in Arizona" and pursue work there.[54] She had little choice but to wait.

Faribault also rebelled. As she entered young adulthood, Cora Winona increasingly collided with mission regulations. Perhaps she—like many American Indian students at boarding schools—bristled at the staff's expectations, particularly of the young women.[55] School personnel at Window Rock repeatedly rebuked her for drinking. Describing Faribault's teenage years as "one escapade after another," people in charge of her care blamed the young woman's heredity. "Her heritage is bad, pathetically sad," Ruth Harmon asserted, emphasizing that Cora Winona had been a child born out of wedlock to institutionalized Native parents. Disappointedly, Harmon continued, "as she reached adolescence the traits of her parents became apparent, and now you have a dipsomaniac to handle."[56] At one point, the Child Welfare Court was contacted to intervene with Faribault, although the exact circumstances remain unclear.[57] One mission employee who had known Faribault for years concluded that additional experts—social workers and clergymen—were needed to help manage her.[58]

The revelation in early 1945 that Cora Winona Faribault had become pregnant prompted a flurry of conversations with Good Shepherd representatives and a new round of interventions.[59] Only recently arrived in Phoenix, the teenager had been working for room and board while also taking classes at a local public high school.[60] Mission and school administrators envisaged a singular, domestic path ahead of her, pressing the young woman to disclose the likely father's name and urging her to marry him or another willing suitor.[61] Ultimately, none of these outcomes came to pass. Absent nearby kin on whom she could rely, and with limited other resources, the expectant mother and those advising her wondered alike where she would live as her pregnancy advanced and who would help her. Returning to Window Rock would have been rejected summarily; Indian boarding schools typically excluded and expelled pregnant students. Fort Defiance staff also did not appear to want Faribault to give birth at the mission. Administrators quickly dispatched her plans to graduate high school. "Of course she is stopping [her studies] at once," one mission observer assured the others.[62] As with her mother Elizabeth's pregnancy in 1926, those supervising and surveilling Cora Winona used the logic of settler ableism to deem her pregnancy as evidence of her inherent defectiveness, considering her a problem that had to be solved. For mission and school authorities, solutions to the problem required fellow "experts"—peers trained to staff other kinds of institutions—who would know best what Faribault needed and would be positioned to ensure that the teenager conformed to expectations. It went without question that more institutional intercession was needed.[63] Guided by mission representatives, Faribault was consigned to the Phoenix Florence Crittenton Home.[64]

The home for unwed mothers that Faribault entered in the spring of 1945 was part of a national network of residential care established by Christian evangelicals in the early 1890s and endorsed by the U.S. Congress.[65] To Faribault, institutional benevolence and coercion mingled familiarly at the house on Garfield Street. She saw daily the "seven foot woven wire fence, mounted with three strands of barbed wire sloping inward," that surrounded the building. The padlocked iron gate was, according to Crittenton's director, "kept locked day and night."[66] Even its administrator admitted that the Phoenix facility was like "a virtual jail."[67] The Crittenton Home's multiple interlocking purposes—as a shelter to unwed pregnant females and to juveniles deemed delinquent by the court, a temporary school and vocational training space, a mission outpost, and a health clinic—pointed toward regimentation and an emphasis on Christian femininity.[68] Cora Winona Faribault and the others housed at Phoenix's Crittenton Home likely followed a longstanding schedule: "From 7 am to 9 pm our girls are taught self-control; sportsmanship; consideration; courtesy; honesty and cleanliness; to love and worship God and a belief in prayer; to love and admire all things beautiful that God has given us and to be grateful for all blessings."[69] On Saturdays, there were obstetrical examinations.[70]

During her time at the Crittenton Home, Cora Winona Faribault strained against the isolation from the people who had known her since childhood.[71] She maintained correspondence with classmates serving abroad in the war, probed for details about her girlfriends at the Navajo Methodist High School, and planned to attend their graduation.[72] As she entered her third trimester, Faribault also increasingly pursued her birth family's dislocated history. She requested records of her mother's death, believing she had caused it during childbirth. Consultations with the Crittenton doctor had honed her fears that she, too, might have a dangerous medical condition, that "the same thing might happen to me."[73] The BIA superintendent at Sisseton swiftly dismissed Faribault's health concerns, noting that her own delivery had been unremarkable and that her mother had "suddenly passed away at the Asylum" two years afterward. He signed off by reminding the enrolled tribal member to send her child's birth certificate for the agency to record and expressed confidence that she would "recover quickly" and that both mother and child would "do well."[74]

It would appear that Cora Winona Faribault envisioned a different trajectory for her life than had the Good Shepherd Mission staff or BIA administrators. As her Dakota relatives had for generations, Faribault drew links between kinship and place. Penning her imagined future in a letter just weeks before her baby was born, the teenager emphasized her desire for a closer connection to her maternal ancestral home, to Sisseton. "I hope to return there to live someday," she wrote.[75]

On May 27, 1945, Cora Winona Faribault gave birth to her first child, whom she named David Howard Faribault.[76] Mother and son remained at the Phoenix Home for the next year.[77] As was common policy at Crittenton Homes, Faribault received childcare support at the same time she was expected to learn a marketable trade.[78] It is probable that she attempted to complete her high school education while a resident at the home, but the local institutions rebuffed her efforts. Shortly after David's first birthday, Cora Winona Faribault returned to the Fort Defiance area, intending to work and support her family.[79] By June 1946, she was living in a dormitory and working as a laundress at the Navajo Medical Center in Fort Defiance.[80] Establishing herself and her child, however, proved untenable. One of Faribault's descendants later surmised that the community at Fort Defiance "didn't accept her and the baby. She realized she wouldn't have a good life for her or the baby."[81] Extant letters depict the significant stress Winona Faribault experienced as she considered her present and her future.

Seeking to find stability and support for her child, Cora Winona Faribault returned to the Phoenix Florence Crittenton Home in the fall of 1946. Standard protocols would have prevented her from an extended stay. Despondent, the young mother approached Social Services.[82] As was increasingly common at the time, the Social Services adviser advocated placing her American Indian child into a white adoptive family.[83] The boy's mother, like most women in similar situations at the time, was encouraged also to consent to a closed adoption, meaning that the birth parents' names would remain confidential and sealed.[84] As a procedural matter, the social worker would have insisted on an alleged or actual father's name. Cora Winona Faribault may have tried to adapt to these pressures, including the reality of relinquishing her one-year-old, by claiming a particular patrilineage for the boy. Faribault's son was recorded with a Diné last name but an anonymous father.[85] As decisions about David's future increasingly were made by others, Cora Winona's place in his story became obscured.[86] Her decision to leave Arizona for the Los Angeles area not long after likely was shaped in part by the cumulative losses in Fort Defiance, Window Rock, and Phoenix.[87]

The white couple from Scottsdale who eventually adopted David—Edward and Myrtie Abrahams—never met the woman who appeared only as "Winona Faribault" in the court record. The Abrahams probably had been told that the child was part Indian and his documented last name gestured to a Diné father.[88] They likely concluded that his mother was white.[89] David's Dakota relatives still are unsure how much he knew about their shared ancestry. As with many adopted children, David expressed a spectrum of feelings about his birth family.[90] At times, he declined opportunities to learn more about his roots and his adoption, but on other occasions, he expressed interest in knowing more about his heritage. According to his childhood friend Steve Roth, David had looked for his father, whom he believed was Native American, "but the court records were sealed."[91] As an adult, David became a volunteer with Navajo Nation, his older brother Edward Abrahams later explained, because "he was dedicated to helping others find their way and maybe come to know a world they did not understand nor how to cope with its complexities."[92] It remains unknown whether David tried to find his birth mother, or how much he even remembered about her.[93]

Those who knew Cora Winona Faribault described the deep mix of grief and curiosity about her son that continued to wash over her.[94] Her eldest daughter recounted, "It was very hard on her to give up the boy. . . . She was brokenhearted from the loss."[95] Perhaps hoping that her firstborn had joined the military—as so many of her high school classmates had—she repeatedly visited the Long Beach Naval Shipyard, scanning faces for signs of recognition.[96] An in-person reunion was never realized in her lifetime. Cora Winona Faribault died in Los Angeles in 1964.[97]

David's other siblings—Cora Winona's younger children—mostly grew up unaware that their mother had another son. Echoing their Uncle Solomon and own mother a generation earlier, Caroline Jean Kiger-StClair and Faith O'Neil began looking for the older brother listed in Sisseton rolls as "David Faribault." "I had the feeling that he was alive," O'Neil remembered, but "I didn't know anything about him."[98]

With the help of a professional investigator, Cora Winona's younger children eventually found news of their sibling. The discovery was bittersweet. David, they learned, had died of cancer a few years earlier.[99] Turning and returning to the inherited memories of Cora Winona and David stirs continued feelings of regret, hope, and wonderment in the family. Faith O'Neil began

Cora Winona Faribault O'Neil pauses from hanging laundry in her backyard to pose for the camera, ca. 1959. Her geometric-patterned halter dress, black high-heeled mules, and carefully coiffed, short, wavy hair exemplify what her daughter Faith called "an impeccable sense of style." Courtesy of Faith O'Neil.

piecing together her family's story from before Elizabeth's forcible removal to Canton, through Cora's upbringing in orphanages and mission schools, to after her mother's detention at the Crittenton Home. A familiar pattern of recovering and remembering began to surface.

Seated at the kitchen table in the home where Cora Winona had raised her, Faith O'Neil placed her hand on a thick scrapbook. Plastic sleeves surrounded the postcards of locations she had visited while researching family history. On nearby pages, copies of letters to archives, historical societies, and the U.S. military mirrored one another: "I am trying to locate a half-brother who I have never known. His name is 'DAVID FARIBAULT': May 1945." Simply, his sister continued, "That is the only information I have about him."[100] Anticipating bureaucratic barriers, O'Neil had begun adding, "If you cannot release information to me and you are able to contact him in some way please tell him I am his half sister and he may write or call me collect."[101] Reaching for family, she asserted her claim: "We have the same mother." Cora Winona's daughter turned the scrapbook pages.

Tucked alongside allotment maps and copies of her mother's handwritten letters are photographs that O'Neil, pausing, revisited slowly. One of Cora Winona, likely taken in the 1950s, captures her in an impeccable dress, pinning laundry on the clothesline, her high-heeled shoes sinking slightly into the grassy backyard. Another, more haunting black-and-white image shows her seated in front of the house, looking off in the distance.[102] Images of Faith O'Neil as a child, paternal grandparents standing nearby, stare back. Newspaper clippings and photographs of David, found on the Internet, followed. The weight of the scrapbook pulled the contents closer to one another. Still, for O'Neil, the swelling archive remains incomplete.

Chapter 6: **Remembering**

*I think about my grandmother a lot. She was afraid that
nobody would care about her. . . . She probably thought
during her life that nobody would care when she was
gone because she already wasn't valued at Canton. . . .
Her family cared and tried to get her out, but since they
couldn't, she worried that she never mattered, that she
wouldn't matter. . . . I want her to know that I won't ever
forget her. It's more than that: I'll always remember her.
I know she remembers me, too.*
—Faith O'Neil, reflecting on her grandmother,
Elizabeth Alexis Faribault

Stepping from her car, Faith O'Neil breathed deeply, questions trailing after
her. Flanked by her friends Lucy Smego and Manfred Hill, she climbed
the steps leading up and into the Craftsman bungalow that had housed
Superintendent Hummer and his family during his tenure at Canton Asylum.[1] Elizabeth Faribault's granddaughter paused in the living room, remembering her ancestor tending to an elderly Levi Hummer. O'Neil thought of her
grandmother cleaning these floors and laundering the family's belongings
up until her own child—Cora Winona (Faith's mother)—was born. Tracing
her grandmother's footsteps, Faith O'Neil searched for signs of Elizabeth
Faribault and answers to her own questions.

As she approached the stairs to the basement, O'Neil was overcome.
Fear, grief, and longing wailed forth. She wept. "Grandma if you're with me
please talk to me," Faribault's granddaughter pleaded, "I've come a long
way to look for you again."[2] A question followed her gaze down the stairway:
what had happened to Elizabeth here? She already knew part of the answer—
"Something awful."[3] Past and present blurred as she sought to reconstruct
moments from her grandmother's time within this house. Moments when
the superintendent would have been alone with her. Moments that Elizabeth
Faribault's descendant feared and needed to remember.

The years of Harry Hummer's proximity to Elizabeth Faribault, his knowledge of her, and his claims on her and on her behalf outraged her descendant. "There isn't a word in English yet that is awful enough to describe
him and what he did," O'Neil asserted.[4] "I think you used my grandmother
like a slave and kept her from her own family and her own people," she

yelled out loud, hoping her message would carry to the late superintendent. She persisted, anger mounting. "Her name was *Elizabeth Alexis Faribault*. And I believe you got my grandmother."[5] O'Neil's voice strained while naming trauma her ancestor endured, "She wanted so much to get back to her family."[6] Supported by the BIA, Dr. Hummer always blocked the way. Faith O'Neil has continued to hold Hummer responsible for Elizabeth Faribault's death. She holds him responsible for the trajectory of her family's story, for her mother Cora's birth. The visit to Canton, like other rememberings, has brought hurt and continued questions.

Back in her home in California, Faith O'Neil picked up a black-and-white photograph from the 1920s. The mother and daughter stand in the foreground on what appears to be a late spring day. A portion of a water tower rises up in the background, brick buildings flanking it. Elizabeth Faribault stands erect, her right arm at her side. Her bobbed haircut shadows part of her face. Her expression appears both intense and obscured: is she angry, exhausted, resigned? Young Cora Winona holds firmly to her mother's left hand. A bonnet covers most of her hair, save for a small lock sweeping down the center of her forehead. A buttoned coat covers most of her white shirt and white stockings. The toddler looks back directly at the camera, unsmiling.[7]

Faith O'Neil returned the gaze. Murmuring that Cora—her parent—"had her mother's arms; they both have such long arms," the Faribault descendant nodded approvingly.[8] The "cynical look" on the elder Faribault's face pulled O'Neil back to the moment on film. Thinking about the hostile environment of the locked wards, she noted that her grandmother "took care of my mother when she was a baby. She was very attentive to my mother."[9] Looking at her grandmother and mother, Faith O'Neil wondered who had stood behind the camera. She wanted to know too: How did her two institutionalized family members experience all of their moments together before and since the shutter had clicked?

O'Neil placed the photo back on the table. Her decision to shield the photograph from public view reflects an intentional act of honoring. Recognizing how few choices Elizabeth Faribault could make independently while incarcerated at Canton, her granddaughter has insisted that the image remain private. Each morning and evening, O'Neil looks upon the picture and remembers all her ancestors. She thanks Nellie Kampeska for helping sustain her grandmother during their shared detention. "Lizzie Red Owl," O'Neil acknowledged, "brought my mother up for . . . the remaining time she was at Canton."[10] Some of the kin relations remain cloudy. Fathers. Grandfathers. The people inhabiting her family story, as Faith O'Neil has experienced them, create a complicated web of relationships—imposed, contested, contradictory, missing, treasured, yearned for, and imagined. For her and many others for whom institutionalization is a cross-generational lived history, there is no full account or a full accounting.[11] "It makes me wonder how many relatives I have living around me that I don't even know about," O'Neil has said matter-of-factly.[12]

An array of Faribault family keepsakes surround the vintage photograph, including a copy of Elizabeth's 1922 letter to relative David Mazakute. Faith O'Neil has memorized one of the lines—"is ci koda tuwena waamiciyataninsni"—and its English translation.[13] "You said that nobody ever thought about you or cared about you," O'Neil said to the letter, to her grandmother.[14] She has read Faribault's handwriting, the letter's contents, and the stories between the lines as a kind of remembering into the future. Elizabeth's granddaughter answered back, her own voice, presence, and searches countering the erasure Canton Asylum inflicted on them both. "We won't forget you," O'Neil assured her ancestor, "we're trying to make things better for you."[15] She has often wondered what loved ones called her grandmother during her lifetime. In the silence wrought by institutionalization, O'Neil has offered a new Dakota name: Mićaŋté ("my heart").[16] Smiling at Elizabeth, at the belonging between them, O'Neil affirmed, "I am so happy to be your granddaughter."[17]

Faith O'Neil has continued to seek Faribault family history—her history. As she described it, the search for kin and memories of them has been both "intense" and "incomplete." "I went looking for David," his sister explained, "and I found out about Grandma. Elizabeth."[18] Remembering for this family has pulled to many places: the Sisseton Reservation, Canton, Fort Defiance, a scattering of marked and unmarked gravesites. Searching for her grandmother's remains, trying to find out what happened to her at Canton and how she died, has continued to infuse O'Neil's life. "She's always with me in spirit," O'Neil said, her eyes flashing as she nodded. "I'll never quit searching."[19]

Many descendants have shared the reality of living with unanswered and unanswerable questions, and, even so, they have continued seeking. Faribault's kin looked for connections to their ancestors beyond the walled perimeters of Canton Asylum and state and national archives. For others, including the family of O-Zoush-Quah, many of the stories were close to home.

———

Jack Jensen (Prairie Band Potawatomi) stood at a distance, taking in the landscape of calico fabric and embroidered names of his kin on the quilt.

Surrounding sky blue medallions, small pink and peach daisies unfurl alongside other plants in burnt yellow, bright red, and soft green. Names and patterned petals spread across the squares like a family garden. Some call the quilt pattern Dresden Plate, but a slightly older name seems more apt: Grandmother's Sunburst.[20] Caught like a cotton skyscape in midmovement, the four-foot-by-six-foot span of swirling colors and names appears animated, like planets rotating, orbiting one another, continuing beyond the fabric edges of their universe.

The family quilt's story extends far beyond the current edges too. Like many Native American women who came of age in the late nineteenth century, Jensen's great-grandmother O-Zoush-Quah had honed her beading and sewing skills under the watchful gaze of her female elders, their craftsmanship and stories intermingling with her own.[21] In subsequent decades, O-Zoush-Quah's own daughters likely swayed in baby hammocks made from their relatives' piecework.[22] As the girls grew up, they would watch their mother transform scraps of fabric into new shapes, absorbing lessons about family and quilting.[23]

Shortly after the BIA forcibly removed O-Zoush-Quah to Canton in 1908, her daughters drew on these memories to sustain themselves and to support their mother. On behalf of the family, Shack-To-Quah (Nettie Hale Tork) wrote to the Canton staff, registering their desire for O-Zoush-Quah's return. Explaining that "of late years she's not worked on beads, but did piece quilts," her children asked that she be given supplies to do patchwork as a means of passing the infinite time and loneliness of her detention.[24] In letters referenced but not preserved, O-Zoush-Quah's daughters may have explicitly conveyed, too, that they wanted her quilt pieces sent to them. It is likely that the Potawatomi elder intuitively knew this to be true. Daughter Pah-Kish-Ko-Quah kept her mother's hand-sewn sunbursts all of the years of her exile.[25]

At her home on the Potawatomi Reservation, Pah-Kish-Ko-Quah created additional quilt squares. Filling hours marked by fabric strips, worn scissors, thread, and imagination, Mary Hale Jensen—as she was known to many of her neighbors—rounded out additional medallions and petals, penciling names of family members on the backs of flour sacks before stitching them on the top layer.[26] In all likelihood, she began with her mother's English name—Maggie Hale—adding herself and her siblings around the central plate. Fingers running across cloth and thread, the mother and daughter left traces for others to find and follow generations later.

For O-Zoush-Quah's descendants, the quilt is a storyteller, an archive, medicine.[27] As Jack Jensen explained, imagining is an act of healing. In her hands, the institutionalized Potawatomi woman grew a quilt that could cloak or hold her children, her grandchildren, her great-grandchildren, and beyond. Jensen imagined his grandmother Mary visiting with the quilt pieces, layering them in a cardboard box in the 1920s, imagined her son Francis quietly looking at the family portrait of O-Zoush-Quah that hung on the living room wall.[28] He wondered: Did Mary resist sewing the squares together as she waited, hoping that her mother would still return to assist in this final assembling? After both women had died (O-Zoush-Quah in 1943, Pah-Kish-Ko-Quah in 1968), the box remained untouched for nearly five decades. Jensen could picture the quilt squares passing down from attics to younger hands until the fall of 2017, when he inherited them.[29]

Looking at the contents of the box spread across the dining room table and considering the possibility of assembling different patterns brought him back to haunting questions. Like his father, Francis, Jack Jensen had long wondered about O-Zoush-Quah, "what she had done to be taken away."[30] An awareness of the violence common within asylums troubled him as well. What had she endured? From his ancestor's vantage point, institutionalization had meant something completely different than the archival reports Jensen had read.[31] He realized that his elders never forgot the Potawatomi healer and never accepted that the U.S. government knew better than they what was best and right. O-Zoush-Quah's present absence shifted, her challenges to asylum staff and locked wards becoming legible everyday acts of defiance, refusal.[32] Nodding at the revelation, Jensen stated plainly, "the problem was never the person—O-Zoush-Quah—or being Potawatomi."[33] In the name of Western medicine and care, he recognized, the BIA had taken O-Zoush-Quah away from her family and tribe.

Like his great-grandmother before him, Jack Jensen was drawn to work as a healer. For most of his adult life, he pursued a career in orthopedic surgery away from Potawatomi lands, people, and traditions. Returning to Indigenous practices as an older adult created new spaces to address cross-generational wounds. Jensen's father, Francis, had shared with his eldest son O-Zoush-Quah's healing eagle feathers. The plumes—dark tips and dappled vanes—fanned outward; soft leather strands wrapping the quills draped downward, swaying gently in Jensen's hand. In a vision quest, his connection with his great-grandmother strengthened. She welcomed him, claimed him, and remembered him.[34] Since then, Jensen has continued to meet O-Zoush-Quah in dreams, in stories, in family photographs, and in her healing feathers that he stewards now. Through remembering, Jensen has remained engaged in a healing process that includes his ancestors past and others yet to come.[35]

The choice to compose a full quilt from the inherited pieces extended this family's story. A half-sunburst anchoring the top portion of the quilt now explicitly names the ancestor around whom the patchwork has grown: orange needlepointing spells out "O-Zoush-Quah." Rising from the bottom hem, a half-sunburst answers, completing the circle pattern. In pink embroidery, "Pah-Kish-Ko-Quah" / "Mary Hale Jensen" is honored.[36] The threaded tributes and their placement in the design tie O-Zoush-Quah closely to her family, countering what years of institutionalization had wrought. Incorporated into one of the medallions, Jensen also had added "Bodewadmi" as well as its English translation, "Keepers of the Fire." Explicitly connecting ancestors with the name Potawatomi call themselves, the assembled quilt expands, telling new stories within older ones.[37]

Ellen Lofland and Jack Jensen exhibit the brightly colored piecework made by Jensen's ancestors and assembled into a quilt by Lofland. Photograph taken by Alexanderportraits.com, 2019. Courtesy of Jack Jensen.

On a fall weekend in 2019, Jack Jensen invited others to join him in celebrating the quilt and its story. He displayed what he has called the "ancestry project" at his ranch outside of Houston, an invitation to seek connections with sacred spaces, dreams, ancestors, and history.[38] As with many ceremonies honoring Indigenous relations, stories join people across families, communities, generations, and nations.

———

Thirty years earlier and hundreds of miles away, Lakota activist-journalist Harold Iron Shield, hand outstretched, welcomed other ceremony attendees.[39] Familiar faces nodded their recognition or smiled invitations to newcomers. The group then turned, walking slowly toward the unmarked graves.[40] An inscription on a modest bronze plaque nearby registered 120 names of American Indians buried in the Canton Asylum cemetery.[41] Iron Shield and the others began to pray. Many people shared stories. Elders recalled spiritual men and women they had known who were exiled to the Asylum's locked wards, individuals who never returned. Some offered memories passed down to them about young people being taken away to the Indian Asylum. Others remembered teachers at boarding schools wielding the specter of Canton in the face of resistant children.[42] Seeking to restore "a spiritual connection to our relatives who died," the journalist from Standing Rock and the others who had joined him affirmed, "These ancestors know they are not forgotten, that their memories are cherished and held up, that what happened to them will no longer be hidden from view."[43] Surrounding the cemetery, manicured hills and putting greens reflected the afterlife of the Indian Asylum: in 1948, the town converted the property into the Hiawatha Golf Course.[44] Over the two decades that Iron Shield coordinated ceremonies—from 1987 until 2007—on the former campus of the Asylum, Native kin from across the United States, along with their supporters, gathered to remember the people buried between the fourth and fifth holes.

For many kin, this kind of remembering is a returning—to stories, to people, and to places that hold both. Some descendants have described their first visit to the Asylum grounds as "a return." They followed the traces of their ancestors' lives and presence at Canton, threads that tie them also to this site. It is a fraught reunion.

As many family members have experienced it, the Indian Asylum was "more of a prison atmosphere for Indian people who resisted living on the reservation," a place "erected to imprison spiritual leaders and students of government boarding schools who did not conform to government policies of the early 1900's."[45] In Canton Asylum, one relative asserted, the BIA had "a place to send their troublemakers, and cemented their omnipotent power over our Nations."[46] It followed a familiar pattern: "This is a classic example of what the government did to Indians," Harold Iron Shield remarked.[47] Kin mourned that "many of those who are incarcerated suffered from beatings, sexual abuse and inhumane conditions."[48] Standing on the site where her Mandan, Hidatsa, and Arikara Nation ancestors had been forcibly detained, Pemina Yellow Bird imagined them crossing the threshold into the Main Building. "They must have been frightened, deeply traumatized, at finding themselves locked up in such a cold, hateful and foreign place, so far from home and family."[49] Looking across the graves and noting that "a lot of people from different tribes are buried here," Ivan Looking Horse (Cheyenne River Sioux Tribe) added, "A lot of them died horrible deaths."[50] Story by story, the legacy of institutionalization at Canton extended beyond tribal and temporal boundaries, cascading into the present day. As Iron Shield explained at the tenth annual ceremony he facilitated, "Many of the family members still are living in pain and grief over this unjust situation."[51]

Standing on the former asylum grounds, Harold Iron Shield (second from left) addresses a group in 1998 about Native people's lived experiences there. Through educational events such as this, honoring ceremonies, and his many newspaper articles, the activist-journalist sought to reaffirm "a spiritual connection to our relatives who died" at the Canton Asylum. For Iron Shield and others, reclaiming the cemetery has remained an active expression of Native self-determination. Photograph by Lloyd Cunningham. Courtesy of the Argus Leader. *Relatives of Harold Iron Shield granted permission for use of this image.*

When repatriation and psychiatric survivor activist Pemina Yellow Bird accepted Iron Shield's invitation to attend an honoring ceremony in 2000, she carried with her ties to broader social movements and overlapping communities targeted by settler interventions.[52] Cemeteries like Canton's, Yellow Bird claimed, laid bare the damaging impact of wide-ranging U.S. institutions, including those that specifically targeted American Indians (such as boarding schools and orphanages) as well as psychiatric hospitals in whose walled campuses Native and non-Native people had long struggled and often perished.[53] The human rights advocate from Fort Berthold recognized the Indian Asylum's unmarked gravesites surrounded by a golf course as the material and symbolic process of elimination and replacement. Yellow Bird's collaborator Pat Deegan, a national leader in state hospital cemetery restoration and reclamation work, similarly viewed the harms perpetuated by institutionalization at Canton as distinctive but also familiar. She joined her colleague at the ceremony in support of the "collective recovery as devalued people."[54] For Pemina Yellow Bird, a commitment to Native self-determination guides the path forward. "We must then *tell* our stories of loss, of violation, of what happened to us, and we must at long last grieve those things; we must determine how the past informs us, is part of who we are, and how it walks with us every day of our lives as Native people." She added pointedly, "We must determine for ourselves, based on our own original teachings and instructions, what we must do to care for ourselves."[55]

As a living process, rituals commemorating the people institutionalized at Canton continue to take different forms. Organized walks, drumming and prayers, and visits by Native nations delegations have marked important kinship connections over the years.[56] In the wake of Harold Iron Shield's death in 2008, others have planned gatherings in small and large scale. For several years, Lavanah Judah, whose relatives were confined at both Canton Asylum and St. Elizabeths Hospital, coordinated ceremonies at the South Dakota cemetery.[57] Reaching across differences and trying to build strong and enduring cross-tribal ties has been at times, according to the Yankton advocate, "painful, hard work."[58] As Judah and others acknowledge, the honoring events have not included everyone with shared Indigenous connections to the Indian Asylum.[59] As is often the case with social movement efforts, organizing remains a work in progress. Still, observances honoring the hundreds of people involuntarily committed to Canton and the thousands more impacted by institutionalization have provided focal points to fortify community relations that had been frayed or broken. For American Indian historians Kay

Davis and Anne Gregory, who met at one of the Canton gatherings, practices of remembering have generated new kinship ties as well as new ways to understand their Indigenous pasts and possible futures.

Anne Gregory attended the 2013 honoring ceremony in Canton longing to know more about her ancestor, feeling heartbroken by some of what she had already found, and keenly aware that the story was incomplete.[60] She lingered at the gravesite of Emma Gregory, hoping to close the distance that violence, time, and geography had placed between them. Joining others afterward, Anne Gregory was drawn to Kay Davis's map, its vectors of colored threads spreading out from each reservation that had members forcibly institutionalized at the federal asylum. Anne traced a line from Creek Nation to Canton, marking Emma's experience. "My great-great-grandmother, Emma Gregory, is buried in the cemetery," the Oregon relative explained, gesturing toward the area beyond the split-rail fence behind them. Davis smiled knowingly, a quiet invitation. Anne continued, "She has one of the more terrible experiences in Canton." She added, shaking her head, "Emma Gregory was listed in one of the reports for being left in a room with no windows, strapped to a bed for very long periods of time, getting no normal sun or fresh air. She received not just poor care but also neglect."[61] Anne reflected on the revelation of Emma's institutionalization and the rippling ramifications it has had on her own life. They were "echoes that travel through a family over generations when something violent happens."[62]

Kay Davis nodded in recognition and began sharing details gathered during her own genealogical research of Emma Gregory. Discrepancies between their understandings of the Creek woman's past surfaced, and the two moved closer, as if to bridge the historical fissures. Returning to another center on the map, the historian from Nett Lake threaded archival work back to her own family story. Learning as a teenager that her father was an enrolled member of the Bois Forte Chippewa, Davis was drawn to better understand genealogy—her own and her tribe's. She earned a degree in Native American studies and applied that training to tribal-acknowledgment work.[63] The process had honed her skills in the archives; it also underscored the distance between sources generated and preserved by the U.S. government and the lived histories of American Indians.[64] Kay Davis's insights resonated with Anne Gregory, who felt that the conversation united both their individual stories and their broader Indigenous histories. On the grounds where their ancestors had been detained and had perished, a spark passed from elder to younger: Anne Gregory headed back to Oregon to pursue an undergraduate degree in history and Native American studies.[65] "I wanted to do what Kay had done," she later reflected. "I wanted to pursue genealogy and research to empower Native families."[66]

As Anne Gregory and Kay Davis experienced it on that spring day in 2013, remembering is a practice that creates new connections across geographies and generations.[67] In this genealogy of learning, reciprocity, and self-determination, Gregory now claims kinship not only to her Creek ancestor detained at Canton Asylum but also to Harold Iron Shield, Pemina Yellow Bird, Kay Davis, and countless other Indigenous witnesses, survivors, and storytellers. "It's like a circling," she explained in conversation, her voice trailing off.[68] Native ancestors past, present, and emerging fill the quiet.[69] Their active presence attests that the ongoing settler project of erasure and replacement, while profoundly destructive, has not fully succeeded.

Davis, Gregory, and numerous other Indigenous people directly affected by Canton Asylum and institutionalization know that theirs is a story of violence, trauma, and tragedy. It is also necessarily a story of survival, resistance, and transformation, a living process that Anishinaabe scholar-author Gerald Vizenor calls "survivance." He writes, "Survivance is the continuance of stories, not a mere reaction, however pertinent. . . . Survivance stories are renunciations of dominance, detractions, obtrusions, the unbearable sentiments of tragedy, and the legacy of victimry."[70] Many relatives of people incarcerated at the Indian Asylum have described their continued existence as the counterstory to institutionalization's sustained violence. Writing to other Bois Forte Chippewa Tribe members, Davis once detailed her day-to-day practice of survivance through her role as their historian: "So life is busy, doing the work of love, history of our people, and meeting with many of you." Kinship sustained this lifework. "I appreciate your help, your encouragement, and most of all, your desire to maintain the records of our Tribe," she declared.[71]

Gregory's dreamscape ahead has led to the classroom. The entangled history of institutionalization and settler colonialism is an axis along which her teaching of Indigenous North American history travels. "What I usually do . . . is bring to class a postcard that used to get handed out," she explained. The iconic early twentieth-century image has "white scratch-writing on the bottom" identifying the Canton Asylum for Insane Indians.[72] "I introduce it as a physical place, I ground it in the history of the place," Gregory continued, "and then introduce the people and the dynamics."[73] She tells the students about her great-great-grandmother Emma, the world she inhabited in the locked wards, and her unsurprising and horrifying death from tuberculosis.

Connecting history to the present day, Gregory shares the challenges in piecing together her family's story—"the practical implications of genocide."[74] For her, remembering Emma Gregory immediately brings to mind survivance. "I think about this a lot," she noted, her voice picking up tempo. "As a teacher and mentor . . . I end up taking it forward." She paused before adding, "Some days I think it's the only thing you can do."[75]

Epilogue: **Telling**

*Indigenous survival as people is due to centuries of
resistance and storytelling passed through the generations.
. . . This survival is dynamic, not passive. Surviving
genocide, by whatever means, is resistance: non-Indians
must know this in order to more accurately understand the
history of the United States.*
—Roxanne Dunbar-Ortiz, *An Indigenous Peoples History
of the United States*

In the summer of 2016, Faith O'Neil accepted the invitation of Mary Garcia
(Tohono O'odham Nation) to come to Arizona and share her family's story with
Gila River Indian Community leaders. Mentored by Tohono O'odham elders
in traditional healing, Garcia had been collaborating with educators, health
advocates, environmentalists, and Native leaders across the United States to
foster sustainable healing practices for communities harmed by violence.[1] The
two women had met a year earlier, in 2015, at an honoring ceremony at Canton.[2]
Unaccustomed to public speaking, O'Neil expressed concern that she might
disappoint or that she might not be believed.[3] Garcia assured and clarified, noting that Tohono O'odham Nation and Gila River Indian Community members
also had kin forcibly institutionalized at Canton Asylum. Telling stories, teaching others about their lived pasts, was fundamental to promoting community
well-being, Garcia emphasized. "We need this information to identify what
happened to us—to our relations," the traditional singer and healer continued,
"and through those shared events . . . that will support . . . healing efforts."[4]

On a clear day in June, the two women sat waiting before the meeting,
awash in the stories that had carried them there. Feeling Elizabeth Faribault's presence, Garcia began to tell O'Neil: "Your grandmother, Elizabeth,
is standing right near you. She's in a long dress. And she wants you to know
that you are where you need to be." Faith locked eyes with Mary, nodding with
recognition. More words tumbled forth. Garcia later recounted that Elizabeth
Faribault "gave Faith the name 'Shining Star, my Bright Star.'" The Dakota ancestor also reminded her granddaughter of her purpose. "Never ever forget.
. . . You're put together so that you can share and be able to do this, because
it needs to be done."[5] The message echoed in their mutual tears, longing,
and gratitude. Faith O'Neil and Mary Garcia breathed deeply, feeling to their
bones that stories bind them across generations with ancestors.[6]

In this close-up portrait from 2015, Faith O'Neil wears a deerskin dress and dangling rose-beaded earrings, her windblown hair brushing her right shoulder, a resolute expression on her face. For O'Neil, this image captures her commitment to finding her grandmother, Elizabeth Faribault, who was forcibly taken to Canton Asylum in 1915. Courtesy of Faith O'Neil.

A few minutes later, inside a brightly lit meeting room flanked by tables, Garcia introduced O'Neil to the cultural council members.[7] Faith O'Neil began her story. "I told the elders about my mother being born at Canton. My grandmother spending most of her life there," she later recalled. "Someone said that they had relatives there, too," she added. Like her, "They want their loved ones back."[8] As she offered more details about her family and the impact the Indian Asylum had on all of them, O'Neil felt enveloped with memories and feelings. "It's very emotional for me to talk about it to others,"

*Mary Garcia, wearing a bright orange-red dress with black-and-white ribbon trim,
stands in front of a monument in Botachee, Saskatchewan, Canada, 2019.
She visited the Metis Reserve for the Missing and Murdered Women's
Tribute as part of her work supporting sustainable healing practices for
communities harmed by violence. Courtesy of Mary Garcia.*

she explained. Some elders sought guidance on how they could find their ancestors' stories. Others wondered aloud how O'Neil carried the responsibilities inherent in knowing these histories. Faribault's granddaughter nodded
as she described how learning about Elizabeth's life now propels her own
story. Mary Garcia and the others thanked her, explicitly recognizing Faith
O'Neil's story as a gift that contributed to Gila River Indian Community's
own self-determination and healing work. "It's like a healing for me, too, I
believe," Faith O'Neil concluded.[9]

As many people impacted by institutionalization see it, their storytelling is a component of medicine, of regeneration, and of enduring kinship. Narrating these stories—what Mary Garcia also has called "truth-telling"—counters the structures and cycles of violence that settler colonialism maintains. "When I talk to Faith," Garcia added, collective understanding strengthens their insights and their sense of kinship. "She's from that experience" and "still carries that . . . the memories, the effects . . . knowing that these individuals did that to her grandmother, her mother."[10]

Learning more about the people who lived side by side with their kin at the Indian Asylum, descendants frequently report, makes each story bigger than they had been in isolation. In this expanding shared history, heartbreak, recognition, and comfort stitch memories and families tightly together. Recalling her visit to the Canton Asylum cemetery, Mary Garcia remembered the graves of Indigenous healers from many nations and bearing witness to the incarcerated children who still haunted her dreams and visions. She thought of Faith O'Neil and others standing nearby, their pasts and present intertwining. Recognizing the many others tied to this story has reminded Garcia and O'Neil of the humanity denied, claimed, and carried across time and space.

Storytelling by the people whom institutionalization has harmed underscores another truth: the violence of Canton Asylum was *collective* as well as *individual*. "This story is not the only one," Mary Garcia has insisted. The institution's reach then and now is propelled by the ongoing structures of settler colonialism. Other relatives of Canton's institutionalized people have repeated similar refrains: what happened to their kin at the Indian Asylum is inextricably tied to other forms of settler efforts to eliminate Indigenous people, lifeways, and histories, including the widespread abuses and deaths of boarding-school children, missing and murdered Indigenous women and girls, and the disproportionately high rates of incarcerated Native people.[11] Canton Asylum is one point along an arc of Native people's history marked by living and dying and surviving amid settler colonialism. "I want to get people together to realize that it's not just our tribe but it's every single Indigenous person," Mary Garcia explained, her voice rising, "It's all connected."[12]

It is also unfolding. There is ongoing work to name, to heal, and to enable future tellings. This adds urgency to Garcia's truth-telling. As she has understood it, "these stories are kind of a key to everything": to counter erasure, to honor ancestors, to be self-determining people.[13] As many Indigenous elders have underscored, once stories are shared, it is up to the readers and listeners to respond—to feel the stories, grasp them, and allow them to guide us into action.[14] As Pemina Yellow Bird has affirmed, "I, for one, also prayed for the strength and guidance I would need to tell the story . . . tell it again and again, so that our people could empower and heal ourselves through the telling and that we would use the memory . . . as a rallying point."[15] In her dreamscape, and in those of many other descendants, this telling-healing galvanizes Native communities and nations and imagines pathways into Indigenous futures.[16]

NOTES

Abbreviations

BIA	Bureau of Indian Affairs
CA	Canton Asylum for Insane Indians
CCF	Central Classified Files
CPL	Canton Public Library, Canton, SD
KA	Keshena Agency
NARA-CP	National Archives and Records Administration, College Park, MD
NARA-D	National Archives and Records Administration, Denver
NARA-DC	National Archives and Records Administration, Washington, D.C.
NARA-FW	National Archives and Records Administration, Fort Worth
NARA-KC	National Archives and Records Administration, Kansas City, MO
PA	Potawatomi Agency
RCUA	Records of the Consolidated Ute Agency
RG	Record Group
SA	Sisseton Agency
SDSA	South Dakota State Archives

Introduction

1. "Weather," 7.

2. The name of the Office of Indian Affairs changed in 1947 to the Bureau of Indian Affairs. This book will primarily refer to the bureau by its current name. For histories of the BIA, see Kvasnicka and Viola, *Commissioners of Indian Affairs*; and Philp, *John Collier's Crusade for Indian Reform*.

3. E. B. Merritt to Ed. S. Johnson, April 1, 1921, Box 296, SA, 722.1, CCF 1907–39, RG 75, NARA-DC; H. R. Hummer to Commissioner, June 1, 1915, ibid.; E. B. Merritt to Supt. Mossman, May 13, 1915, ibid.; E. B. Merritt to H. R. Hummer, May 13, 1915, ibid.

4. John Noble to Commissioner, November 22, 1916, Box 296, 722.1, SA, CCF 1907–39, RG 75, NARA-DC.

5. John Noble to Commissioner, November 22, 1916.

6. Telegram, Selkirk, clerk in charge, to Commissioner, BIA, May 8, 1915, Box 296, SA, 722.1, CCF 1907–39, RG 75, NARA-DC.

7. Telegram, Supt. Mossman to Commissioner, May 12, 1915, Box 296, SA, 722.1, CCF 1907–39, RG 75, NARA-DC. See also E. B. Merritt to Supt. Mossman, May 10, 1915, ibid.

8. Dr. W. I. Longstreth to E. D. Mossman, December 10, 1915, Box 296, SA, 722.1, CCF 1907–39, RG 75, NARA-DC.

9. E. B. Merritt to Supt. Mossman, May 13, 1915, Box 296, SA, 722.1, CCF 1907–39, RG 75, NARA-DC; E. B. Merritt to H. R. Hummer, May 13, 1915, ibid.; H. R. Hummer to Commissioner, June 1, 1915, ibid.

10. These themes align with what Vine Deloria Jr. (Standing Rock Sioux Tribe) describes as a "bunch"—topics that "are not neat, clean, and clear areas of concern. Rather they are intangible and emotional aspects of American Indian concerns that are not often

reduced to a structural framework with a larger area of policy considerations." Deloria, "Introduction," *American Indian Policy in the Twentieth Century,* 7.

11. "RBC Taylor Emerging Writer Award Leanne Simpson."

12. Riney, "Power and Powerlessness," 44; Putney, "Canton Asylum," 3–4; Middleton, "Supplanting the Medicine Man," 141. For more on histories of carceral architecture, see Spens, *Architecture of Incarceration.*

13. Self-determination takes many forms, and Native American and Indigenous studies scholars have considered wide-ranging examples and dimensions. See, for example, Barker, *Sovereignty Matters;* Chang, "Enclosures of Land and Sovereignty," 108–19; Barker, *Native Acts;* A. Cobb, "Understanding Tribal Sovereignty," 115–32; D. Cobb and Fowler, *Beyond Red Power;* P. Smith and Warrior, *Like a Hurricane;* Champagne, "Self-Determination and Activism among American Indians," 32–35; D. Cobb, *Native Activism in Cold War America;* Kirwan, "'Mind the Gap,'" 42–57; and T. Anderson, Benson, and Flanagan, *Self-Determination.*

14. Wolfe, "Settler Colonialism and the Elimination of the Native," 387–409. See also Kauanui and Wolfe, "Settler Colonialism Then and Now."

15. See, for example, "Christopher Estate Sold to United States for Indian Asylum"; and "Prosperity at Canton," 1.

16. Kelton, *Cherokee Medicine, Colonial Germs;* Cameron, Kelton, and Swedlund, *Beyond Germs;* Ostler, *Plains Sioux and U.S. Colonialism.* See also Yellow Bird, "Wild Indians," accessed December 17, 2014. For a study of cross-generational trauma, resilience, and healing among Diné people, see Goodkind et al., "'We're Still in a Struggle,'" 1019–36.

17. P. Deloria, "From Nation to Neighborhood," 343–82; Chang, "Enclosures of Land and Sovereignty," 108–19; Kauanui and Wolfe, "Settler Colonialism Then and Now"; Fixico, *Termination and Relocation;* V. Deloria and Lytle, *Nations Within;* Ostler, *Plains Sioux and U.S. Colonialism;* Lomawaima, "Federalism," 273. A useful online resource for those interested in coalitional decolonization work is *Unsettling America: Decolonization in Theory and Practice.*

18. As some historians have argued, European colonization and domination in North America contributed directly to the decimation of Native populations. According to one estimate, fewer than 237,200 American Indians were living in the United States by 1900. Thornton, *American Indian Holocaust and Survival,* 42–43, 64. See also Berger, *Long and Terrible Shadow,* 28–29, chap. 3 passim. Estimates of Indigenous populations pre- and post-1492 remain highly contentious. See, for example, Denevan, *Native Population of the Americas in 1492;* and Thornton, "Population History of Native North Americans," 9–50. Federal attacks on Indigenous nations' medical-spiritual autonomy (another site of sovereignty battles) have ranged from disparagement and dismissal to outright legal bans on Indigenous practices. See Goodkind et al., "'We're Still in a Struggle,'" 1033. See also D. Lewis, *Neither Wolf nor Dog.*

19. For more on sovereignty, see Kauanui, "Precarious Positions," 1–27; A. Cobb, "Understanding Tribal Sovereignty," 118 and passim; Barker, *Sovereignty Matters;* Womack, Justice, and Teuton, *Reasoning Together;* V. Deloria and Lytle, *Nations Within;* Mallon, *Decolonizing Native Histories;* Biolsi, "Imagined Geographies"; Kirwan, "'Mind the Gap,'" 42–57; and Churchill, *Struggle for the Land.* For details why settler colonialism is a useful framework to historians, see Hoxie, "Retrieving the Red Continent," 1153–67. For more on

white settler disavowal of Indigenous people and presence and on forms of resistance, see Bergland, *National Uncanny*; Joy Porter, "Progressivism and Native American Self-Expression in the Late Nineteenth and Early Twentieth Century," in Smithers and Newman, *Native Diasporas*, 273–93; and Ramírez, *Colonial Phantoms*.

20. See, for example, L. Smith et al., "Indigenous Knowledge, Methodology, and Mayhem," 131–56; O'Brien, *Firsting and Lasting*; Smithers, *Science, Sexuality, and Race*; and Jacobs, *Generation Removed*. J. Kēhaulani Kauanui draws critical attention to "indigeneity" as a related but distinct concept from "settler colonialism." See Kauanui, "'A Structure, Not an Event'"; and Kauanui, "Tracing Historical Specificity," 257–65.

21. O'Brien, *Firsting and Lasting*; L. Smith, *Decolonizing Methodologies*, 33; Bergland, *National Uncanny*; Simpson and Smith, *Theorizing Native Studies*; Jacobs, *White Mothers to a Dark Race*; Smithers and Newman, *Native Diasporas*; Tuck, "Suspending Damage"; Fixico, "Ethics and Responsibilities in Writing American Indian History," 88–99; Woolford, *This Benevolent Experiment*; Ramírez, *Colonial Phantoms*.

22. See, for example, DeJong, *"If You Knew the Conditions,"* 67; Dilenschneider, "Invitation to Restorative Justice"; Leahy, *They Called It Madness*; Kilpatrick, "Spirit Descending," 92–96; Joinson, *Vanished in Hiawatha*; Young, "Keepers of Canton Native American Asylum Don't Want People to Forget"; and Prucha, *Great Father*, 858. For additional critiques of whiteness as a constructed historical, racial category, see Painter, *History of White People*; Omi and Winant, *Racial Formation in the United States*; Lipsitz, *Possessive Investment in Whiteness*; Feagin, *White Racial Frame*; and Rasmussen et al., *Making and Unmaking of Whiteness*.

23. See, for example, Putney, "Canton Asylum"; Sweet, "Controversial Care"; Leahy, *They Called It Madness*; Dilenschneider, "Invitation to Restorative Justice," 105–28; Joinson, *Vanished in Hiawatha*; and Willis, Dean, and Larsen, "First Mental Hospital for American Indians." Notable exceptions to this include Yellow Bird, "Wild Indians," accessed December 17, 2014; Riney, "Power and Powerlessness"; and Whitt, "False Promises." Jennifer Soule fuses artistry with an analysis of settler violence in her poems "Hiawatha Asylum for Insane Indians" and "How to Get Committed to the Hiawatha Asylum for Insane Indians."

24. Critical disability studies scholar Chris Chapman identifies similar rhetorical patterns and contexts of settler colonialism and ableism in the long reach of Canada's Indian residential schools in "Colonialism, Disability, and Possible Lives."

25. It appears that many materials already were lost not only through poor record keeping but also through the general devaluing of the people who were incarcerated at Canton (and of their families). For more on dynamics of power and archives, see Trouillot, *Silencing the Past*; and Fuentes, *Dispossessed Lives*.

26. I am grateful to Lisa Kahaleole Hall, Eli Clare, Pemina Yellow Bird, Faith O'Neil, Napos, Lavanah Judah, Katherine Ott, Bobby Buchanan, Jessica Cowing, Adria Imada, Caroline Lieffers, Sarah Whitt, Corbett O'Toole, and Regina Kunzel for extended conversations about the ethical aspects of this kind of research. See also Reaume, "Posthumous Exploitation?"; Burch and Richards, "Methodology"; Nielsen and Burch, "Disability History"; Roman et al., "No Time for Nostalgia!," 17–63; and Fuentes, *Dispossessed Lives*.

27. A. Cobb, "Understanding Tribal Sovereignty," 115–32.

28. Dr. Wallace Isaac Longstreth to E. D. Mossman, December 10, 1915, Box 296, SA, 722.1, CCF 1907–39, RG 75, NARA-DC.

29. H. R. Hummer to Commissioner, November 18, 1918, Box 296, SA, 772.1, CCF 1907–39, RG 75, NARA-DC; H. R. Hummer to Commissioner, July 8, 1918, Folder 121232-1916, ibid.; H. R. Hummer to Commissioner, March 20, 1917, ibid.; E. B. Merritt to John S. Noble, December 11, 1916, ibid.; E. B. Merritt to John Noble, November 27, 1916, Box 296, SA, 722.1, CCF 1907–39, RG 75, NARA-DC; E. B. Merritt to Alec Murray, December 27, 1918, Folder 121232-1916, ibid.; H. R. Hummer to Commissioner, January 22, 1927, Box 17, CA, ibid.; E. B. Merritt to Mr. Johnson, April 1, 1921, Box 296, SA, 722.1, ibid.; H. R. Hummer to Commissioner, March 21, 1921, ibid.; H. R. Hummer to Commissioner, September 29, 1921, ibid.

30. Elizabeth Fe Alexis to Commissioner, May 22, 1922, Box 16, CA, CCF 1907–39, RG 75, NARA-DC.

31. Like many disability studies scholars, I use the term "bodymind" to resist simple binaries (i.e., "body vs. mind") and to underscore the interdependence of physical and mental processes. For more on the concept of bodymind, see Kafer, *Feminist, Queer, Crip*; Price, *Mad at School*; Clare, *Brilliant Imperfection*; Schalk, *Bodyminds Reimagined*; and Imada, "A Decolonial Disability Studies?" For more on mad studies and mad activism, see the website *Mad in America*.

32. For more on the history of Western biomedicine and what disability studies scholars often call a "medical model of disability," see Scotch, "Medical Model of Disability"; Clare, *Brilliant Imperfection*; Nielsen, *Disability History of the United States*; Kudlick, "Social History of Medicine and Disability History," 105–24; and Kudlick, "Comment: On the Borderland of Medical and Disability History," 540–59. Disability studies scholar Ellen Samuels offers additional reflections on biocertification and fantasies of human measurements in *Fantasies of Identification*.

33. Anthropologist James B. Waldram offers helpful critiques of non-Native cultural perceptions of Indigenous forms of medicine in his book *Revenge of the Windigo*. See also C. King, "The Good, the Bad, and the Mad," 37–47; Stevenson, *Life Beside Itself*; DeJong, "*If You Knew the Conditions*," 14; Kanani, "Race and Madness"; Trafzer, *Fighting Invisible Enemies*; Arnold, *Imperial Medicine and Indigenous Societies*; P. Allen, *Sacred Hoop*; Walker, DeMallie, and Jahner, *Lakota Belief and Ritual*; Pengra and Godfrey, "Different Boundaries, Different Barriers," 36–53; P. Allen, *Grandmothers of the Light*; LaDuke, *Recovering the Sacred*; and Inglis, "Disease and the 'Other,'" 385–406.

34. Lovern and Locust, *Native American Communities on Health and Disability*, 51; Locust, *American Indian Beliefs Concerning Health and Unwellness*; Johnston, "Native American Traditional and Alternative Medicine," 195–213; P. Allen, *Sacred Hoop*; Gonzales, *Red Medicine*; Mohatt and Eagle Elk, *Price of a Gift*; Crawford O'Brien, *Coming Full Circle*; Senier, "Rehabilitation Reservations"; Koithan and Farrell, "Indigenous Native American Healing Traditions," 477–78; Portman and Garrett, "Native American Healing Traditions," 453–69; P. Allen, *Grandmothers of the Light*; Angel, *Preserving the Sacred*; Pengra, "Lakota Quality of Life."

35. Yellow Bird, "Wild Indians," accessed December 17, 2014; Yellow Bird interview, November 12, 2019; Waldram, *Revenge of the Windigo*; Senier, "Rehabilitation Reservations"; Weaver, "Perspectives on Wellness," 5–17; Whitt, "False Promises"; Gough,

"Colonization and Madness." I also thank Pemina Yellow Bird, Menominee elder Napos (David Turney Sr.), and Rosebud Sioux Tribe archaeologist Ben Rhodd for insights on Indigenous medicines compared to Western psychiatric concepts.

36. Yellow Bird, "Wild Indians," accessed December 17, 2014.

37. Cowing, "Obesity and (Un)fit Homes"; Cowing, "Settler States of Ability." For more on disability justice and critiques of settler ableism, see Sins Invalid, *Skin, Tooth, and Bone*; Mingus, *Leaving Evidence* (blog); Clare, *Brilliant Imperfection*; and T. Lewis, "Ableism 2020."

38. As with other systems of power, ableism emerges and manifests differently across time and places. Scholars and activists also offer expansive definitions and critiques of ableism. See Lieffers, "Imperial Ableism"; T. Lewis, "Ableism 2020"; Michalko and Titchkovsky, *Rethinking Normalcy*, 84, 251–52; Rohrer, "Ableism"; Kafer, *Feminist, Queer, Crip*; Campbell, *Contours of Ableism*; Dolmage, *Academic Ableism*; Scuro, *Addressing Ableism*; Nario-Redmond, *Ableism*; Taylor, *Beasts of Burden*; Schweik, "Disability and the Normal Body"; and Hunt-Kennedy, *Between Fitness and Death*. Environmental historian Traci Voyles's concept of "wastelanding"—"a racial and spatial signifier that renders an environment and the bodies that inhabit it pollutable"—also intersects with settler ableism. Voyles, *Wastelanding*, 9.

39. This is also true of "sanism," commonly defined as systemic discrimination and oppression toward people who are—or are perceived to be—mad, mentally ill, or insane. For more on sanism, see B. Lewis, "Mad Fight"; Wolframe, "Madwoman in the Academy"; and LeFrançois, Beresford, and Russo, "Destination Mad Studies."

40. See, for example, Smithers, "'Pursuits of the Civilized Man,'" 245–72; Whitt, "False Promises"; TallBear, "Dossier: Theorizing Queer Inhumanisms," 230–35; Trafzer and Weiner, *Medicine Ways*. For late-nineteenth-century and twentieth-century examples of settler colonialism and ableism, as well as Native resistance, see C. King, "The Good, the Bad, and the Mad," 38; Schweik, "Disability and the Normal Body"; and Porter, "Progressivism and Native American Self-Expression." Linda Tuhiwai Smith details both the crucial role of counterstories and the influence of settler colonialism on historical practices in *Decolonizing Methodologies*. For more on ableism and foundational ideas in North American history, including competence, normalcy, deviance, and citizenship, see Kafer, *Feminist, Queer, Crip*; Clare, *Exile and Pride*; Michalko and Titchkovsky, *Rethinking Normalcy*; Erevelles, "(Im)Material Citizens"; Nielsen, *Disability History of the United States*; and Rembis, *Defining Deviance*.

41. Portions of this paragraph appear in Burch, "Disorderly Pasts," 362–85.

42. Waldram, *Revenge of the Windigo*; W. Anderson, *Colonial Pathologies*; Kern, "Sugarcane and Lepers," 78–100; Bashford, *Imperial Hygiene*; Tuck, "Suspending Damage"; Lunbeck, *Psychiatric Persuasion*, 122–30; Carocci, "Sodomy, Ambiguity, and Feminization," 73.

43. LeFrançois, Menzies, and Reaume, *Mad Matters*; Cahn, "Border Disorders"; Clare, *Brilliant Imperfection*; Kilty and Dej, *Containing Madness*; Burch and Joyner, *Unspeakable*; Rembis, *Defining Deviance*; Menzies and Palys, "Turbulent Spirits," 149–75; Samuels, *Fantasies of Identification*. See also Metzl, *Protest Psychosis*; B. Lewis, "Mad Fight"; and Lunbeck, *Psychiatric Persuasion*.

44. For a thoughtful reflection on this point, see Goodkind et al., "'We're Still in a Struggle,'" 1022. See also Tuck, "Suspending Damage."

45. For more on collective struggle, trauma, and ableism, see Erevelles, "Thinking with Disability Studies"; and Burch, "Disorderly Pasts." For more on multigenerational kinship, Indigenous self-determination, and settler colonial violence, see Andersen and O'Brien, "Feminism, Gender, and Sexuality," 183–226; Morgensen, "Theorising Gender, Sexuality, and Settler Colonialism," 2–22; Jacobs, *White Mother to a Dark Race*; and de Finney, "Indigenous Girls' Resilience in Settler States," 10–21.

46. Historian Mark Levene has called these forms of slow and sometimes subtler forms of violence "creeping genocide." Levene, "Chittagong Hill Tracts," 339–69. See also Levene, *Genocide in the Age of the Nation State*.

47. H. R. Hummer to Commissioner, September 29, 1926, Box 17, CA, CCF 1907–39, RG 75, NARA-DC.

48. In her study of activism, Indigenous ancestors, and haunting settler colonial spaces, historian Victoria Freeman has explained ancestors' living presence this way: "The relationship between ancestors and descendants could best be described as based on reciprocity, one of the most fundamental Indigenous values, and one that promotes strength and continuance." Freeman, "Indigenous Haunting in Settler Colonial Spaces," in Boyd and Thrush, *Phantom Past, Indigenous Presence*, 232.

49. Barker, *Native Acts*, 224–28; Jacobs, *Generation Removed*, xxxiii; Lesser, "Caddoan Kinship Systems," 260–71; Pickering, *Lakota Culture, World Economy*, 6; Kimmerer, *Braiding Sweetgrass*, 21, 37; Galloway, "'The Chief Who Is Your Father,'" 254–78; Mintz and Kellogg, *Domestic Revolutions*; Child, *Boarding School Seasons*; Hyde, *Empires, Nations, and Families*; Justice, *Our Fire Survives the Storm*; Child, *Holding Our World Together*. Beth Piatote (Nez Perce) further notes: "During assimilation period the Indian family home relations served as the locus of settler-national efforts to diminish or eliminate the tribal-national polity. Policies such as child removal, compulsory boarding school, marriage regulation, and land allotment shattered Indian families and homeland alike." Piatote, *Domestic Subjects*, 173.

50. Other examples include a daughter and mother from the Western Navajo Agency in Tuba City, Arizona; spouses from Crow Creek Sioux Reservation, South Dakota; siblings from the Chippewa Laona Agency in Wisconsin; Cherokee siblings from Union Agency, Muskogee, Oklahoma; and three generations of a Menominee family from Keshena, Wisconsin. For more on the ways that "family" as a heteropatriarchal concept has served settler colonialism both ideologically and materially, see Morgensen, *Spaces between Us*; L. Hall, "Strategies of Erasure," 273–78; and A. Smith, "Queer Studies and Native Studies." See also social theorist Patricia Hill Collins, "It's All in the Family," 62–82.

51. Charles Werner to Commissioner, November 11, 1910, RCUA, 44011, NARA-D. A more detailed explanation of this family's experience appears in chapter 2.

52. Portions of this paragraph appear in Burch, "Disorderly Pasts," 362–85.

53. Record of Marriage for Jesse Faribault and Mary Marlow, October 27, 1919, Registered No. 480, Sisseton, Roberts County, South Dakota Division of Census and Vital Records, Pierre; Marriage Index, 1905–14, and Marriage Certificates, 1905–49, South Dakota Department of Health, Pierre. In the early 1920s, Mary Marlow Faribault tended the home shared with Solomon, Annie, and Howard—Jesse and Elizabeth's children. I thank Joe Rabon for sharing George Leo Marlow's family history.

54. For example, Davis interviews, June 8–10, 2014; handmade map, ca. 2010–14, personal collection of Kay Davis; Gregory interviews, May 9, 2012, February 23, 2015, July 3, 2017, December 28, 2018, July 19, 2019; Gregory family photographs, personal collection of Anne Gregory; J. Jensen interviews, April 22, 23, 2017; October 3–5, 2019; bandolier, ca. 1890s, by O-Zoush-Quah; family quilt, Ancestry Project, ca. 1900–2019, personal collection of Jack Jensen; Faribault family scrapbook, 1960s–2019, personal collection of Faith O'Neil; Marlow family photographs, 1890s–1940s, personal collection of Joe Rabon; Mitchell interview, April 8, 2014; and Garcia telephone interviews, June 30, August 22, November 20, 2015, January 21, July 6, November 1, 2016, September 11, 2019, January 3, 28, 2020. For more on Native cultural innovations as a living tradition, see, for example, Ortiz, "Towards a National Indian Literature"; Wilson, *Remember This!*; Teuton, *Red Land, Red Power*, 24–25 and passim.

55. For more on the powerful role of place in Native American history and culture, see Johnson, "American Indians, Manifest Destiny, and Indian Activism"; Carlson, *The Power of Place, the Problem of Time*; Tuck and McKenzie, *Place in Research*; Lerma, *"Indigeneity and Homeland"*; C. Allen, *Blood Narrative*; and Lyons, *X-Marks*. See also Kaufman, *Place, Race, and Story*.

56. K. Tsianina Lomawaima describes these kinds of insights and historical sources as "the gifts." Lomawaima, *"To Remain an Indian,"* 12. Historian Ava Chamberlain describes some of this methodology as an "indirect approach" that "shifts from an overemphasis on individuals to people inhabiting authentic relationships within families." Chamberlain, *Notorious Elizabeth Tuttle*, 2–3. See also Stevenson, *Life Beside Itself*; Boyd and Thrush, *Phantom Past, Indigenous Presence*, 230; Carlson, *The Power of Place, the Problem of Time*, 112; and Burghardt, *Broken*.

57. For more on the concept of "present absence," see Morrison, "Unspeakable Things Unspoken," 123–63; Gordon, *Ghostly Matters*; Shanley, "Talking to the Animals," 32–45. Scholars often cite Shanley's use of present absence from her presentation "Indigenous Intellectual Sovereignties: A Hemispheric Convocation," delivered at a conference at the University of California, Davis, April 8–10, 1998.

58. See, for example, Vizenor, *Manifest Manners*; Vizenor, "Aesthetics of Survivance: Literary Theory and Practice," in *Survivance*.

59. Vizenor, *Manifest Manners*, vii.

60. See, for example, Justice, "Go Away, Water!," 147–68; J. Miller, "Kinship, Family Kindreds, and Community," 139–51; Jacobs, *Generation Removed*. Mark Rifkin provides insights into the inherent limits of kinship frameworks within a settler context. See Rifkin, *When Did Indians Become Straight?* Anishinaabe writer Basil Johnston details his family's experiences with residential boarding schools, kinship ties, disability, and the power of storytelling in his memoir *Crazy Dave* (1999).

61. Definitions of "kin" include, "the group of persons who are related," and, "one's kindred, kinsfolk, or relatives, collectively." *OED Online*, Oxford University Press, s.v. "kin," accessed September 2014, www.oed.com (subscription required). For demographic histories, see Thornton, *Studying Native America*; and Jacobs, *Generation Removed*.

62. Portions of this paragraph appear also in Burch, "Disorderly Pasts," 362–85.

63. For more on Diné Nation history, see Iverson, *Diné*.

64. *Fourteen Years' Work among "Erring Girls"*; "Home for the Erring," 9; Kunzel, *Fallen Women, Problem Girls*.

65. Abrahams, "Inquiry Answers Re. David Abrahams," June 24, 2017.

66. For more on Indigenous children and adoption, see Jacobs, *Generation Removed*; and Briggs, *Somebody's Children*.

67. This process coincided with interventions by the U.S. government in the lives of other and overlapping groups, such as children and orphans, individuals accused of crimes, disabled persons, and poor people, through what geographer Jake Kosek calls "intimate entanglements"—seemingly disparate places, people, and issues that broad historical forces closely knit together. Kosek, *Understories*.

68. Briggs, *Somebody's Children*; Jacobs, *Generation Removed*; Kunzel, *Fallen Women, Problem Girls*; Holt, *Indian Orphanages*; Adams, *Education for Extinction*; Chang, *Color of the Land*; Jacobs, *White Mothers to a Dark Race*; Haskins, *One Bright Spot*. As American Indian studies scholar Brenda J. Child (Red Lake Ojibwe) and others have shown, spaces of removal and containment, such as reservations, boarding schools, and orphanages, profoundly shaped generations of Native Americans. Child, *Boarding School Seasons*; Biolsi, "Birth of the Reservation," 28–53.

69. For more on the relational dimensions of institutionalization, see Rembis, *Defining Deviance*; Burghardt, *Broken*; Clare, *Brilliant Imperfection*; Carey, *On the Margins of Citizenship*; Hechler, "Diagnoses That Matter"; Parsons, *From Asylum to Prison*.

70. *Lexico*, s.v. "institutionalization," accessed June 2017, https://www.lexico.com/en /definition/institutionalization; *OED Online*, s.v. "institutionalization," accessed September 2014, www.oed.com (subscription required).

71. See, for example, Hernández, *City of Inmates*; Rembis, *Defining Deviance*; Ben-Moshe, Chapman, and Carey, *Disability Incarcerated*; Parsons, *From Asylum to Prison*; Rothman, *Discovery of the Asylum*; Kunzel, *Fallen Women, Problem Girls*; Nielsen, *Disability History of the United States*; Burch and Joyner, *Unspeakable*; Christianson, *With Liberty for Some*; Leong and Carpio, "Carceral States," vii–xviii; Rothman, *Conscience and Convenience*; Porter and Wright, Confinement of the Insane; Lasch, *World of Nations*; Szasz, *Manufacture of Madness*; Appleman, "Deviancy, Dependency, and Disability," 417–78; Herman, *Kinship by Design*; Burghardt, *Broken*; Willie, Kramer, and Brown, Racism and Mental Health; Child, *Boarding School Seasons*; Holt, *Indian Orphanages*; Adams, *Education for Extinction*; Chang, *Color of the Land*; Jacobs, *White Mothers to a Dark Race*; D. K. Miller, "Spider's Web," 385–408; and Haskins, *One Bright Spot*.

72. Leong and Carpio, "Carceral States," vii–xviii; Perreira, "Unsettling Archives," 327–34; Hernández, *City of Inmates*; Mendoza, "Caging Out, Caging In," 86–109.

73. Rembis, *Defining Deviance*; Ben-Moshe, Chapman, and Carey, *Disability Incarcerated*; Parsons, *From Asylum to Prison*; Burch and Joyner, *Unspeakable*; Jarman, "Coming up from Underground," 9–29. In many ways, this disability studies–anchored interpretation complements and expands what historian Douglas K. Miller has coined "settler custodialism." Miller, "Spider's Web," 388.

74. *English Oxford Living Dictionaries*, s.v. "Institutionalization." See also *OED Online*, Oxford University Press, s.v. "institutionalize," accessed June 2017, www.oed.com (subscription required); and Yellow Bird, "Wild Indians," accessed December 17, 2014.

75. For example, James Herman, "Statement on Treatment of Patients at Canton Insane Asylum," received June 17, 1915, Box 5, CA, CCF 1907–39, RG 75, NARA-DC, 3; Susan Wishecoby to H. R. Hummer, June 14, 1925, Box 17, ibid.; letter, Peter Thomson Good Boy, trans. John Brown, February 19, 1917, Box 9, CA: Individual Patient Files, 1914–16, Decimal 414-580, Program Mission Correspondence, 1914–34, RG75, NARA-KC. I thank Mary G. Vickmark for her assistance in researching her relative Susan Wishecoby.

76. See, for example, Goffman, "Characteristics of Total Institutions"; and Goffman, *Asylums.*

77. See, for example, Reaume, "Mad People's History," 170–82; Rembis, *Defining Deviance*; Braslow, *Mental Ills and Bodily Cures*; McCandless, *Moonlight, Magnolias, and Madness*; Lunbeck, *Psychiatric Persuasion*; Grob, *The Mad among Us*; Deutsch, *Mentally Ill in America*; Jimenez, *Changing Faces of Madness*; Lasch, *World of Nations*, 7–12; Stiker, *History of Disability*; and Burch and Joyner, *Unspeakable.*

78. See, for example, Parsons, *From Asylum to Prison*; Jacobs, *Generation Removed*; Grob, "Public Policy and Mental Illnesses," 425–56; Stern, *Eugenic Nation*; and Michael Rembis, "The New Asylums: Madness and Mass Incarceration in the Neoliberal Era," in Ben-Moshe, Chapman, and Carey, *Disability Incarcerated*, 139–59.

79. Daniel M. Cobb insightfully critiques memorialization and reclaiming in the past in "'The Remembered/Forgotten' on Native Ground," in Cobb and Sheumaker, *Memory Matters*, 19–27.

80. Anthropologist Guillermo Delgado-P offers "re-membering" as a process of recovering, coalition, Indigenous self-determination, and decolonization. Delgado-P, "Makings of a Transnational Movement," 36–38.

81. Faith O'Neil, commentary to "Institutional Racism: American Indians, Asylums, and Dislocated Histories, 1900–2012," UCLA Disability Studies Program event, April 2015; O'Neil interviews, March 6, June 25–26, 2012, March 12, October 29, November 11, 24, 2014, April 6–7, 2015, March 8, 2016, March 29, 2019; Richards and Burch, "Dreamscapes for Public Disability History"; Yellow Bird interviews, October 14, 2013, March 8, 2015, July 22, 2019; Gregory interviews, May 9, 2012, February 23, 2015, July 3, 2017, December 28, 2018, July 19, 2019; J. Jensen interviews, April 22, 23, 2017; J. Jensen telephone conversations, February 17, 2017; Napos interviews, July 18–19, 2015; Napos telephone interviews, June 16, July 5, 16, October 25, 2015, January 6, February 23, March 6, 13, December 18, 2016, May 5, 2017; BigFoot telephone interview, April 29, 2014; Rhodd conversations, August 17, 2017, November 9, 2019.

82. Lomawaima, *"To Remain an Indian,"* 15.

83. *OED Online*, s.v. "disorder," accessed September 5, 2018, www.oed.com (subscription required). See also *Merriam-Webster*, s.v. "d isorder," accessed September 5, 2018, https://www.merriam-webster.com/dictionary/disorder.

84. O'Brien, *Firsting and Lasting*; Kelman, *Misplaced Massacre*; Lomawaima, *"To Remain an Indian."*

Chapter 1

1. The author thanks Kay Davis for extended conversations about the map. After she walked on in December 2017, her family shared the photos of Kay and the map and granted permission for them to be included in this book.

2. Davis interviews, June 8–10, 2014; Davis email correspondence, May 20, 2013–June 17, 2015.

3. Davis interviews, June 8–10, 2014; Davis, Oral History Interview Information Sheet, July 7, 2017; Davis email correspondence, May 20, 2013–June 17, 2015; Dexter interview, April 5, 2017. Using a wide range of archival and nonarchival materials, I created a database of figures, trends, and timelines, among other information, related to the Canton Asylum. Some facts in this paragraph come from that database, hereafter cited as Burch, digital database.

4. Davis interviews, June 8–10, 2014; Davis, Oral History Interview Information Sheet, July 7, 2017; Davis email correspondence, May 20, 2013–June 17, 2015.

5. Davis interviews, June 8–10, 2014; Davis, Oral History Interview Information Sheet, July 7, 2017.

6. Driskill, "Introduction," in *Asegi Stories*, 3. See also Mahuika, "Re-storying Māori Legal Histories"; and Achebe, *Home and Exile*, 79.

7. For more on broad historical studies of settler violence and genocide, see Hixson, *American Settler Colonialism*; Ostler, "'Just and Lawful War,'" 1–20; and Dunbar-Ortiz, "Introduction," in *Indigenous Peoples' History of the United States*, 1–14.

8. White strands from other Great Sioux Nation reservation lands overlap this threaded trajectory, fanning out across the Great Plains and the map's borders.

9. I thank Tamara St. John, Dianne Desrosiers, and the Sisseton Tribal Historic Preservation Office for their assistance with research on Alexis, Faribault, and Sisseton-Wahpeton Oyate history.

10. Related government documents suggest she was born there as early as 1857. U.S. Census rolls place Mary Alexis in Minnesota prior to 1862. See, for example, Twelfth Census of the United States, 1900, RG 29, NARA-DC, Lawrence (town), Roberts (county), South Dakota, Roll 1554, p. 1B, Enumeration District 0284, microfilm #T623, 1854 rolls; Mary Alexis, SA, 1922, Indian Census Rolls, RG 75, NARA-DC, M595, Roll 511, line 5, microfilm; Mary Alexis, SA, 1899, ibid., Roll 508, p. 1, line 14; Mary Alexis, SA, 1913, ibid., Roll 509, line 5. Manzakoyakesuim had a son, Henry, born in 1886, but he did not survive. Alexis family, SA, 1888, ibid., Roll 507, lines 1–4. The family was in Spirit Lake (also known as Devils Lake), Dakota Territory, in 1889. Zihkanakoyake and Manzakoyakesuim, Devils Lake Agency, 1889, Indian Census Rolls, RG 75, NARA-DC, M595, Roll 94, p. 39, microfilm. For more on histories of the Great Sioux Nation, see Ostler, *Plains Sioux and U.S. Colonialism*; Utley, *Last Days of the Sioux Nation*; and Nurge, *Modern Sioux*.

11. The couple had parted ways. Zihkanakoyake remained at Spirit Lake. Manzakoyakesuim moved to and remained at the Sisseton Reservation.

12. Devens, "'If We Get the Girls, We Get the Race,'" 160. Oneroad and Skinner also affirm that the Dakota language was the primary means of communication on the reservation in the nineteenth century. See Oneroad and Skinner, *Being Dakota*, 11.

13. See Devens, "'If We Get the Girls, We Get the Race,'" 165; Hansen, *Encounter on the Great Plains*; Hyman, *Dakota Women's Work*; Young Bear and Theisz, *Standing in the Light*; Rhodd conversations, August 17, 2017, November 9, 2019. One enrollment list from 1900 suggests that seventeen-year-old Elizabeth had married a Sioux man from Manitoba, Edward Walkingcloud, and that the couple was living with her siblings and mother. Twelfth Census of the United States, 1900, RG 29, NARA-DC, Lawrence (town),

Roberts (county), SD, Roll 1554, p. 1B, Enumeration District 0284, microfilm #T623, 1854 rolls. Descendants of the people referred to in U.S. documents as Mary Alexis and Elizabeth Faribault know few details about the women's immediate kin before the mid-1800s, and the fragmentary sources they possess primarily reflect white settlers' interpretations rather than Dakota people's.

14. Historian Christina Snyder describes ways that names marked different chapters in peoples' lives and the infiltration across the nineteenth century of European-derived names. Snyder, *Great Crossings*, 70, 78. See also Young Bear and Theisz, *Standing in the Light*. Historian Karen V. Hansen describes historic debates over settler names for Native people in *Encounter on the Great Plains*, 87–90.

15. Lawson, "Indian Heirship Lands," 217–18. For more on the history of allotments, see Chang, "Enclosures of Land and Sovereignty," 108–19; D. Lewis, *Neither Wolf nor Dog*, 16–19, 53–60, 97–105, 139–41; Chang, *Color of the Land*; Prucha, *Great Father*; Valandra, *Not without Our Consent*, 100–107; Berthrong, "Legacies of the Dawes Act," 31–53; McDonnell, *Dispossession of the American Indian*; Prucha, *American Indian Policy in Crisis*; and Hansen, *Encounter on the Great Plains*, chap. 3. For more on allotment policies, see Churchill, *Struggle for the Land*; and Biolsi, "Birth of the Reservation." For more on Dakota Nation history, see, for example, Gibbon, *The Sioux*; and Westerman and White, *Mni Sota Makoce*.

16. See, for example, Jacobs, *Generation Removed*; Child, *Boarding School Seasons*; Adams, *Education for Extinction*; Archuleta, Child, and Lomawaima, *Away from Home*; Fear-Segal, *White Man's Club*; and Iverson, *Plains Indians of the Twentieth Century*.

17. Devens, "'If We Get the Girls, We Get the Race,'" 160.

18. This was common across the Sisseton Reservation. In 1911, for example, virtually all of the churches on the reservation were ministered by Native clergymen who conducted services almost exclusively in the Dakota language. Meyer, *History of the Santee Sioux*, 322; Sneve, *That They May Have Life*, 31–32.

19. Solomon (b. 1901 or 1902), Stephen (b. 1903), Annie (b. 1904), Howard (b. 1909), and Gilbert (b. 1911). The name of one of the infants who died remains unknown. SA, 1912, Indian Census Rolls, RG 75, NARA-DC, M595, Roll 509, lines 1–6, microfilm; SA, 1911, ibid., line 7; SA, 1910, ibid., line 20; SA, 1913, ibid., lines 16–21. It is unclear how or when the couple lost their son Gilbert, but he likely had died by 1914.

20. Joseph DuBray to L. McCoy, Indian Office, June 15, 1918, Box 296, SA, 722.1, CCF 1907–39, RG 75, NARA-DC.

21. For example, the federal government established the Courts of Indian Offenses in 1883, which especially targeted traditional ceremonies. The 1885 Major Crimes Act granted federal courts jurisdiction "over Indians who commit any of the listed offenses," which profoundly undermined Native self-governance. The Major Crimes Act—18 U.S.C. § 1153.

22. This form of government had been in place since the 1880s, and had longer roots in Dakotah traditions.

23. Across his career as an agent for the BIA, Mossman consistently sought to curtail Indigenous practices. See for example Gooding, "'We Come to You as the Dead,'" 1–14; Troutman, "The 'Dance Evil,'" In *Indian Blues*, 58, 66, 71; D. R. Miller, "Mossman Administration," 233–49.

24. United States Congress, Senate Committee on Indian Affairs: Claims of Sisseton and Wahpeton and Sioux Indians, "Hearing before the Committee on Indian Affairs, United States Senate, Sixty-third Congress, Second session on S. 113."

25. Treuer, *Rez Life*, 77.

26. Comaroff and Comaroff, *The Dialectics of Modernity on a South African Frontier*, 332; Arnold, *Imperial Medicine and Indigenous Societies*; Inglis, "Disease and the 'Other,'" 385–406; Roman et al., "No Time for Nostalgia!," 17–63; Hunt-Kennedy, *Between Fitness and Death*; Waldram, *Revenge of the Windigo*. Maureen Trudelle Schwartz, a scholar of Indigenous people and biomedicine, has added that, "As a result, contemporary medical pluralism everywhere involves hierarchical relations among medical subsystems . . . the aim was for allopathic medicine and Christianity to dominate and replace the indigenous systems." Schwartz, "I Choose Life," 28.

27. Teuton, "Disability in Indigenous North America," 574. See also Gonzales, Kertész, and Tayac, "Eugenics as Indian Removal," 53–67; Kanani, "Race and Madness"; Voyles, *Wastelanding*, 8–10, Bieder, *Science Encounters the Indian*, chap. 3, 153, 162, 208; Schweik, "Disability and the Normal Body"; Frost, *Never One Nation*; Hoxie, *Final Promise*, 127–28, 181–82.

28. See, for example, H. R. Hummer's 1913 essay, "Insanity Among the Indians." Critiques of settler ableist frameworks can be found in Teuton, "Disability in Indigenous North America"; Grech, "Decolonising Eurocentric Disability Studies"; Edney, "Mapping Empires, Mapping Bodies"; Harley, "Deconstructing The Map"; Lieffers, "Imperial Ableism"; Stern, *Eugenic Nation*, 85–86; Leonard, *Illiberal Reformers*; Currel and Cogdell, *Popular Eugenics*; Szasz, *Insanity*.

29. Oneroad and Skinner, *Being Dakota*, 14.

30. Elizabeth Alexis to Commissioner, May 22, 1922, Box 16, CA, CCF 1907–39, RG 75, NARA-DC.

31. See, for example, Burch and Joyner, *Unspeakable*; Ben-Moshe, Chapman, and Carey, *Disability Incarcerated*; Braslow, *Mental Ills and Bodily Cures*; Rossiter and Clarkson, "Opening Ontario's 'Saddest Chapter,'" 1–30; Szasz, *Insanity*, 250–51, 315–17; Grob, *Mental Illness and American Society*.

32. For example, H. R. Hummer to Commissioner, March 20, 1917, Folder 121232-1916, Box 296, SA, 722.1, CCF 1907–39, RG 75, NARA-DC; E. B. Merritt to John S. Noble, December 11, 1916, ibid.; E. B. Merritt to Alec Murray, December 27, 1918, ibid.; H. R. Hummer to Commissioner, November 18, 1918, ibid.; H. R. Hummer to Commissioner, July 8, 1918, Folder 121232-1916, ibid.; H. R. Hummer to Commissioner, January 22, 1927, Box 17, CA, CCF 1907–39, RG 75, NARA-DC.

33. Yellow Bird, "Wild Indians," accessed December 17, 2014. Another thoughtful critique of settler colonialism, Indigenous resistance, and history is Paul Kelton's *Cherokee Medicine, Colonial Germs*.

34. P. Allen, *Off the Reservation*, 42. See also P. Allen, *Grandmothers of the Light*; Lovern and Locust, *Native American Communities on Health and Disability*, 51; Locust, *American Indian Beliefs Concerning Health and Unwellness*; Trafzer, *Fighting Invisible Enemies*; Crawford O'Brien, *Coming Full Circle*; Walker, DeMallie, and Jahner, *Lakota Belief and Ritual*; Manitowabi and Maar, "Coping with Colonization," 145, 154–155; Angel, *Preserving the Sacred*; P. Allen, *Sacred Hoop*; Pengra and Godfrey, "Different Boundaries, Different

Barriers," 36–53; Kills Small, "Lakota." I also thank Menominee elder Napos for many conversations about Menominee medicine and commonalities with other Native medicine, understandings of well-being and its relationship to Native self-determination. Longtime archaeologist for Rosebud Sioux Tribe Ben Rhodd also provided extensive explanations of Lakota language, culture, and history.

35. Jesse Faribault to Commissioner, August 9, 1918, Folder 12132-1916, Box 296, SA, 722.1, CCF 1907–39, RG 75, NARA-DC.

36. Mary Alexis to Commissioner Charles Burke, September 13, 1921, Folder 12132-1916, Box 296, SA,722.1, CCF 1907–39, RG 75, NARA-DC.

37. Elizabeth Alexis to Commissioner, May 22, 1922, Box 16, CA, CCF 1907–39, RG 75, NARA-DC.

38. See, for example, Mrs. Ed I. Whiting Sr. to BIA (petitioning for the discharge of her brother, referred to as James Herman), July 24, 1914, Box 14, CA, CCF 1907–39, RG 75, NARA-DC; BIA Commissioner to Mrs. Ed I. Whiting Sr., August 25, 1914, ibid.; Charles Fisher to BIA (petitioning for the discharge of his wife), December 16, 1918, ibid.; and Mary L. Davis to BIA (petitioning for the discharge of her mother), June 4, 1917, ibid.

39. Letter, Jesse Faribault, June 12, 1918, Folder 121232-1916, Box 296, SA, 722.1, CCF 1907–1939, RG 75, NARA-DC.

40. Mary Alexis to Royal Johnson, January 10, 1927, Box 17, CA, CCF 1907–39, RG 75, NARA-DC.

41. Fourteenth Census of the United States, 1920, RG 29, NARA-DC, Tom Reynolds, p. 4A, Enumeration District 37, lines 13–18, microfilm #T625, 2076 rolls; Kiowa Agency, 1917, Indian Census Rolls, RG 75, NARA-DC, M595, Roll 214, nos. 600–5. I thank Franklin Longhat and Fawn Jerz for permitting me to include their family's story in this book.

42. W. C. Barton to Commissioner, April 22, 1922, Box 641, Kiowa Agency, 722.1, CCF 1907–39, RG 75, NARA-DC.

43. W. C. Barton to Commissioner, April 22, 1922.

44. J. A. Buntin to Commissioner, April 24, 1922, Box 641, Kiowa Agency, 722.1, CCF 1907–39, RG 75, NARA-DC; H. R. Hummer to J. A. Buntin, May 8, 1922, ibid.

45. H. R. Hummer to J. A. Buntin, May 8, 1922.

46. "Amelia Moss" 39213, Saint Elizabeths Hospital form, January 15, 1934, Box 4, CA, CCF 1907–39, RG 75, NARA-DC; J. A. Buntin to H. R. Hummer, May 22, 1922, Box 15, ibid.; H. R. Hummer to J. A. Buntin, May 8, 1922. Perspectives on a range of perceived mental disabilities presented a murky picture, both then and now. Hummer may have been suggesting that he and other medical professionals regularly applied this definition. Yet while leading American eugenicists in the 1920s commonly grouped people deemed "imbecile" and "insane" under broader categories of "defective," most drew distinctions between what they considered to be cognitive impairments versus psychiatric disorders. The proliferation of colonies for the feebleminded separate from psychiatric facilities, for instance, both encouraged and responded to medically imposed and policed boundaries. Conflating imbecility with insanity, however, was an effective means of convincing people like Superintendent Buntin to incarcerate the young girl at Canton.

47. For example, Buntin, in a 1929 response to a survey about Kiowa Agency members held at Canton Asylum, told the BIA that only Amelia Moss, "who is really a child with very little mental capacity" was there. J. A. Buntin to Commissioner, October 14, 1929,

Box 641, Kiowa Agency, 722.1, CCF 1907–39, RG 75, NARA-DC. By this time, the superintendent was in communication with the Oklahoma Institute for the Feeble Minded. The institution had been opened since 1910 and admitted young boys and girls, but perhaps Buntin had not known about the state school. It is equally possible that Moss's Indigeneity and citizenship status disqualified her from admittance to the Oklahoma institution. With the passage of the 1924 Indian Citizenship Act, individuals like Moss were legally considered citizens of the United States. It is probable that her family and others who may have known the girl advocated for her return to the community, or at least to a place closer to them. Relatives regularly petitioned the BIA with such requests. Longhat interviews, May 3, August 1, 2014; Jerz interviews, January 27, April 1, 2017, January 9, 2020.

48. Financial factors may have played a role in Moss's retention at Canton. The Indian Asylum was a federal institution with federal funding. State institutions regularly resisted admitting Native people, arguing that the U.S. government was responsible for this population. Even though the Oklahoma institution was expanding rapidly in the late 1920s, they may not have had a vacancy available to a person institutionalized at Canton. Another scenario may have played out. In similar instances, Hummer often interceded, asserting his professional expertise and claiming that an individual was best served at his South Dakota asylum. He usually prevailed.

49. "Amelia Moss" 39213, Saint Elizabeths Hospital form, January 15, 1934, Box 4, CA, CCF 1907–39, RG 75, NARA-DC.

50. Longhat interviews, May 3, August 1, 2014. According to Longhat, Moss returned to Caddo Nation before she died. He recalled her speaking in Caddo with her brother—Longhat's father—on his family's porch. Longhat's sister, Fawn Jerz, did not meet Moss but affirms that other siblings shared similar accounts of her. Jerz interviews, January 27, April 1, 2017, January 9, 2020.

51. See Simpson, "On Ethnographic Refusal," 67–80; Simpson, *Mohawk Interruptus*; and Tuck and Yang, "Unbecoming Claims," 811–18.

52. Senate Committee on Indian Affairs, *Asylum for Insane Indians*, 55th Cong., 2nd sess., February 11, 1898, S. Rpt. 567, 2, https://babel.hathitrust.org/cgi/pt?id=uc1.$b63 5600&view=2up&seq=736. For more on Pettigrew and South Dakota politics in the late nineteenth and early twentieth century, see Risjord, *Dakota*.

53. W. W. Gooding to C. N. Bliss, Secretary of the Interior, July 23, 1897, in Senate Committee on Indian Affairs, *Asylum for Insane Indians*, 55th Cong., 2nd sess., February 11, 1898, S. Rpt. 567, 5, https://babel.hathitrust.org/cgi/pt?id=uc1.$b635600&view=2up &seq=738. See also Laudenschlager, "Infamous Institution"; Putney, "Canton Asylum"; and Sweet, "Controversial Care."

54. Construction started in early August and was completed at the end of 1901. Arms, "Asylum for Insane Indians"; "Tale of Two Cities," 4E; Peterson telephone interviews, July 29, 2017, August 3, 2019; "Asylum for Insane Indians," *Boston Daily Globe*, 35; "An Asylum for Insane Indians," New York Daily Tribune, 4; "Appointed Asylum Superintendency," 11; "Arizona News," 5; "Asylum for Insane Indians," *Norfolk (NE) News*, 5; "National Hospital for Insane Indians," 3; "Canton's New Asylum," 3; "Asylum for Insane Indians," Sioux Valley (SD) News, 1; "Pettigrew Hard to Please," 3; "Home for Insane Red Men," *Holt County Sentinel* (Oregon, MO), 8; "Bidding for Construction of Asylum," 1; "Prosperity at Canton," 1; "Insane Indians Are Gathered in an Asylum from All Over the

Country"; "Only Asylum for Insane Indians in U.S.," 18; "News and Gossip from Washington Departments," 4; Willis, Dean, and Larsen, "First Mental Hospital for American Indians"; *History of Lincoln County, South Dakota*, 36–38.

55. "Appointed Asylum Superintendent," 11; "The Leader," 4; "Real Estate," 4; Yellow Bird, "Wild Indians," accessed December 17, 2014; Putney, "Canton Asylum," 3; "Gifford, Oscar S.," 323; Saxman, "Canton Asylum," 40–42; "O. S. Gifford Gets It!," 1; Stawicki, "Haunting Legacy"; "Hiawatha Asylum for Insane Indians Was Only of Its Kind," 5.

56. "Gifford, Oscar S.," 323; "Gifford, Oscar Sherman," *Biographical Directory of the United States Congress*; *History of Lincoln County, South Dakota*.

57. "Asylum for Insane Indians," *Sioux Valley News*, 1. See also "Prosperity at Canton," 1; Bhatara, Gupta, and Brokenleg, "Images in Psychiatry," 767; Putney, "Canton Asylum"; Saxman, "Canton Asylum," 40–42; "Tale of Two Cities," 4E, 6E; Egan, "Historians Revive Stories of Dakota Territory," 4B; Laudenschlager, "Infamous Institution."

58. The author thanks Smithsonian National Museum of American History intern Mariana Bellante for sharing her research work on Lincoln County history.

59. Olson, *Norwegian, Swedish, and Danish Immigrants*, 16.

60. Lovoll, *Norwegians on the Prairie*, 4 (summarizing Ingred Semmingsen). See also Hansen, *Encounter on the Great Plains*, 60–73; G. Olson, "Yankee and European Settlement"; Blegen, *Norwegian Migration to America*, 499–501.

61. Iconically—if hyperbolically—depicted in Norwegian American author and Canton resident Ole Edvart Rølvaag's *Giants of the Earth* (1924), Norwegian pioneers in the Dakotas lived the "Manifest Destiny" dream. Rugged determination and vast fertile land, in this storytelling, enabled protagonist Pers Hansa and his family to tame the West. As in the novel, many Norwegians traveled in kin groups to places like Lincoln County, playing central roles in establishing towns like Canton.

62. See "Birds-eye View of Canton," 2; Peterson telephone interviews, July 29, 2017, August 3, 2019; Canton, SD, photographs, personal collection of Omar F. Peterson, Canton, South Dakota; and Canton, SD, photographs, personal collection of Manfred Hill.

63. Lovoll, *Norwegians on the Prairie*, 6. See also Risjord, *Dakota*, 137–38; Hansen, *Encounter on the Great Plains*, 60–61 and chap. 2 passim; and Blegen, *Norwegian Migration to America*.

64. Barkanp, *Immigrants in American History*, 541.

65. Thompson, "Indian Legend of Hiawatha," 128–40; Schoolcraft, *Myth of Hiawatha*, 2–51; Davis, "How Indian Is Hiawatha?," 5–25; Hewitt, "Hiawatha," 546; Hewitt, "Nanabozho," 19; Clifton, *Invented Indian*, 83–84; Lockard, "Universal Hiawatha," 110–25.

66. See Holt, *Indian Orphanages*, 198; Trachtenberg, *Shades of Hiawatha*; Feagin, *White Racial Frame*; P. Deloria, *Playing Indian*; Lipsitz, *Possessive Investment in Whiteness*; and Painter, *History of White People*. See also Mihesuah, *American Indians*, 77–79.

67. For many white settlers, Hiawatha took on paternalistic and stereotypical qualities too. Holt, *Indian Orphanages*, 198–99; Maddox, *Citizen Indians*, 21–22, 31, 34; Lockard, "Universal Hiawatha," 110–25.

68. It was and is an unexceptional story. Across the United States in the nineteenth and twentieth centuries, many towns, libraries, church missions, and golf courses have invoked Hiawatha in their names. For more on the broader process of settler colonialism that this reflects, see O'Brien, *Firsting and Lasting*.

69. "Gain in Indian Insanity," 44. See also "No Indian Lunatics," 19; "Insane Asylum for Indians," 5; Hummer, "Insanity among the Indians."

70. "Gain in Indian Insanity," 44. The quote is from the article, not directly from Oscar Gifford.

71. "Gain in Indian Insanity," 44.

72. "Gain in Indian Insanity," 44. See also Turner, "Insane Indians," 147–48.

73. "Gain in Indian Insanity," 44.

74. See, for example, Asylum for Insane Indians, *Annual Report*, 1920, SDSA, 2; Asylum for Insane Indians, *Annual Report*, 1922, SDSA, 2; Superintendent, Kiowa Agency, to H. R. Hummer, July 1, 1921, Box 15, CA, CCF 1907–39, RG 75, NARA-DC; Superintendent, Fort Yuma Indian School, to H. R. Hummer, June 30, 1921, ibid.; Superintendent, Coshute Indian School, to H. R. Hummer, June 29, 1921, ibid.; H. R. Hummer to Commissioner (list of applications for admissions), June 2, 1921, ibid.; Asylum for Insane Indians, *Annual Report*, 1925, SDSA, 2. "The management of this institution, believing the same is not fulfilling its entire function, because it is not caring for *all* of the insane Indians in the United States, has prepared a tentative program of expansion." H. R. Hummer, circular, June 21, 1921, Box 15, CA, CCF 1907–39, RG 75, NARA-DC. See also "Asylum Needs Larger Quarters," 17.

75. See, for example, "Home for Insane Red Men," *Portsmouth (NH) Herald*. This 1906 article emphasizes the campus's many trees and pastoral scenes in its description of the "home for the unfortunate."

76. The building was 184 feet long and 114 feet wide at the center. Arms, "Asylum for Insane Indians." An architectural drawing of Canton Asylum's floorplan can be found in Middleton, "Supplanting the Medicine Man," 141.

77. "New Hospital Building at Indian Insane Asylum," 1. See also Laudenschlager, "Infamous Institution."

78. "New Hospital Building at Indian Insane Asylum," 1. See also Herbert T. Hoover, "Canton Asylum" (Vermillion, SD, 1984), Canton Insane Asylum File, CPL. The Hospital Building was located east of the Main Building. *Sioux Valley (SD) News*, July 23, 1915, ibid., 4.

79. Examples include Leahy, *They Called It Madness*; Joinson, *Vanished in Hiawatha*; Dilenschneider, "Invitation to Restorative Justice," 105–28; and Benson, "Keepers of the Canton Indian Asylum Share History." See also the romance novel based on Canton Asylum history, Eagle, *Sunrise Song*; and "Hiawatha Asylum's Dark Past Featured in Romantic Novel," 5.

80. PA, Indian Census Rolls, 1908, RG 75, NARA-DC, M595, Roll 393; PA, Indian Census Rolls, 1920, RG 75, NARA-DC, M595, Roll 210, p. 19.

81. According to one story, a vision of a menacing county sheriff rising up through the floor of the home, threatening to severely beat him, compelled Seh-Tuk to hide in the fields during the day. Admission note, "Willie (John S.) Mitchell, #39252," January 4, 1934, Box 4, CA, CCF 1907–39, RG 75, NARA-DC; Mitchell interview, April 8, 2014; Mitchell email correspondence, December 18, 2013, April 14, 2014. I thank Prairie Band Potawatomi Tribal Historian Gary Mitchell for his guidance and support in writing his family's story.

82. Henry Roe Cloud to H. C. Woolley, February 15, 1934, Folder M, Box 221, Correspondence Relating to Individuals, 1895–1936, M-N, Series 8, PA (Mayetta, KS), RG 75, NARA-KC.

83. See St. Elizabeths Hospital form, "Willie (John S.) Mitchell, # 39252," January 15, 1934, Box 4, CA, CCF 1907–39, RG 75, NARA-DC.

84. Occupational list, 1934, Indian Insane Int. Dept., Records Relating to the Department of the Interior 1902–43, Box 1, Entry 13, RG 418, NARA-DC. A cover letter accompanying the list, dated January 9, 1934, was sent from William G. Cushard, medical officer, to Dr. H. C. Wooley, on St. Elizabeths Hospital letterhead. Thanks to Carla Joinson and Maureen Jais-Mick for confirming the citation.

85. Jasper Cross to H. R. Hummer, March 18, 1930, Folder M, Box 22, Correspondence Relating to Individuals, 1895–1936, Series 8, PA (Mayetta, KS), RG 75, NARA-KC.

86. Jasper Cross to C. M. Blair, May 26, 1933, Folder M, Box 22, Correspondence Relating to Individuals, 1895–1936, Series 8, PA (Mayetta, KS), RG 75, NARA-KC.

87. Riley Guthrie to John S. Mitchell, April 2, 1942, Box 4, CA, CCF 1907–39, RG 75, NARA-DC; Prandoni email correspondence, February 8, 2017. I especially thank Dr. Jogues Prandoni for his assistance with research questions related to Seh-Tuk and others transferred from Canton to St. Elizabeths and elsewhere.

88. Seh-Tuk apparently was readmitted to St. Elizabeths on January 4, 1950; his new medical file was numbered 63909. Hospital records show that he was discharged on September 13, 1961. Prandoni email correspondence, February 8, 2017.

89. Many scholars define specific periods as "the era[s] of removal." See Merrell, *Indians' New World*; Tiro, *People of the Standing Stone*; and Gray, "Limits and Possibilities." The Alabama Department of Archives and History has a website devoted to the "Indian Removal Era."

90. See, for example, Blackhawk, *Violence over the Land*; Dunbar-Ortiz, *Indigenous Peoples' History of the United States*; Jacobs, *White Mothers to a Dark Race*; and Hixson, *American Settler Colonialism*.

91. See, for example, Rembis, *Defining Deviance*; Ben-Moshe, Chapman, and Carey, *Disability Incarcerated*; Hernández, *City of Inmates*; Burch and Joyner, *Unspeakable*; Archuleta, Child, and Lomawaima, *Away from Home*; Adams, *Education for Extinction*; Hyer, *One House*; Lunbeck, *Psychiatric Persuasion*; McCandless, *Moonlight, Magnolias, and Madness*; McLennan, *Crisis of Imprisonment*; Fear-Seagal, *White Man's Club*; Kunzel, *Fallen Women, Problem Girls*; Burch and Joyner, "Disremembered Past"; and Chase, *Caging Borders and Carceral States*.

92. Gary Mitchell wrote extensively about Potawatomi history and culture. See, for example, Mitchell, "Boarding Schools and the Potawatomi"; and Mitchell, *Stories of the Potawatomi People*. He also posted regularly to his column on *The Native Blog* and made the short video "Prairie Band Potawatomi: Preserving Language & Culture." Mitchell passed away in 2015. I thank his wife, Voncile Mitchell, for supporting this project.

93. Mitchell interview, April 8, 2014.

94. Judah interviews, December 28, 2011, February 12, May 12, 2012, May 10–11, June 17, 2013, April 27, 2014; September 19, 2019; Judah correspondence, June 29, July 2, 7,

13, 2011, February 12, April 7, May 3, 18, July 12, 2013, August 6, November 14, 2015, April 8, 2016, January 18, 2017.

95. Geographer Ned Kaufman's concepts of "story site" and "storyscapes" could apply to the former grounds of the Canton Asylum. He defines storyscapes as sites, broadly conceived, that bring "socially valuable stories to mind: stories of history, tradition, and shared memory." Kaufman, *Place, Race, and Story*, 38–39.

96. See O' Brien, *Firsting and Lasting*.

Chapter 2

1. Caldwell telephone interview, April 14, 2014; W. R. Bebout to H. P. Marble, May 3, 1917, Box 162, KA, 722.1, CCF 1907–39, RG 75, NARA-DC; W. R. Bebout to H. P. Marble, October 13, 1917, ibid.; Twelfth Census of the United States, 1900, RG 29, NARA-DC, Menominee Indian Reservation, Shawano, Wisconsin, Roll 1817, p. 33, Enumeration District 198, lines 8–12, microfilm#T623, 1854 rolls; Green Bay Agency, 1899, Indian Census Rolls, M595, RG 75, NARA-DC, Roll 173, p. 10, line 14, and p. 2, line 18, microfilm; Green Bay Agency, 1908, Indian Census Rolls, M595, RG 75, NARA-DC, p. 9, lines 7–8; Thirteenth Census of the United States, 1910, RG 29, NARA-DC, Menominee Indian Reservation, Shawano, Wisconsin, Roll T624_1738, pp. 29A and 31A, Enumeration District 0163. These references come from BIA documents and underscore sovereignty battles between Menominee Nation and the United States. For broader histories of Menominee Nation, see Beck, *Siege and Survival*; Beck, *Struggle for Self-Determination*; Spindler, *Menominee Women and Culture Change*; and Spindler and Spindler, *Dreamers without Power*. I thank Frank Caldwell Jr. for granting me permission to write about his family and for sharing information with me. I also thank Menominee Nation Tribal Historian David Grignon and elder Napos for their guidance in this work.

2. W. R. Bebout to Commissioner, October 13, 1917, Box 162, KA, 722.1, CCF 1907–39, RG 75, NARA-DC.

3. W. R. Bebout to Keshena superintendent H. P. Marble, May 3, 1917, Box 162, KA, 722.1, CCF 1907–39, RG 75, NARA-DC.

4. W. R. Bebout to Commissioner, October 13, 1917. Historian Ronald Takaki has argued that "the crucial term is *reformatory*. The 'discovery of the asylum' in white society had his counterpart in the invention of the reservation for Indian society. Based on the 'principle of separation and seclusion,' the reservation would do more than merely maintain Indians: it would train and reform them." Takaki, *Iron Cages*, 186 (emphasis in original). For more on the violent application and enforcement of colonial gender systems on Indigenous people, see Lugones, "Heterosexualism and the Colonial/Modern Gender System," 186–209. For other examples of settler medicine, pathology, and Indigenous communities, see W. Anderson, *Colonial Pathologies*.

5. Rifkin, *When Did Indians Become Straight?*, 7. See also Voyles, *Wastelanding*; Brown, *States of Injury*; Stoler, *Carnal Knowledge and Imperial Power*; Stoler, *Haunted by Empire*; Kilty and Dej, *Containing Madness*; Gilmore, "Fatal Couplings of Power and Difference," 15–24; and Biolsi, "Birth of the Reservation," 28–53. For more on histories of whiteness and its manifestations, see Lipsitz, *Possessive Investment in Whiteness*; Feagin, *White Racial Frame*; and Painter, *History of White People*.

6. This was a common pattern. See Cahill, *Federal Fathers and Mothers*; Piatote, *Domestic Subjects*; Voyles, *Wastelanding*; and Jacobs, *White Mothers to a Dark Race*. For more on settler depictions of Native people, see Ross, *Inventing the Savage*; Berkhofer, *White Man's Indian*; Hixson, *American Settler Colonialism*; Briggs, "The Race of Hysteria"; Unger, *Destruction of American Indian Families*; V. Deloria and Lytle, *American Indians, American Justice*; Lyons, *X-Marks*; Rose, "Savages," in *Hidden Histories*, 27–36; and Emmerich, "'Save the Babies!'"

7. Mrs. H. P. Marble, "The Field Matron in Indian Work," in *Report of the Thirty-fourth Annual Lake Mohonk Conference on the Indian and Other Dependent Peoples* (N.p., 1916), 106–7. Also cited in Bieder, *Native American Communities in Wisconsin*, 163.

8. Historian Margaret Jacobs adds, "Prior methods of child rearing were under attack and in fact officials often justified the removal of Indian children to boarding schools based on supposedly deficient Indian child-rearing and aberrant family models." Jacobs, "Diverted Mothering," 180. Brenda Child (Red Lake Ojibwe) and other historians additionally have noted ways that traditional Indigenous kinship, gender roles, and domestic life differed significantly from settler colonial customs and have long been a central target of imperialist campaigns. See, for example, Mintz and Kellogg, *Domestic Revolutions*; Child, *Boarding School Seasons*; Hyde, *Empires, Nations, and Families*; Cahill, *Federal Fathers and Mothers*; Unger, *Destruction of American Indian Families*; and Emmerich, "'Save the Babies!'" For more on the overlaps of gender, Indigeneity, and institutionalization, see Rimke, "Sickening Institutions," 15–39.

9. W. R. Bebout to Commissioner, October 13, 1917, Box 162, KA, 722.1, CCF 1907–39, RG 75, NARA-DC.

10. Teuton, "Disability in Indigenous North America," 574. See also Gonzales, Kertész, and Tayac, "Eugenics as Indian Removal," 53–67; Smithers, *Science, Sexuality, and Race*, chap. 4; and Lieffers, "Imperial Ableism."

11. The parents' documented names vary. The 1900 and 1914 Indian census rolls, for example, list "Robert Burch" also as "Acaneca (Steve)" and "A-Ca-Nee-A," and list "Ruth Bent Burch" as "Mary," "Peachigavits," and "Sec-Pe-On." Daughter Wepiwicenaget (Jane) also was referred to as "Wopiwicunaget." Susan appears in some Indian rolls as "Sawwapeget." Southern Ute Agency, 1900, Indian Census Rolls, RG 75, NARA-DC, M595, Roll 545, nos. 1–13; Southern Ute Agency, 1914, ibid.

12. The 1900 U.S. census notes that neither elder daughters nor their parents wrote or spoke English. The younger siblings, who also were listed as attending school, were described as understanding English. Twelfth Census of the United States, 1900, RG 29, NARA-DC, Southern Ute Reservation, La Plata, Colorado, p. 6, Enumeration District 0155, lines 21–29, microfilm #T623. Osburn, *Southern Ute Women*; Osburn, "'To Build Up the Morals of the Tribe,'" 10–27. Osburn and other scholars have emphasized the high value placed on pregnant mothers and children in Southern Ute communities and the comparative sexual autonomy women enjoyed at the turn of the twentieth century. See, for example, Young, *Ute Indians of Colorado in the Twentieth Century*, 92. The author thanks Eddie Box Jr., Traditional Leader of the Southern Ute Indian Tribe, for permitting me to include his family's story in this book.

13. Charles Werner to Commissioner, November 11, 1910, RCUA, 44011, NARA-D.

14. Charles Werner to Commissioner, November 11, 1910.

15. Charles Werner to Commissioner, November 11, 1910. According to historian Katherine Osburn, Werner regularly punished Ute people, particularly women, who defied his expectations of appropriate gender behavior. For example, he denied some infants from being enrolled in the tribe if he did not recognize the parents as legally married. Osburn, *Southern Ute Women*, 93–94. As historian Elizabeth Lunbeck and many others have argued, young women whose gender and sexual behavior did not conform to white settler norms commonly were targeted for institutionalization during the early twentieth century. See, for example, Lunbeck, *Psychiatric Persuasion*; and Rembis, *Defining Deviance*.

16. H. R. Hummer to Dr. McChesney, October 4, 1912, File 006-Burch, Box 4, Decimal Files, 1879–1952, RCUA, CCF 1907–39, RG 75, NARA-D; H. R. Hummer to Commissioner, August 16, 1913, Box 19, CA, CCF 1907–39, RG 75, NARA-DC; W. B. Fry to H. R. Hummer, September 9, 1912, Series 723-005, Correspondence-Utes, RG 75, NARA-D; H. R. Hummer to W. B. Fry, September 12, 1912, ibid.; H. R. Hummer to W. B. Fry, September 20, 1912, ibid.; H. R. Hummer to Superintendent at Ignacio, CO, September 23, 1912, ibid.; Charles Werner to Commissioner, January 3, 1911, ibid.

17. Werner to Commissioner, August 6, 1912, CCF-SU, 722.1-9047-1910, as cited in Osburn, *Southern Ute Women*, 94n30.

18. H. R. Hummer to Commissioner, March 10, 1913, Box 13, CA, CCF 1907–39, RG 75, NARA-DC; H. R. Hummer to Superintendent, Southern Ute Indian School, March 10, 1913, File 006-Burch, Box 4, Decimal File, Series 723, RCUA, CCF 1907–39, RG 75, NARA-D.

19. "Report Regarding Susan Burch," April 1, 1913, Box 154, Decimal File, Series 723, RCUA, RG 75, NARA-D.

20. Stephen Abbott to Commissioner, May 9, 1913, File 006-Burch, Box 4, 44015, Decimal File, 1879–1952, RCUA, RG 75, NARA-D.

21. According to BIA correspondence the child was placed in her grandparent's home and raised primarily by them. Superintendent, Southern Ute Agency, to Commissioner, October 31, 1913, File 006-Burch, Box 4, Decimal File, 1879–1952, RCUA, RG 75, NARA-D; Superintendent Abbott to Commissioner, June 19, 1913, ibid. Census rolls identify the little girl with her father. See, for example, Southern Ute Agency, 1914, Indian Census Rolls, RG 75, NARA-DC, M595, Roll 545, lines 1–2, microfilm.

22. Cora Burch Allen was the among the only children born at Canton who survived into adulthood. In 1932, she married a man referred to as John Williams. Two years later, the couple had a daughter, Emily. Sawwapeget's elderly parents, Cora Allen Burch's grandparents, lived nearby. Southern Ute Agency, 1916, Indian Census Rolls, RG 75, NARA-DC, M595, Roll 77, lines 1–5 and 9–13, microfilm; Consolidated Ute Agency, 1935, ibid., Roll 78, p. 33, line 3; Fourteenth Census of the United States, 1920, RG 29, NARA-DC, Ignatio, La Plata, Colorado, Roll 165, p. 1A, Enumeration District 169, microfilm #T624; Sixteenth Census of the United States, 1940, RG 29, NARA-DC, Bayfield, La Plata, Colorado, Roll T627_466, p. 5B, Enumeration District 34–20. See also Stephen Abbott to Commissioner, June 19, 1913.

23. Osburn, *Southern Ute Women*, 95; Superintendent Southern Ute Indian Agency to H. R. Hummer, July 10, 1913, File 006-Burch, Box 4, Decimal Files, Series 7223, RCUA, CCF 1907–39, RG 75, NARA-D; Superintendent Southern Ute Agency to Superintendent Hummer, August 23, 1913, ibid.

24. According to the superintendent of Southern Ute Agency, the removal of Susan and Jane devastated Steven Burch. Explaining that he already had "lost two girls in S. Dakota," Burch petitioned the BIA in 1917 to release his son from boarding school so he could return to the family. Letter to Frederick Snyder (superintendent, Santa Fe School), June 15, 1917, File 006-Burch, Box 4, Decimal File, 1879–1952, RCUA, CCF 1907–39, RG 75, NARA-D.

25. See, for example, Superintendent Marble to BIA, February 5, 1917, Box 162, KA, 722.1, CCF 1907–39, RG 75, NARA-DC; W. R. Bebout to H. P. Marble, September 26, 1917, Box 163, ibid.; and Ferdinand Shoemaker to BIA, December 10, 1913, Box 162, ibid. The government's rationale reflected popular white American mainstream and scientific ideas at the time. Lovett, *Conceiving the Future*; Forbes, *Africans and Native Americans*; Haller, *Outcasts from Evolution*; Teuton, "Disability in Indigenous North America," 574; Jutel, "Sociology of Diagnosis," 278–99.

26. J. Smith, *Eugenic Assault*, 11, 71–82; Smithers, *Science, Sexuality, and Race*; Gonzales, Kertész, and Tayac, "Eugenics as Indian Removal," 53–67; Whitaker, *Mad in America*. Psychiatry, particularly in colonial contexts, shared similar qualities. See Swartz, "Black Insane in the Cape," 399–415; Swartz, "Colonialism and the Production of Psychiatric Knowledge at the Cape"; and Marks, "Every Facility That Modern Science and Enlightened Humanity Have Devised," 263.

27. For more on eugenics and the targeting of families, see Larson, *Sex, Race, and Science*; Stern, *Eugenic Nation*; Lombardo, *Three Generations, No Imbeciles*; Leonard, *Illiberal Reformers*; and Lovett, *Conceiving the Future*. For more on medicine and imperialism, see Inglis, "Disease and the 'Other.'"

28. According to sociologist Lutz Kaelber, South Dakota passed its sterilization law in 1917, but the first recorded sterilizations began near the end of the 1920s. Between that time and the 1960s, 789 South Dakotans were sterilized. Most—nearly two-thirds—were women labeled as having mental disabilities. Of all states with sterilization laws, South Dakota performed the fifteenth-largest number of surgical sterilizations. Canton Asylum, like St. Elizabeths Hospital, was a federal institution, so surgical sterilizations were not recorded at either facility. The head of St. Elizabeths, William Alanson White (who had supervised Dr. Hummer during the future Canton superintendent's residency at St. Elizabeths), was staunchly opposed to eugenic sterilization. These factors likely contributed to the absence of such procedures at Canton Asylum at a time when state facilities increasingly deployed them. Kaelber, "Eugenics." For more on sterilizations of Indigenous women, see Kluchin, *Fit to Be Tied*; and Voyles, *Wastelanding*, 140–44. U.S. and regional sterilization histories include Kevles, *In the Name of Eugenics*, 47–48, 93–94, 107–11; Hansen and King, *Sterilized by the State*, 254; Stern, *Eugenic Nation*, 1–10, 99–114; Larson, *Sex, Race, and Science*, 33–39; Bruinius, *Better for All the World*; Whitaker, *Mad in America*, 56–60; and Dowbiggin, *Keeping America Sane*.

29. Burch, digital database. Hummer advocated for Agnes Caldwell to remain institutionalized in order to restrict her from mothering more children: "I recommend that she be kept under proper surveillance for her own good and as well as posterity." H. R. Hummer to Commissioner, November 8, 1920, Box 14, CA, CCF 1907–39, RG 75, NARA-DC.

30. As historian James Moran explains, "The strict separation of patients at the asylum by sex was . . . the socio-spatial division completely unfamiliar to those cared for

in the community." Moran, "Architecture of Madness," in Topp, Moran, and Andrews, *Madness, Architecture, and the Built Environment*, 164. For more on eugenic policies and institutions, including segregation and sterilization, see Rembis, *Defining Deviance*; Larson, *Sex, Race, and Science*, 24, 46–47, 106; Whitaker, *Mad in America*, 56–62 and chap. 3; Kevles, *In the Name of Eugenics*, 92–93; Bruinius, *Better for All the World*; Stern, *Eugenic Nation*, 30, 85–87; Leonard, *Illiberal Reformers*; and Birnbaum, "Eugenic Sterilization," 951–58. Comparatively little has been recovered and acknowledged about the pervasive forced sterilizations of Native people, especially women, even in the late twentieth century. The extent to which eugenicists sterilized American Indians before the 1950s remains mostly unknown to scholars. Lawrence, "The Indian Health Service and the Sterilization of Native American Women," 400–419.

31. For many people across the United States and elsewhere, detention in psychiatric facilities during the late 1800s and across much of the 1900s spanned full lifetimes. For more on the histories of warehousing and incarceration, see Spens, *Architecture of Incarceration*; Parsons, *From Asylum to Prison*; Ben-Moshe, Chapman, and Carey, *Disability Incarcerated*; Appleman, "Deviancy, Dependency, and Disability," 417–78; Radford and Park, "'Convenient Means of Riddance,'" 369–92; Hernández, *City of Inmates*; McLennan, *Crisis of Imprisonment*; and Nichols and Swiffen, *Legal Violence and the Limits of the Law*.

32. Expectations about labor productivity and adherence to capitalism also pervade the story. According to the superintendent, the person referred to as "Susan" and her immediate family did not seem to do what the BIA wanted them to do with their allotted land. The administrator pathologized their nonconformity, claiming that the sisters "exhibit insanity to some extent." Charles Werner to Commissioner, November 11, 1910, RCUA, 44011, NARA-D.

33. Osburn, *Southern Ute Women*, 94; Osburn, "'And as the Squaws Are a Secondary Consideration,'" 328.

34. Letter, W. C. Barton, April 22, 1922, Box 641, Kiowa Agency, 722.1, CCF 1907–39, RG 75, NARA-DC.

35. J. A. Buntin to H. R. Hummer, May 22, 1922, Box 15, CA, CCF 1907–39, RG 75, NARA-DC; "Amelia Moss," Saint Elizabeths Hospital patient 39213, January 15, 1934, Box 4, ibid. Matron Lucie Jobin, Canton Asylum's only Native staff member at the time, went to retrieve the child. The author thanks Kathryn Leslie for sharing background history on her ancestor Lucie Jobin.

36. For more on asylum architecture and management, see Miron, *Prisons, Asylums, and the Public*.

37. See, for example, Topp, Moran, and Andrews, *Madness, Architecture, and the Built Environment*; Yanni, *Architecture of Madness*; and Spens, *Architecture of Incarceration*.

38. In this way, Canton Asylum was unlike other institutions of assimilation, representing an overlapping but distinct form of erasure. Indefinite, often-permanent incarceration disrupted or severed the typical family lifespan and generation. For more on the Indian Service and "surrogate families," see Cahill, "'Seeking the Incalculable Benefit of a Faithful, Patient Man and Wife,'" 71–92. My work also draws on feminist disability scholar Alison Kafer's insights about the ableist cultural drive to eliminate disabled people and disabled futures. See Kafer, *Feminist Queer, Crip*.

39. BigFoot telephone interview, April 29, 2014.

40. H. R. Hummer to Commissioner Merritt, November 18, 1918, Box 296, SA, 722.1, CCF 1907–39, RG 75, NARA-DC. For more on trachoma and the Office of Indian Affairs, see Benson, "Blinded with Science," 52–75.

41. H. R. Hummer to Commissioner, June 22, 1922, Box 16, CA, CCF 1907–39, RG 75, NARA-DC; H. R. Hummer to Commissioner, September 29, 1921, Folder 121232-1916, Box 296, SA, 722.1, ibid.

42. For example, Commissioner to H. R. Hummer, October 11, 1921, Folder 121232-1916, Box 296, SA, 722.1, RG 75, NARA-DC; E. B. Merritt to Mr. Ed. S. Johnson, April 1, 1921, ibid.; E. B. Merritt to H. R. Hummer, December 12, 1918, ibid.; and E. B. Merritt to Jesse Faribault, August 30, 1918, ibid.

43. H. R. Hummer to Commissioner, July 8, 1918, Box 296, SA, 722.1, CCF 1907–39, RG 75, NARA-DC.

44. H. R. Hummer to BIA, October 21, 1919, Box 14, CA, CCF 1907–39, RG 75, NARA-DC. See also H. R. Hummer to BIA, November 8, 1920, ibid.

45. H. R. Hummer to BIA, December 30, 1918, Box 14, CA, CCF 1907–39, RG 75, NARA-DC.

46. There is no record of any officials claiming that Native men needed to be institutionalized because they might reproduce. This particular form of medicalized intervention focused on women.

47. In one interview, Superintendent Gifford, for example, asserted, "It is a peculiar fact that Indians desert unfortunates." "Gain in Indian Insanity," 44. For details on home care of people deemed insane in the late nineteenth and early twentieth centuries, see McCandless, Moonlight, Magnolias, and Madness.

48. W. R. Bebout to Commissioner, October 13, 1917, Box 162, KA, 722.1, CCF 1907–39, RG 75, NARA-DC. Claiming concern for her family, H. R. Hummer recommended Caldwell's continued detention. Many historians have detailed this settler logic. See, for example, Jacobs, Generation Removed; Barker, Native Acts, 224–28; Piatote, Domestic Subjects; Dunbar-Ortiz, Indigenous Peoples' History of the United States; and Smithers, Science, Sexuality, and Race.

49. See, for example, W. R. Bebout to Commissioner, December 18, 1916, Box 162, KA, 722.10, CCF 1907–39, RG 75, NARA-DC; W. R. Bebout to Commissioner, October 13, 1917, ibid.; W. R. Bebout to H. R. Marble, May 7, 1917, ibid.; and Fernindand Shoemaker (physician expert) to Commissioner, December 10, 1913, ibid. Agents claimed, too, that the family caring for Peter Clafflin wanted him sent to Canton Asylum and that this dislocation would benefit the reservation generally. W. R. Bebout to H. R. Marble, May 3, 1917, ibid.

50. Many scholars have drawn attention to the ways the U.S. government and colonial settlers have especially targeted Indigenous kinship structures. See, for example, Jacobs, Generation Removed; Piatote, Domestic Subjects; and Dunbar-Ortiz, Indigenous Peoples' History of the United States. Indigenous studies scholar Joanne Barker has argued, "The notion that indigenous peoples are weaker than, wards, dependent, and limited in power in relation to their colonial states has perpetuated dominant ideologies of race, culture, and identity." Barker, Sovereignty Matters, 16.

51. As critical race theorist Patricia Hill Collins has explained: "Racial ideologies that portrayed racial/ethnic groups of intellectually underdeveloped, uncivilized children

require parallel ideas that constrict whites as intellectually mature, civilized adults. When applied to race, family rhetoric that deemed adults more developed than children, and thus entitled to greater power, uses naturalized ideas about age and authority to legitimate racial hierarchy to distribute national rights, entitlements and responsibilities." Collins, "It's All in the Family," 19.

52. H. R. Hummer to Commissioner, July 8, 1918, Box 296, SA, 722.1, CCF 1907–39, RG 75, NARA-DC. Hummer also specifically charged that Elizabeth was better off at Canton than with her spouse, Jesse. H. R. Hummer to Commissioner, December 2, 1916, Folder 121232-1916, ibid.

53. H. R. Hummer to Commissioner, December 30, 1918, Box 14, CA, CCF 1907–39, RG 75, NARA-DC; H. R. Hummer to Commissioner, November 6, 1920, ibid.

54. H. R. Hummer to J. A. Buntin, November 18, 1918 (re. M. Magpie), Box 94, Tongue River Agency, CCF 1907–39, RG 75, NARA-DC; H. R. Hummer to Commissioner, November 4, 1918, ibid.

55. Stephen Abbott to Commissioner, May 9, 1913, File 006-Burch, Decimal Files, Series 723, RCUA, CCF 1907–39, RG 75, NARA–D.

56. Cahill, *Federal Fathers and Mothers*.

57. Agnes Caldwell was described as having done "general housework at Dr. Hummer's home." Occupational list, 1934, p. 3, Indian Insane Int. Dept., Records Relating to the Department of the Interior 1902–43, Box 1, Entry 13, RG 418, NARA-DC.

58. Elizabeth Alexis to Commissioner, May 22, 1922, Box 16, CA, CCF 1907–39, RG 75, NARA-DC.

59. See, for example, Agnes Caldwell to Commissioner, October 29, 1920, Box 14, CA, CCF 1907–39, RG 75, NARA-DC; Agnes Caldwell to Commissioner Cato Sells, August 17, 1919, ibid.; Agnes Caldwell to H. R. Hummer, December 11, 1919, ibid.; Agnes Caldwell to Commissioner, November 10, 1920, ibid.

60. Wong, "Diverted Mothering," 69.

61. Elizabeth Alexis to Commissioner, May 22, 1922.

62. Agnes Caldwell to BIA, February 24, 1920, Box 15, CA, CCF 1907–39, RG 75, NARA-DC; Agnes Caldwell to BIA, November 10, 1919, Box 14, ibid.

63. Agnes Caldwell to Commissioner, March 10, 1920, Box, CA, CCF 1907–39, RG 75, NARA-DC.

64. Agnes Caldwell to Cato Sells, October 3, 1920, Box 15, CA, CCF 1907–39, RG 75, NARA-DC.

65. Affidavit, L. M. Hardin, November 19, 1909, Box 5, CA, CCF 1907–39, RG 75, NARA-DC, 3. Other staff who provided domestic service included Mrs. William Wiley, Mrs. Cecil (Chamberlin) Hendricks, and Mary Magwire.

66. For more on ways that the U.S. government idealized and institutionalized the nuclear-family structure, see Cahill, *Federal Fathers and Mothers*; Jacobs, *Mothers to a Dark Race*; and Piatote, "Indian/Agent Aporia," 45–62, 359.

67. The matron's duties involved daily inspections of the wards and oversight of laundry and meals. Norena Hummer's disdain for the other employees rippled across the campus. Initially kept to mutterings and complaints behind closed doors, staff eventually came forward when Dr. L. M. Hardin, the only other doctor on the premises at the time, petitioned the BIA for her and her husband's removal in 1909. Extensive evidence

of Norena Hummer's dereliction of duty were provided, including insufficient rations for staff and the Native people institutionalized at Canton, unsanitary living conditions in the wards, and hostility toward individuals under her supervision. Dr. Hummer and the BIA ultimately invoked family roles and expectations as a way to divert scandal and formal dismissal: noting that Norena Hummer was pregnant during the time of the allegations, she was allowed to resign. The move reaffirmed the status quo: she was expected to maintain the role of matron to her own family without competing obligations of institutional work, supporting her husband, who continued to oversee both his house-hold and the Indian Asylum. Near the time they moved into the cottage, the couple lost another child, a baby daughter, in 1913. See affidavit, L. M. Hardin, November 19, 1909; and Joinson, *Vanished in Hiawatha*, 115.

68. Asylum for Insane Indians, *Annual Report*, 1910, SDSA, 8–9.

69. "Local," 5. Another article at the time claimed, "We learn there is being con-structed at the Indian Asylum grounds an elegant and commodious residence building," *Sioux Valley (SD) News*, August 20, 1915, Canton Insane Asylum File, CPL.

70. Other staff members directly benefited from close affiliation to the Hummer family and household. The Christopher sisters, Randy and Clara, for instance, regularly expressed personal loyalty to the superintendent. Early in Hummer's tenure, Randy was elevated from a general laborer to matron. Clara, who joined the staff as a dining room girl, eventually enjoyed a status comparable to matron. Canton's administrator regularly advocated for wage increases for Clara Christopher, and she—unlike her peers—was not required to seek permission to leave the premises. She also was relieved from certain cleaning duties in the 1920s. For more on Clara Christopher, see Christopher interview, April 10, 1979.

71. Ione Landis, "Statement Regarding Harry Hummer, Superintendent of the Canton Insane Asylum," 1915, Box 5, CA, CCF 1907–39, RG 75, NARA-DC; statement by Norman Ewing, (1915), ibid.; Sweet, "Controversial Care," 50–56.

72. Landis, "Statement Regarding Harry Hummer." Landis was dismissed on January 22, 1915.

73. Cato Sells to H. R. Hummer, May 15, 1916, Box 5, CA, CCF 1907–39, RG 75, NARA-DC, 3.

74. Economic factors, coupled with cultural expectations, fueled this outcome. The federal government did not want staff providing domestic labor for Superintendent Hum-mer. At the same time, the BIA wanted to reduce harassment—or at least complaints about it—but administrators chose not to fire the superintendent. Instead, they removed the white female staff from a location of ongoing threat: the Hummer bungalow. Follow-ing this logic, having Native women provide the domestic work resolved both problems: There was less financial and other resource drain, while harassment and potential com-plaints of harassment by Native women were not considered authentic problems. When Elizabeth Faribault complained about her treatment working for Hummer and his family, for example, the BIA and the superintendent did not interpret the letter as a complaint about workplace harassment or unfair conditions, instead viewing her expressions as symptoms of mental disability and dismissing them accordingly.

75. H. R. Hummer to Commissioner, January 14, 1920, Box 14, CA, CCF 1907–39, RG 75, NARA-DC; H. R. Hummer to Commissioner, January 16, 1920, ibid.; E. B. Merritt to

H. R. Hummer, January 21, 1920, ibid. In a letter to Commissioner Merritt on March 20, 1917, Hummer claimed that Elizabeth was unchanged, "chronically insane with no chance for ultimate recovery and this is about as good a home as she could possibly find." H. R. Hummer to Commissioner, March 20, 1917, Folder 121232-1916, Box 296, SA, 722.1, ibid.

76. E. B. Merritt to H. R. Hummer, January 21, 1920.

77. An earlier version of this information appears in Burch, "'Dislocated Histories,'" 141–62.

78. H. R. Hummer to Commissioner, January 14, 1920; H. R. Hummer to Commissioner, September 29, 1921, Folder 121232-1916, Box 296, SA, 722.1, RG 75, NARA-DC. Hummer specifically invoked Faribault's second attempt in this letter as well as other perceived infractions during her detention.

79. Elizabeth Alexis to Commissioner, May 22, 1922, Box 16, CA, CCF 1907–39, RG 75, NARA-DC.

Chapter 3

1. Written references to O-Zoush-Quah vary in the archival record and include "Ozow-shquah," "Ozowshquay," and "Mrs. Maggie Hale." Her name will appear consistently in the main text of this book as "O-Zoush-Quah" in deference to family members' wishes. J. Jensen email correspondence, January 29, June 6, 2019, January 19, 2020; J. Jensen telephone conversations, March 9, 2018, January 19, 2020.

2. This photograph belonged to Francis Jensen, O-Zoush-Quah's grandson. Francis's son, Dr. Jack Jensen, received the photograph from his father, and it now hangs in his home in Houston, Texas. The image was shared with permission from Francis and Jack Jensen. Missing from the portrait was O-Zoush-Quah's other adult daughter, Shuck-To-Quah (Nettie), who likely was living with husband John Tork nearby on the Potawatomi Reservation. F. Jensen interviews, April 7, 8, 2014; F. Jensen telephone conversations, January 30, April 1, July 21, September 5, October 20, 2014; bandolier, ca. 1890s, by O-Zoush-Quah; J. Jensen interviews, April 22, 23, 2017; J. Jensen email correspondence, March 26, July 2, September, 12, 2018, January 29, June 6, 2019; January 19, 2020.

3. Information on Anna and Nettie Hale comes from the Twelfth Census of the United States, 1900, RG 29, NARA-DC, Wakarusa, Douglas, Kansas, Roll 479, Enumeration District 0174, lines 3–4, microfilm #T623, 1854 rolls. For more on the Haskell Institute, see Milk, *Haskell Institute*. For a broad overview of Potawatomi history, see Mitchell, "Boarding Schools and the Potawatomi"; and Mitchell, Stories of the Potawatomi People. See also Clifton, *Prairie People*.

4. Nettie Tork to Oscar S. Gifford, March 12, 1909, Box 13, CA, CCF 1907–39, RG 75, NARA-DC.

5. Nettie Tork to Oscar S. Gifford, March 12, 1909.

6. Nettie Tork to H. R. Hummer, March 22, 1909, Box 13, CA, CCF 1907–39, RG 75, NARA-DC.

7. For a general overview of beliefs about health, wellness, and American Indian identities, see Locust, *American Indian Beliefs Concerning Health and Unwellness*; and Weaver, "Perspectives on Wellness," 5–17.

8. Nettie Tork to H. R. Hummer, March 22, 1909.

9. According to his grandchildren, Nash-Wa-Took played a central role in Mayetta's annual fair and rodeo. Wearing the elaborate garments O-Zoush-Quah had made for him, the Hale family patriarch continued to foster close ties to Potawatomi ways, including annual festivals and rodeos. His daughters and son also attended these festivities, his grandchildren delighting in the gatherings. Jensen and Jensen, "Reclaimed Heritage," 30–31; F. Jensen interviews, April 7, 8, 2014.

10. Family Bible, ca. 1880s–, personal collection of Jack Jensen; O-Zoush-Quah and Jensen family photographs, 1890s–2019, ibid.

11. In an annotated list of people detained at Canton around 1912, "Ozowshquay" was described as doing "a small amount of beadwork." Annotated list, n.d., Box 2, CA, CCF 1907–39, RG 75, NARA-DC. See also F. Jensen interviews, April 7, 8, 2014; J. Jensen interviews, April 22, 23, 2017; and J. Jensen, telephone conversation, March 9, 2018.

12. See, for example, Braman, *Doing Time on the Outside*; Comfort, *Doing Time Together*; Ben-Moshe, Chapman, and Carey, *Disability Incarcerated*; Hernández, *City of Inmates*; Burghardt, *Broken*; and D. K. Miller, "Spider's Web."

13. Disability studies scholar Alison Kafer's theory of disability as political and relational offers an important way to understand what Faribault and her kin experienced. Kafer, *Feminist, Queer, Crip*.

14. For cogent explanations of kinship connections and obligations, cultural regeneration and recovery, and literary traditions, see Justice, *Our Fire Survives the Storm*.

15. The experiences of O-Zoush-Quah and her family, as with many others, aligns with Indigenous studies scholar Lisa Kahaleole Hall's contention that relationships are contextual and contingent. I thank Lisa Kahaleole Hall for our many conversations about this insight. See also J. Miller, "Kinship, Family Kindreds, and Community," 141; Gish Hill, *Webs of Kinship*; DeMallie, "Kinship," 306–56; Justice, "Go Away, Water!," 147–68; and Jacobs, *Generation Removed*. For insights into the inherent limits of kinship frameworks within a settler context, see Rifkin, *When Did Indians Become Straight?*

16. As historian Colette Hyman explains in her critique of settler colonialism across the nineteenth and twentieth centuries, "These events necessarily alter the work of Dakota women: bearing and caring for the next generation; feeding, clothing, and sheltering the older generations; and working not only for physical survival but for cultural and spiritual survival as well." Hyman, *Dakota Women's Work*, 12.

17. This was typical during Superintendent Gifford's tenure as well as Superintendent Hummer's.

18. H. R. Hummer, "Asylum for Insane Indians: Elizabeth Faribault," October 1, 1926, Folder 2331, Box 17, CA, CCF 1907–39, RG 75, NARA-DC. The next report, from November 1, 1926, follows the regular format and information that preceded Cora Winona's birth.

19. H. R. Hummer to Commissioner, September 29, 1926, File 45757, Box 17, CA, CCF 1907–39, RG 75, NARA-DC.

20. Sarah Deer details how sexual assaults and sexual violence is a fundamental component of settler colonialism that particularly targets Indigenous women. Deer, *Beginning and End of Rape*.

21. For more on Sisseton-Wahpeton history, see Oneroad and Skinner, *Being Dakota*; and Brown, "Biographic Sketch of Chief Gabriel Renville."

22. Rose Renville to Royal C. Johnson, January 10, 1927, Box 17, CA, CCF 1907–39, RG 75, NARA-DC; H. R. Hummer to Mrs. S. H. Renville, December 3, 1926, ibid.

23. Royal C. Johnson to Charles H. Burke, January 14, 1927, Box 17, CA, CCF 1907–39, RG 75, NARA-DC.

24. Rose Renville to Royal C. Johnson, January 10, 1927.

25. As cited in Rose Renville to Royal C. Johnson, January 10, 1927.

26. H. R. Hummer to Commissioner, September 29, 1926. Faith O'Neil—Faribault's granddaughter and Cora's daughter—shared her grandmother's viewpoint. She asserted strongly that Hummer mistreated her grandmother and was to blame for Elizabeth's pregnancy. Reflecting on the consequences of Hummer's actions, O'Neil added: "The ruin of so many Indian lives. My relatives." O'Neil, personal audio recording, August 14, 2012.

27. At the time of Cora Winona's birth, Elizabeth Faribault and Willie Dayea apparently disputed the claim of Dayea's paternity. The only extant sources are from Superintendent Hummer and the asylum staff, whom he directed to compose letters regarding the child's birth. Hummer's confident assertion to the BIA that Dayea fathered the little girl contrasts with the descriptions of cloudy paternity he offered later in correspondence with Faribault's oldest son, Solomon. Allegations that institutionalized men impregnated institutionalized women fit a broader pattern at Canton and most other state-run psychiatric and carceral facilities. Superintendents Gifford and Hummer both consistently disregarded claims by women that male staff fathered their children. Administrators at St. Elizabeths Hospital similarly assumed that an institutionalized man impregnated an Oglala Lakota woman held in their locked wards in the 1930s. This patterned interpretation reinforced settler ableist-eugenic logics that rendered Indigenous people problems, buffered institutions and staff from allegations of harm and mismanagement, and buttressed claims for the need to sustain institutionalization and institutional structures. See, for example, L. L. Culp to Commissioner, March 1, 1934, Box 4, CA, CCF 1907–39, RG 75, NARA-DC; L. L. Culp to Commissioner, February 26, 1934, ibid.; H. R. Hummer to John M. Thompson, August 18, 1928, SA, ibid.; H. R. Hummer to Commissioner, March 2, 1928, Box 17, CA, ibid.; Winfred Overholser to James G. Townsend, November 17, 1937, Folder 7448, ibid.; CA abstract, Willie Dayea, 1933, Box 3, ibid.; H. R. Hummer to BIA, March 26, 1921, Box 7, ibid.; and Burch, "'Dislocated Histories,'" 157–59.

28. H. R. Hummer to Commissioner, January 22, 1927, Box 17, CA, CCF 1907–39, RG 75, NARA-DC.

29. Burch, digital database. According to archival sources, two children were removed to orphanages. Staff began plans to move one other infant ("Baby Enaspah"), but the baby died before the transfer occurred.

30. Mary Alexis to Commissioner Charles Burke, September 13, 1921, Folder 121232-1916, Box 296, SA, CCF 1907–39, RG 75, NARA-DC.

31. For example, "List of patients now at the Asylum for Insane Indians, Canton, South Dakota, who have who have been received since July 1925," November 22, 1929, Folder 56470, Box 18, CA, CCF 1907–39, RG 75, NARA-DC.

32. The name "Cora" became especially popular after the publication of American writer James Fenimore Cooper's The Last of the Mohicans (1826). The novel's dark-haired heroine was named Cora Munro. The other baby who survived Canton also was named

Cora. It is possible, though unlikely, that this first name was imposed by Canton staff rather than selected by the mothers.

33. Hyman, *Dakota Women's Work*, 133.

34. Hyman, *Dakota Women's Work*, 133. Colette Hyman also noted that Dakota children commonly were referred to as *wakanyeza* ("sacred little beings"). Hyman, *Dakota Women's Work*, 13. See also Oneroad and Skinner, *Being Dakota*, 88.

35. See, for example, H. D. Jenckes, Report, August 31, 1917, Folder 82331, Box 35, Pipestone, 722.1, CCF 1907–39, RG 75, NARA-DC; Asylum for Insane Indians, *Annual Report and Census*, 1921, SDSA; Asylum for Insane Indians, *Annual Report and Census*, 1924, ibid.; Asylum for Insane Indians, *Annual Report and Census*, 1926, ibid.; H. R. Hummer to Commissioner, September 12, 1917, Folder 82331, Box 35, Pipestone, 722.1, CCF 1907–39, RG 75, NARA-DC; H. R. Hummer to Commissioner (regarding Abraham Hopkins), March 28, 1929, Box 12, CA, ibid. Eleven-year-old Margaret DeCouteau was institutionalized in 1916. H. R. Hummer to Commissioner, August 7, 1916, Box 296, SA, 722.1, CCF 1907–39, RG 75, NARA-DC; H. R. Hummer to Commissioner, October 15, 1924, Box 10, CA, ibid; Commissioner to L. L. Culp, December 16, 1933, Box 3, ibid.

36. Ben Meader, "Visualization 2," Canton Asylum for Insane Indians: GIS Visualizations, unpublished document for Susan Burch. There were at least twenty identified Lakota people from Pine Ridge and another twenty members of Rosebud Sioux Tribe. Meader, Map 2, Canton Asylum for Insane Indians: GIS Visualizations, unpublished document for Susan Burch, 25.

37. Accounts vary on the number of nations whose people were incarcerated at Canton. According to journalist Steve Young, it was upward of sixty-three; other authors have estimated it closer to fifty. See, for example, Young, "Shameful Past," 30; Leahy, "Canton Asylum," 75.

38. See, for example, Susan Wishecoby to H. R. Hummer, June 14, 1925, Box 17, CA, CCF 1907–39, RG 75, NARA-DC; unsigned report, October 23, 1929, Box 6, CA, Program Mission Correspondence, 1914–34, RG 75, NARA-KC; unsigned report, "Case No. 152: Peter Thompson Good Boy," February 15, 1917, Individual Patient Files, 1910–16, Box 9, ibid.; "Translation by John Brown," February 19, 1917, ibid.; and H. R. Hummer to Commissioner (describing Nellie Kampeska writing Elizabeth Faribault's letter), December 31, 1918, Folder 1252-1916, Box 296, SA, 722.1, CCF 1907–39, RG 75, NARA-DC. Reports from St. Elizabeths Hospital—where some people later would be confined—continued to reference people taking care of one another. Two examples: One Cherokee man took care of "untidy" hallmates at Canton and at St. Elizabeths regularly fed, bathed, and clothed another man who had been detained previously at Canton as well. Admission note, Watt McCarter, January 3, 1934, Box 4, CA, ibid. A Turtle Mountain Chippewa elder was described as taking a "motherly interest" in a younger Native woman on her ward. St. Elizabeths Hospital admissions note, Madeline Dauphinais, January 15, 1934, ibid.; "Report Regarding Susan Burch," January 1, 1913, Box 154, Decimal Files, Series 723-005, RCUA, RG 75, NARA-D.

39. For more on Indigenous kinship as a verb rather than merely a noun, see Justice, "Go Away Water!," 150–51. Disability literary scholar Benjamin Reis, in *Theaters of Madness*, details efforts by institutionalized people in nineteenth-century New York to carve out spaces of cultural expression, relationships, and personhood.

40. As anthropologist Ella Deloria (Yankton Dakota) explained, "By kinship all Dakota people were held together in a great relationship that was theoretically all-inclusive and co-extensive with the Dakota domain." Deloria, *Speaking of Indians*, 24–25. For more on Dakota kinship, see also DeMallie, "Kinship"; and Rumi, "Mitákuye Owás'į (All My Relatives)."

41. Affidavit, Nellie Kampeska, January 22, 1919, Box 14, CA, CCF 1907–39, RG 75, NARA-DC.

42. See, for example, see Fixico, *American Indians in a Modern World*, 5–6; Walker, DeMallie, and Jahner, *Lakota Belief and Ritual*, 198–200; and Holt, *Indian Orphanages*, 23. See also Jacobs, "Diverted Mothering," 185n.

43. Milwaukee Public Museum, "Kinship." See also DeMallie, "Kinship."

44. Elizabeth Alexis to David Mazakute, January 2, 1922, Box 16, CA, CCF 1907–39, RG 75, NARA-DC.

45. Describing the impact of written language and literacy for Dakota people during battles with the United States during the 1860s, historian Collette Hyman has explained, "Letters could not compensate for the physical, emotional, and spiritual burdens of separation, and letter writing could no way re-create a living community among the Dakota. It did, however, give them knowledge about relatives several hundred miles away. With the centrality of tiospaye among the Dakota, communication through letters allowed for some fragmentary nurturing of familial bonds." Hyman, *Dakota Women's Work*, 114. K. Tsianina Lomawaima's historical study of the Chilocco Boarding School as a "story of Indian students—loyal to each other, linked as family, and subversive in their resistance," resembles in some ways the inner workings at Canton Asylum. Lomawaima, *They Called It Prairie Light*, xi. For insightful critiques of gender dynamics and institutionalization, including strategies of resistance, see Rembis, *Defining Deviance*.

46. H. R. Hummer to the Department of the Interior, June 30, 1919, Box 14, CA, CCF 1907–39, RG 75, NARA-DC; H. R. Hummer to Commissioner, December 31, 1918, Folder 121232-1916, Box 296, SA, 722.1, ibid.

47. Affidavit, Nellie Kampeska, January 22, 1919, Box 14, CA, CCF 1907–39, RG 75, NARA-DC; H. R. Hummer to Commissioner, January 23, 1919, ibid.

48. Kampeska's discharge is additionally remarkable because the diagnosis Hummer assigned her was considered more chronic, serious, and heritable than many others who were not released, and she was still young and thus presumably capable of having children.

49. It is unknown whether Jesse, Mary, or Elizabeth's other relatives on the outside knew at the time of her escape. It appears that not long afterward, Jesse married Mary Marlow. By the end of 1920, institutional documents listed Elizabeth Faribault as divorced, and ever after she signed letters as "Elizabeth Alexis"—her original documented family name. The frayed familial ties with Jesse compounded Elizabeth's physical dislocation.

50. Mary Alexis to Charles Burke, September 13, 1921, Folder 121232-1916, Box 296, SA, CCF 1907–39, RG 75, NARA-DC; Elizabeth Fairbault to Charles Burke, September 13, 1921, Folder 45525–1922, CA, 722.1, ibid.

51. Hummer presumed that Faribault was headed to Sisseton and her family. H. R. Hummer to Commissioner, September 26, 1921, Box 15, CA, CCF 1907–39, RG 75, NARA-DC.

52. H. R. Hummer to Commissioner, September 29, 1921, Folder 121232-1916, Box 296, SA, 722.1, CCF 1907–39, RG 75, NARA-DC.

53. The original expression is "is ci koda tuwena waamiciyataninsni." I am grateful to the Dakota elders who translated Faribault's letter in 2012.

54. Elizabeth Alexis to David Mazakute, January 2, 1922, Box 16, CA, CCF 1907–39, RG 75, NARA-DC.

55. DeMallie, "Kinship."

56. Elizabeth Alexis to David Mazakute, January 2, 1922. Historian Keith Thor Carlson details the multiple, overlapping, and sometimes contradictory identities Indigenous people simultaneously have lived, alongside contested ideas about memory and place, in *The Power of Place, the Problem of Time*.

57. H. R. Hummer to Commissioner, June 22, 1922, Box 16, CA, CCF 1907–39, RG 75, NARA-DC.

58. Yellow Bird, "Wild Indians," 9, accessed December 17, 2014.

59. H. R. Hummer to Commissioner, March 2, 1928, Box 17, CA, CCF 1907–39, RG 75, NARA-DC.

60. Samuel Silk in 1929 had described Canton's record keeping as inadequate and contradictory, taking issue with multiple diagnoses and reporting practices. Samuel A. Silk to Commissioner (through Richard White), "Report of Survey: Asylum for Insane Indians, Canton, South Dakota," April 13, 1929, Box 1078, 5-1 (California–CA), CCF 1907–36, RG 48, NARA-CP, 59–60 (hereafter referred to as "1929 Silk Report"). Some of Elizabeth Faribault's relatives have specifically noted that the partial, ambiguous, and inconsistent records reflect a system, as well as individual employees and administrators, that harmed their ancestor. O'Neil interviews, March 6, June 25, 2012, March 12, October 29, November 11, 24, 2014, March 8, 2016, April 6–7, May 17, 2015, March 29, 2019.

61. Cora Winona Faribault's continued detention at Canton lends support to the Faribault family's claim that Elizabeth did not get sent back to Peever for burial. Infants at Canton were taken from mothers, but it was not likely that a toddler would be left behind there if her mother's body was returned to a reservation for burial. To keep Cora Winona and return Elizabeth would have required significant administrative effort.

62. See E. Deloria, *Speaking of Indians*, 26, 49; DeMallie, "Kinship."

63. J. Miller, "Kinship, Family Kindreds, and Community," 151.

64. DeMallie, "Kinship," 323. See also Peers and Brown, "There Is No End to Relationship among the Indians," 529–55. Native American historian Margaret Jacobs has explained: "Indigenous communities defined family broadly and designated many caregivers beyond the biological mother and father, particularly grandparents. In many matrilineal Indigenous cultures, a mother's brother played the fatherly role to his nephews and nieces, and a child might consider all his or her maternal aunts as mothers." Jacobs, *Generation Removed*, xxxiii.

65. Unsigned report, October 23, 1929, Box 6, CA, Program Mission Correspondence, 1914–34, RG 75, NARA-KC.

66. Iron Cloud telephone interviews, May 19, 2015, March 27, 2018; Elizabeth Red Owl to Charles Burke, April 18, 1924, Box 17, CA, CCF 1907–39, RG 75, NARA-DC; Elizabeth (Lizzie) Red Owl to Amos Red Owl, March 15, 1926, Box 538, Pine Ridge, ibid.; Elizabeth Red Owl to Commissioner, May 18, 1930, Box 1, CA, ibid. Her parents also yearned for

her return. Amos Red Owl to John Collier, September 15, 1933, Box 18, ibid. See also Commissioner to Amos Red Owl, December 10, 1929, ibid. Amos Red Owl petitioned the BIA commissioner on November 18, 1929, emphasizing that he could take care of Lizzie, that she was his daughter, and that he wanted her to be allowed home. Amos Red Owl to Commissioner, December 10, 1929, ibid. A relative of Lizzie Red Owl, Richard Iron Cloud, would later bring a group of Oglala Lakota youth to swim from Alcatraz to the San Francisco shore as a collective act of survivance and Indigenous self-determination. Their experiences were documented in a film, directed by Nancy Iverson, entitled *From the Badlands to Alcatraz* (2009).

67. On other days, the child would sit and listen to the radio, likely with Lizzie nearby. Unsigned staff report, October 23, 1929, Box 6, CA, Program Mission Correspondence, 1914–34, CCF 1907–39, RG 75, NARA-KC; unsigned staff report, October 25, 1929, ibid.

68. Lizzie Red Owl to Commissioner Burke, April 18, 1924, 4; Elizabeth Red Owl to commissioner, May 18, 1930.

69. As quoted in Joshua Wetsit to John Collier, November 6, 1933, Folder 40642-28, Box 350, SA, CCF 1907–39, RG 75, NARA-DC.

70. Burch, photo of dolls made by Lizzie Red Owl, taken at the CPL; Juel telephone conversations, October 6, 2013, April 4, 2020; Juel informal interview, May 18, 2015.

71. Iron Cloud telephone interviews, May 19, 2015, March 27, 2018; Iron Cloud email correspondence, May 20, 2015. For more on Native American dolls and dollmaking, see Lenz and Kidwell, *Small Spirits*; and Lenz, *Stuff of Dreams*.

72. Young, "Hiawatha Remembered"; Juel telephone conversations, October 6, 2013, April 4, 2020; Juel informal interview, May 18, 2015.

Chapter 4

1. This paragraph is a lightly edited version from Burch, "Disorderly Pasts," 362–85. For general histories of Canton Asylum, see Riney, "Power and Powerlessness"; Putney, "Canton Asylum"; and Saxman, "Canton Asylum." For more on Menominee Nation history, see Beck, *Struggle for Self-Determination*; Ourada, *Menominee Indians*. I especially thank Menominee Nation Tribal Historian David Grignon and elder Napos for their insights and guidance on researching and writing these stories.

2. Samuel Silk described the asylum's building, including the dormitory spaces. "1929 Silk Report," 4.

3. Containment fundamentally framed everyday life at most asylums across the United States during the late nineteenth and early twentieth centuries. See Grob, *Mental Illness and American Society*; Braslow, *Mental Ills and Bodily Cures*; Lunbeck, *Psychiatric Persuasion*; Dwyer, *Homes for the Mad*; Whitaker, *Mad in America*; Rothman, *Discovery of the Asylum*; Porter and Wright, *Confinement of the Insane*; Szasz, *Coercion as Cure*; Rothman, *Conscience and Convenience*; Jimenez, *Changing Faces of Madness*; Scull, *Madhouses, Mad-Doctors, and Madmen*; Szasz, *Manufacture of Madness*; Dowbiggin, *Keeping America Sane*, 75; Scull, *Madness in Civilization*; Deutsch, *Mentally Ill in America*; Goffman, "Characteristics of Total Institutions."

4. Like other carceral institutions, Canton embodied additional levels of containment. Sex-segregated wards imposed social structures that were antagonistic to Native communities. Spouses who were simultaneously detained, as just one example, were

cordoned off to different rooms and wings from one another. For more on sex segregation as a form of institutional sterilization in psychiatric institutions, see Dwyer, *Homes for the Mad*, 25–26; and Whitaker, *Mad in America*, 55–60.

5. As one report implied, negligence contributed significantly to padlocked isolation rooms and to people being shackled to beds and steampipes. Among the additionally secluded people the inspector had observed was a young barefoot boy in a solitary room, subdued in a straitjacket. "Untidiness and dribbling of saliva," staff claimed, motivated this treatment. "1929 Silk Report," 14.

6. John Noble to Commissioner, November 22, 1916, Box 296, SA, 722.1, RG 75, NARA-DC.

7. It appears that Faribault assisted in the laundry and the Hummer household concurrently for some time. Institutional correspondence about the Dakota woman's pregnancy claimed that she and Willie Dayea met in the laundry area. H. R. Hummer to Commissioner, September 29, 1926, Box 17, CA, CCF 1907–39, RG 75, NARA-DC; L. L. Culp to Solomon Faribault, February 26, 1934, Box 4, ibid.; L. L. Culp to Commissioner, February 26, 1934, ibid.

8. Cato Sells to H. R. Hummer, May 15, 1916, Box 5, CA, CCF 1907–39, RG 75, NARA-DC; "Statement Regarding Harry Hummer, Superintendent of the Canton Insane Asylum," n.d., ibid.; affidavit L. M. Hardin, November 19, 1909, ibid., 3. Clara Christopher attested that the chamber work was daily. "In the Matter of Complaints, Canton Asylum, Canton, South Dakota, Statement of Clara Christopher, Laborer," June 8, 1915, ibid.

9. Elizabeth Fe Alexis to Commissioner Burke, May 22, 1922, Box 16, CA, CCF 1907–39, RG 75, NARA-DC.

10. H. R. Hummer, "Asylum for Insane Indians: Elizabeth Faribault (2331)," October 1, 1926, Box 17, CA, CCF 1907–39, RG 75, NARA-DC.

11. H. R. Hummer, "Asylum for Insane Indians: Elizabeth Faribault," November 1, 1926, Box 17, CA, CCF 1907–39, RG 75, NARA-DC.

12. Reliable and efficient, Dayea would have been a likely choice when staff selected teams of people to clear the highway and water areas as well.

13. In 1926, 230 acres of Christopher family farmland was bought to expand the asylum's campus. Commissioner Charles Burke to Secretary of the Interior, October 23, 1926, Box 1078, CA, CCF 1907–36, 5-1, RG 48, NARA-CP. See also "1929 Silk Report," 29; and Meriam and Work, *The Problem of Indian Administration*, 306 (hereafter referred to as *Meriam Report*).

14. See, for example, CA abstract, Willie Dayea, 1933, Box 3, CA, CCF 1907–39, RG 75, NARA-DC.

15. Asylum for Insane Indians, *Annual Report*, 1925, SDSA, 2. Other farmers in the area at this time described long days and continuous work: tilling, seeding, planting, irrigating, harvesting, and storing wheat, corn, and other produce as snow-frozen ground softened in the spring, hardened under late summer heat, and submitted to the return of winter.

16. See, for example, James McLaughlin to Secretary of the Interior, July 21, 1910, Box 1078, 5-1 (California–Canton Asylum), CCF 1907–36, RG 48, NARA-CP; Asylum for Insane Indians, *Annual Report*, 1910, SDSA, 3–4; Asylum for Insane Indians, *Annual Report*, 1911, ibid.; Asylum for Insane Indians, "Narrative: Industries," ibid., 19; Asylum

for Insane Indians, *Annual Report*, 1927, ibid.; *Meriam Report*, 307; V. E. Ball to H. R. Hummer, November 2, 1929, Box 6, CA, Program Mission Correspondence, 1914–34, RG 75, NARA-KC; Occupational list, 1934, Indian Insane Int. Dept., Records Relating to the Department of the Interior 1902–43, Box 1, Entry 13, RG 418, NARA-DC; Putney, "Canton Asylum," 7.

17. See, for example, Dwyer, *Homes for the Mad*, 131–36; Jackson, "In Our Own Voice," 19–21; Reaume, "Patients at Work"; Ernst, *Work, Psychiatry and Society*; Trent, *Inventing the Feeble Mind*; and Deutsch, *Mentally Ill in America*.

18. Burch, digital database.

19. It was a standard contention that this practice reduced the need for more explicit forms of restraint, such as shackles or medications. McCandless, *Moonlight, Magnolias, and Madness*, 272. For other studies of asylums and labor, see Rothman, *Discovery of the Asylum*; Burch and Joyner, *Unspeakable*; and Scull, *Madhouses, Mad-Doctors, and Madmen*.

20. Asylum for Insane Indians, "Labor: Statistical," in *Annual Report*, 1921, SDSA, 24; Asylum for Insane Indians, "Table XIII," in *Annual Report*, 1911, ibid., 32.

21. As with other settler enterprises that often loaned their charges to neighboring businesses, there is evidence to suggest that both of Canton's superintendents supplemented the budget by detailing men like Willie Dayea to nearby highway and agricultural work. Burch, digital database. Other settler institutions with outing and other involuntary-labor practices included Indian boarding schools, prisons, and state asylums. See, for example, Parker, *Phoenix Indian School*; Hernández, *City of Inmates*; Christianson, *With Liberty for Some*, 184–88; Nichols and Swiffen, *Legal Violence and the Limits of the Law*; and Burch and Joyner, *Unspeakable*.

22. This was typical across institutions nationwide. McCandless, *Moonlight, Magnolias, and Madness*, 275.

23. Gregory interviews, May 9, 2012, February 23, 2015, July 3, 2017, December 28, 2018, July 19, 2019; Gregory email correspondence, November 16, 2018. Used with permission from Anne Gregory. For background on Creek Nation history and the Trail of Tears, see Hamill and Cinnamon, "This Strange Journey," 93–111.

24. In 1909, for example, there were twenty people above listed capacity. "Reply to Charges," November 16, 1909, 7, Box 2, CA, CCF 1907–39, NARA-DC.

25. Affidavit, L. M. Hardin, November 19, 1909, Box 5, CA, CCF 1907–39, RG 75, NARA-DC.

26. "Females: Emma Gregory," 1910, Box 2, CA, CCF 1907–29, RG 75, NARA-DC.

27. "List of Canton Inhabitants with Diagnoses," n.d., Box 2, CA, CCF 1907–39, RG 75, NARA-DC. Drs. Hardin and Turner pointed out that Gregory ate well and had no cough or fever, but they were unable to overturn Superintendent Hummer's directives.

28. Spaulding, "Canton Asylum for Insane Indians." Peter McCandless has detailed conditions at southern institutions that especially encouraged disease spread, such as overcrowding, insufficient ventilation and sunlight, and poor plumbing. Canton embodied nearly identical conditions in this regard. McCandless, *Moonlight, Magnolias, and Madness*, 284. Jean A. Keller provides a similar assessment of tuberculosis spread in American Indian boarding schools during the early twentieth century in her work *Empty Beds*.

29. See, for example, affidavit, L. M. Hardin, November 19, 1909, 6; and *Meriam Report*, 307. For more on the history of medical research on tuberculosis, see Tomes, "Germ Theory, Public Health Education, and the Moralization of Behavior," 257; Keller, *Empty Beds*, 151–54.

30. According to Dr. Hardin, the Diné woman with tuberculosis died shortly thereafter, as did the infant child she delivered not long after being committed to the asylum. Affidavit, L. M. Hardin, November 19, 1909, 6. See also W. T. Shelton to Commissioner, October 11, 1909, Box 13, CA, CCF 1907–39, RG 75, NARA-DC.

31. Dr. Hardin said that Emma Gregory did not have a persistent cough or fever and that she was eating well. Affidavit, L. M. Hardin, November 19, 1909, 6.

32. Although general public awareness of the disease's origins increased during this time, carceral institutions, including prisons, psychiatric asylums, and colonies for the feebleminded, remained active locations for tuberculosis outbreaks and fatalities. When Dr. Samuel Silk from St. Elizabeths Hospital inspected the asylum in 1933, he reported: "In the cases of suspected pulmonary tuberculosis no ex-aminations of sputum are performed, and in no case is the diagnosis definitely established. Three patients had active coughs and loss of weight, which would point to that diagnosis. They mingled with the other patients, and no special provision was made for their care." "1933 Silk Report," 12.

33. Affidavit, L.M. Hardin, November 19, 1909; "Emma Gregory," Box 2, CA, CCF 1907–39, RG 75, NARA-DC; BIA to J. A. Self, November 10, 1906, Box 1, Misc. Records Relating to Lunacy Cases, 1904–8, CCF 1907–39, RG 75, NARA-FW; Joseph Murphy, "Report of Charges against the Superintendent," February 1, 1910, Box 2, CA, CCF 1907–39, RG 75, NARA-DC; "Reply to Charges-II," ibid.; H. R. Hummer to Commissioner, "Report on Methods of Combatting Tuberculosis," February 23, 1909, Box 18, ibid.; Inspection of the Asylum for Insane Indians, July 21, 1910, Box 2, ibid.

34. An attendant later attested that Gregory had been fully blocked from leaving the confined space.

35. Joseph A. Murphy to Commissioner, February 1, 1910, Box 2, CA, CCF 1907–39, RG 75, NARA-DC.

36. There were many other men and women who would intimately come to know such spaces. It was commonplace at the Indian Asylum for people to be confined for months at a time in the dormitories and isolation rooms.

37. Gregory interviews, July 3, 2017, December 28, 2018. Anthropologist Paul Farmer argues a similar point in "House of the Dead," 240. For broader studies of the health consequences to Indigenous people because of settler colonialisms, see Kelton, *Cherokee Medicine, Colonial Germs*; and Cameron, Kelton, and Swedlund, *Beyond Germs*. See also Kauanui, "'A Structure, Not an Event.'"

38. Herman was forcibly committed to Canton Asylum on February 28, 1914. H. R. Hummer to Commissioner, March 2, 1914, Box 13, CA, CCF 1907–39, RG 75, NARA-DC. I thank descendants of James Herman for permitting me write about their ancestor and the colleagues at Rosebud's Tribal Historic Preservation Office for their insights and advice in the process of writing this book.

39. James Herman, "Statement on Treatment of Patients at Canton Insane Asylum," received June 17, 1915, Box 5, CA, CCF 1907–39, RG 75, NARA-DC, 8. Years earlier, an observer had complained that "filth and disorder reigned supreme" at the Indian Asylum.

Another had noted that water overflow and body waste had soaked into the soapstone urinal in a men's bathroom, making it unusable and generating an "exceedingly offensive" odor. See J. F. Turner to K. K. Sniffen, January 3, 1910, Box 2, ibid.; "Dr. J. F. Turner, Former Assistant Superintendent," n.d., ibid.; Joseph Murphy, "Section 1: Relations between Superintendent and Employees," February 1, 1910, 7, ibid.; Joseph A. Murphy to Commissioner, "Report of Conditions of Patients," February 1, 1910, Box 11, ibid., sec. 2, p. 2. More than a decade after Herman's testimony, in 1929, medical inspections continued to reference the proliferation of open chamberpots and the related stench in the locked wards. "1929 Silk Report," 6.

40. Report to Commissioner, January 31, 1912, Box 2, CA, CCF 1907–39, RG 75, NARA-DC.

41. Affidavit, Oscar Gifford, August 13, 1907, 4, Box 1, CA, CCF 1907–39, RG 75, NARA-DC; Walter Stevens, "Medical Report," September 1925, Box 10, ibid. See also "1929 Silk Report," 17.

42. Silk also noted that some people had been left in their own excrement for days and even weeks. "1929 Silk Report."

43. See, for example, letter, Peter Thomson Good Boy, trans. John Brown, February 19, 1917, Box 9, CA, Individual Patient Files, 1914–16, Decimal 414–580, Program Mission Correspondence, 1914–34, RG 75, NARA-KC. This source is cited with concurrence from the Rosebud Tribal Historic Preservation Office.

44. See James Herman, "Statement on Treatment of Patients at Canton Insane Asylum," received June 17, 1915, Box 6, CA, CCF 1907–39, RG 75, NARA-DC, 8; Dr. L. F. Michael, "Report to Commissioner," June 12, 1915, ibid., 18–19.

45. Herman, "Statement on Treatment of Patients at Canton Insane Asylum," 3.

46. Herman, "Statement on Treatment of Patients at Canton Insane Asylum," 3. Menominee member Susan Wishecoby similarly documented mistreatment in the wards. A formal letter to Superintendent Hummer in 1925 sought intervention with the staff: "I wish you would please learn them to treat us like human beings not like beast to be teasing all the time." Susan Wishecoby to H. R. Hummer, June 14, 1925, Box 17, CA, CCF 1907–39, RG 75, NARA-DC.

47. James Herman was among the minority of Native people with strong English literacy and personal connections to influential white people outside the asylum. These advantages contributed to the creation, dissemination, and preservation of his affidavit. Norman Ewing, Canton's only Native staff member at the time, secreted Herman's written observations out of the institution and delivered them to BIA officials.

48. For example, H. R. Hummer to Commissioner, December 18, 1909, Box 6, CA, CCF 1907–39, RG 75, NARA-DC; H. R. Hummer to Commissioner, August 6, 1931, Box 6, CA, Program Mission Correspondence, 1910–34, RG 75, NARA-KC; H. R. Hummer to Tom Robinson, May 14, 1932, Box 18, CA, CCF 1907–39, RG 75, NARA-DC; H. R. Hummer to Commissioner, March 26, 1920, Box 6, ibid.; H. R. Hummer to Commissioner, September 27, 1926, Box 17, ibid.; notes, H. R. Hummer, March 18, 1929, Box 6, CA, Program Mission Correspondence, 1910–34, RG 75, NARA-KC; affidavit, Jesse Watkins, November 23, 1909, Box 13, CA, CCF 1907–39, RG 75, NARA-DC; Elizabeth Coleman to Commissioner, July 17, 1926, Box 5, ibid. Historian Scott Riney also details assaults of institutionalized people by staff at Canton in "Power and Powerlessness," 1–3.

49. See, for example, Riney, "Power and Powerlessness," 41–42; Spaulding, "Canton Asylum for Insane Indians," 1007–11; and Sweet, "Controversial Care," 69n102. Samuel Silk noted that even more serious incidents sometimes escaped recording. "1929 Silk Report," 31.

50. Basements, staff quarters, secluded places on the grounds, and women's dormitories were among the identified sites of attacks.

51. Affidavit, Nellie Kampeska, January 22, 1919, Box 14, CA, CCF 1907–39, RG 75, NARA-DC.

52. Affidavit, Nellie Kampeska, January 22, 1919.

53. As cited in H. R. Hummer to BIA, March 26, 1921, Box 7, CA, CCF 1907–39, RG 75, NARA-DC.

54. Other Indigenous women inhabiting single or double rooms, often near stairways, appear in similar accounts of sexual assault at Canton.

55. H. R. Hummer to Department of the Interior, June 30, 1919, Folder 57067, Box 14, CA, 722.1, CCF 1907–39, RG 75, NARA-DC. Legal expert Sarah Deer has shown that rape has been and continues to be a pervasive, sustained result of settler colonialism. Deer, *Beginning and End of Rape*. See also Freedman, *Redefining Rape*.

56. H. R. Hummer to Commissioner, March 26, 1920, Box 5, CA, CCF 1907–39, RG 75, NARA-DC. Pathologizing the victim of sexual assault fits a larger pattern of systemic sexual assault on Native Americans. Deer, *Beginning and End to Rape*; Freedman, *Redefining Rape*.

57. See, for example, records on staff members Berney Christopher, William E. Juel, Louis A. Hewling, and V. E. Ball, CA, CCF 1907–39, RG 75, NARA-DC. Allowing perpetrators to go unpunished also fits a larger settler pattern of sexual violence targeting Native women. Goeman and Nez Denetdale, "Guest Editors' Introduction: Native Feminisms," 9–13; Deer, "Decolonizing Rape Law," 149–67; Deer, *Beginning and End to Rape*; Weaver, "Colonial Context of Violence," 1552–63.

58. E. B. Merritt to H. R. Hummer, February 1, 1919, Box 14, CA, 722.1, CCF 1907–39, RG 75, NARA-DC. Responding to the assault on Caldwell and Amour, the commissioner also had informed Hummer that he "may give William E. Juel and Louis A. Hewling, male employees of the asylum, an opportunity to resign if they desire to do so." Cato Sells to H. R. Hummer, April 5, 1920, Box 5, CA, ibid.

59. Commissioner Merritt, responding to Superintendent Hummer, noted at the time, "In view of the fact that all of the employees indicated in Nellie's charge have left the institution, it is doubtful that anything further should be done." E. B. Merritt to Hummer, February 1, 1919, Box 14, CA, CCF 1907–39, RG 75, NARA-DC.

60. Environmental humanities specialist Rob Nixon has challenged scholars to attend to "violence that is neither spectacular nor instantaneous, but rather incremental and accretive, its calamitous repercussions playing out across a range of temporal scales." Nixon, *Slow Violence*, 2–3.

61. H. R. Hummer to Commissioner (documenting Herman's first breakout), March 24, 1919, Box 13, CA, CCF 1907–39, RG 75, NARA-DC; H. R. Hummer to Commissioner, March 15, 1919, ibid.; H. R. Hummer to Commissioner, February 9, 1920, Box 15, ibid.; H. R. Hummer to Commissioner, October 9, 1919, Box 13, ibid.; H. R. Hummer to Commissioner, August 29, 1922, Box 16, ibid.; H. R. Hummer to Commissioner, January 22,

1919, Box 14, ibid.; H. R. Hummer to Commissioner, October 10, 1919, Box 13, ibid.; H. R. Hummer to Commissioner, June 12, 1920, Box 15, ibid.; telegram, H. R. Hummer to Indian Office, October 23, 1919, Box 13, ibid. James Herman was formally discharged from Canton a few weeks after he had already escaped the campus. H. R. Hummer to Commissioner, October 29, 1919, ibid.; H. R. Hummer to Commissioner, January 14, 1920, Box 14, ibid.; H. R. Hummer to Commissioner, January 16, 1920, ibid.; H. R. Hummer to Commissioner, January 21, 1919, Folder 82331, Box 35, Pipestone, 722.1, ibid.

62. Many relatives on the outside repeatedly pleaded for families to be reunited as well, a resounding pattern of kinship and resistance.

63. As one of numerous examples, an institutionalized man described employees "using us rough," using a "Black Hand" on them, and making "sick people work." Describing others in his locked ward, he added, "Many of them die" because employees "get mad and kill them." The witness directed another Native man to translate his testimony into English and show it to the commissioner. Letter, Peter Thomson Good Boy, trans. John Brown, February 19, 1917, Box 9, CA, Individual Patient Files, 1914–16, Decimal 414–580, Program Mission Correspondence, 1914–34, RG 75, NARA-KC. See also Susan Wishecoby to H. R. Hummer, June 14, 1925, Box 17, CA, CCF 1907–39, RG 75, NARA-DC.

64. Emma Gregory died on Sunday, March 3, 1912. CA cemetery list, Box 4, CA, CCF 1907–39, RG 75, NARA-DC.

65. James Self had received updates on his sister and wrote to the BIA to ask about her condition. See, for example, unsigned letter to J. A. Self, November 10, 1906, Box 1, Misc. Records Relating to Lunacy Cases, 1904–8, RG 75, NARA-FW; H. R. Hummer to Commissioner, March 13, 1912, Box 19, CA, CCF 1907–39, RG 75, NARA-DC; and Gregory interviews, May 9, 2012, February 23, 2015, July 3, 2017, December 28, 2018, July 19, 2019.

66. This individual died on May 4, 1911.

67. Map of CA cemetery, Box 4, CA, CCF 1907–39, RG 75, NARA-DC; Asylum for Insane Indians, "Table 5: Number of Discharges Divided into Yearly Periods," *Annual Report*, 1912, 7.

68. Workers broke ground for the cemetery within months of the asylum's opening.

69. According to archival sources, at least 189 people out of 382 died while institutionalized. Burch, digital database; Soule and Soule, "Death at the Hiawatha Asylum for Insane Indians," 17; Spaulding, "Canton Asylum for Insane Indians."

70. The asylum ledger references 121 individuals, but archival documents confirm that 2 additional people—unnamed, and with no tribal affiliation or date of death recorded—are buried there as well.

71. Judah interview, November 7, 2015; Judah correspondence, November 14, 2015, April 8, 2016, January 18, 2017.

72. Burch, digital database.

73. H. R. Hummer to Commissioner, February 23, 1909, Box 18, CA, CCF 1907–39, RG 75, NARA-DC. Some BIA medical professionals, like Winnebago Agency physician W. J. Stevenson, contended that tuberculosis was "slowly, but surely, solving the Indian problem." Dr. W. J. Stevenson, "Reports of Agents in Nebraska: Report of Omaha and Winnebago Agency," August 24, 1897, in *Report of the Commissioner of Indian Affairs*, 179. Historian Christian W. McMillen has underscored that rampant infections of tuberculosis

and other diseases were never natural or neutral occurrences but the result of particular power structures and human actions. McMillen, "'The Red Man and the White Plague,'" 617. By this time, Western medical researchers had identified that tubercle bacillus, not hereditary illness, caused tuberculosis. See Tomes, "Germ Theory, Public Health Education, and the Moralization of Behavior," 257.

74. Farmer, "House of the Dead," 240; McCandless, *Moonlight, Magnolias, and Madness.*

75. Soule and Soule, "Death at the Hiawatha Asylum for Insane Indians," 17.

76. Medical notes dated April 1, 1913, for the person referred to as Susan Burch described her as "unchanged" mentally; her physical condition was "not satisfactory" because she had "irregular fever and headache. Slight cough. Profuse nasal discharge." "Report Regarding Susan Burch," Box 154, Decimal Files, Series 723-005, RCUA, RG 75, NARA-D.

77. H. R. Hummer to Commissioner, August 16, 1913, Box 17, CA, CCF 1907–39, RG 75, NARA-DC.

78. CA cemetery ledger, Box 4, CA, CCF 1907–39, RG 75, NARA-DC.

79. Numerous people detained at Canton had been held in hospitals, asylums, or sanataria before their dislocation to the Indian Asylum. The US government transferred some from Canton before the BIA closed the Indian Asylum, placing them in other (usually state run) disability-related facilities; others were sent from St. Elizabeths to state hospitals or colonies for the feebleminded. See, for example, Oscar S. Gifford to Department of Interior, January 17, 1903, RG 418, Entry 13, NARA-DC; H. R. Hummer to Commissioner, July 20, 1925, Box 17, CA, CCF 1907–39, RG 75, ibid.; H. R. Hummer to Commissioner, September 26, 1933, Box 18, ibid.; J. M Scanland to H. R. Hummer, December 12, 1921, Box 15, ibid.; H. R. Hummer to Commissioner, January 2, 1921, ibid.; L. L. Culp to Commissioner, January 5, 1934, Box 4, ibid.; "Transferring of Patients from St. Elizabeth's to Canton," 2; Brings Plenty telephone interviews, September 8, 29, 2014; Brings Plenty email correspondence, September 30, 2014; Iron Cloud telephone interviews, May 19, 2015, March 27, 2018; F. Jensen telephone conversations, January 30, April 1, July 21, September 5, October 20, 2014; Judah interviews, June 24, December 28, 2011; and Teeman email correspondence, March 12, April 5, May 19, July 16, 18, 2014.

80. Silk reported that he had "personally examined each patient." He also noted that the interviews were brief. Samuel Silk to commissioner (through Dr. W. A. White), October 3, 1933, Folder 4, Box 3600B, H83-1, CA, SDSA, 1, 15.

81. Untitled handwritten note, H. R. Hummer, January 31, 1930, Box 5, CA, Program Mission Correspondence, 1914–43, RG 75, NARA-KC; telegram, H. R. Hummer to Superintendent Blair, January 31, 1930, ibid.

82. The admissions form for St. Elizabeths in 1934 describes Marlow as having black hair and brown eyes; standing five feet, six inches tall; and weighing 124 pounds. Admission note, George Marlow, December 30, 1933, Box 4, CA, CCF 1907–39, RG 75, NARA-DC.

83. "All the reports on the asylum are reminiscent of the terrible incidents as Charles Dickens leveled against English poor houses and schools." Cited in Herbert T. Hoover, "Canton Asylum," Canton Insane Asylum File, CPL, 2. See also "Hummer Asked to Disregard Closing Order," 1.

84. Public Health Service researcher Ruth Raup argued in 1959, "By the early 1920s, the Indian Bureau had a definite policy of limiting the growth of the Canton Asylum and placing more of the mentally ill Indians in State institutions." According to Raup, the *Meriam Report* added momentum to the process of closing the Indian Asylum. Raup, *Indian Health Program*, 16. See also "Only 125 of 225,000 Indians Insane," 1. Historical works about Collier and the BIA offer only passing references, if any, to Canton's closing. When noted, the interpretation follows a progress narrative that casts Collier as a hero for closing the Indian Asylum and transferring those detained there to St. Elizabeths. See, for example, Kelly, *Assault on Assimilation*; Kvasnicka and Viola, *Commissioners of Indian Affairs*, 277; and Philp, *John Collier's Crusade for Indian Reform*. See also DeJong, *"If You Knew the Conditions,"* 67. For historical examples of transinstitutionalization and the malleability of institutional systems, see Parsons, *From Asylum to Prison*; Ben-Moshe, Chapman, and Carey, *Disability Incarcerated*; and Chow and Priebe, "Understanding Psychiatric Institutionalization."

85. Ewing directly "related a series of truths" to Dr. L. F. Michael during the inspector's visit to Canton in June 1915. In addition to his own observations of mismanagement by Dr. Hummer, Ewing gave the inspector James Herman's written testimony. Ewing corresponded with the physician afterward, reaffirming that abuses were continuing. Norman Ewing to Dr. L. F. Michael, June 18, 1925, Box 6, CA, CCF 1907–39, RG 75, NARA-DC; affidavit, Norman Ewing, June 24, 1915, Box 5, ibid.; Norman Ewing to Commissioner, June 19, 1915. A visit to Washington, D.C., that year enabled Ewing to convey his concerns to Assistant Commissioner Edgar B. Merrit. No administrative changes were made, and Ewing was transferred to Fort Peck, Montana. Affidavit, Norman Ewing (Flying Iron), October 19, 1933, Box 3, ibid. See also Merritt to Ewing, June 30, 1915, Box 5, ibid.; and telegram, Norman Ewing to John Collier, October 16, 1933, Box 3, ibid. On October 18, 1933, Ewing headed to Washington. The Department of the Interior gave a press release that cited his telegram and affidavit attesting to Canton's brutal conditions, describing Ewing as "an important Indian source" and who approved of their effort to close the facility. Telegram, Norman Ewing to John Collier, October 18, 1933, ibid.; Department of the Interior, Memorandum for the Press, October 18, 1933, ibid.

86. Since his transfer, Ewing had honed his activist work, eventually becoming national chairman of the Inter-Tribal Committee. "Says Indians Have Fewer Rights Than Newly Arrived Immigrants," 4; "Chief Flying Iron Makes Plea for Indian's Citizenship Rights," 15; "Sioux Chief Asks Fair Play from U.S. for Indians," 2.

87. Telegram, Norman Ewing to John Collier, cited in Department of the Interior, Memorandum for the Press, October 18, 1933.

88. At the time, Harold Ickes questioned the town's motives: "Those responsible for securing this injunction presumably are actuated by a desire to save for Canton the revenue the continued operation of the institution there means. . . . They appeared to be willing to make a profit out of the degradation of helpless Indians. They do not object to locking up sane human beings in an Indian asylum." Ickes quoted in "Canton Asylum Conditions 'Sickening,'" 1.

89. See, for example, "Dr. Culp, Physician, Will Take Charge," 12; "Hummer Asked to Disregard Closing Order," 1; "Canton Asylum Conditions 'Sickening,'" 1; "Hummer

Denies All Charges," 1; "Brief Filed in Asylum Action," 10; "Moen, Judge Daugherty Offer Argument," 3; "Insane Indians Left at Canton," 8; "Ask Senators to Investigate Conditions at Asylum"; "'Indian Hunters' Impressed at Civilization Fund Out Here," 1; "20 Sane Indians Held in Asylum, Ickes Charges," 1; "Nephew Pres. Taft Counsel for Asylum," 21; Dutcher, "End of Misrule Heralded by Indians," 9-10; "Collier Visits in So. Dakota"; "30,000 Indians Petition to Retain Asylum"; "Ousted Asylum Head to Fight Charges," 1; "Wheeler Gets Results," 4; "Moving the Insane Indians," 6; "Collier Postpones Visit," 6; "Hiawatha Warhoops," 14; "Says U.S. Court Has Power," 5; "Sane Reds Confined in Asylum," 1; "Apparently an Expensive Move," 6; "Gov. Official Here to Make Report to US," 3; "'Sane' Indians Held in Dakota Asylum," N2; and "Asylum Story Listed as Most Important," 1.

90. "Head of Indian Asylum Fired by Ickes," 4; "Dr. Culp, Physician, Will Take Charge," 12; Valandra, "Naming a Committee," 6; "Transfers at Asylum Here Being Made," 1; "Near-By News Notes," 3.

91. John Collier to L. L. Culp, December 16, 1933, Box 3, CA, CCF 1907–39, RG 75, NARA-DC.

92. Collier, "Introduction," in La Farge, *Changing Indian*.

93. "Indian Mental Patients Reach Hospital Here," 4. See also "Indians' 'Inhuman' Asylum Is Closed," 2. The *Santa Cruz News*, under a banner that read "The End of Misrule Is Heralded for Indians," connected Collier's response to Canton Asylum alongside other reforms. See "Asylum Is Abolished," 1.

94. "Surprise Move Came without Warning Here," 1. See also "Plan Removal Canton Indians," 1; "Canton Indians Entrain for Capitol," 1; and Laudenschlager, "Infamous Institution," 336.

95. Hill interviews, May 15, 2012, May 18, 2013, May 14, 2015, February 13, 2017; Hill telephone conversations, September 12, 2014, December 4, 2016, July 18, 2017; Hill interview by Dexter, July 26, 2013. According to one newspaper, the separation of groups being discharged from those being sent to Washington caused distress for many Native people. "Canton Indians Entrain for Capitol," 1. See also L. L. Culp to Commissioner, December 21, 1933, Box 3, CA, CCF 1907–39, RG 75, NARA-DC.

96. "Surprise Move Came without Warning Here," 1.

97. Two others who were ill at the time were transferred in early 1934. "Two More Indian Patients Are Taken to Washington," 23; "Surprise Move Came without Warning Here," 1. See also letter to Dr. William A. White, St. Elizabeths Hospital, January 10, 1934, Box 4, CA, CCF 1907–39, RG 75, NARA-DC.

Chapter 5

1. "Insane Patients Reach Washington," 1; "Indian Mental Patients Reach Hospital Here," 4.

2. St. Elizabeths confined Native Americans before Canton Asylum was established. For more on some of the Indigenous individuals detained at the Government Hospital, see Farr, *Blackfoot Redemption*; Mihesuah, *Ned Christie*; Thomas Ryan to Superintendent, January 10, 1903, RG 418, Entry 13, NARA-DC; A. C. Tonner to A. B. Richardson, June 12, 1902, ibid; A. C. Tonner to Superintendent, February 16, 1903, ibid; note, Oscar Gifford, January 17, 1903, ibid.

3. Otto, *St. Elizabeths Hospital*, 232; Gambino, "Mental Health and Ideals of Citizenship"; McMillen, "Ministering to a Mind Diseased." See also Millikan, "Wards of the Nation"; Clark, *St. Elizabeths Hospital for the Insane*; D'Amore and Eckburg, *William Alanson White*; McMillen telephone interview, April 14, 2017; Prandoni interview, May 12, 2017; and Prandoni email correspondence, July 28, 2011, March 11, April 14, August 20, 2014, January 25, February 1, 8, March 1, 8, 29, November 5, 2017. The author thanks Jorges Prandoni, Matthew Gambino, and Frances McMillen for sharing their expertise on this history.

4. Staff reported this as "presented a dull facial expression." "Mrs. Maggie Hale," (#39216), St. Elizabeths Hospital, January 15, 1934, Box 4, CA, CCF 1907–39, RG 75, NARA-DC.

5. "Mrs. Maggie Hale," (#39216), January 15, 1934.

6. "Mrs. Maggie Hale," (#39216), January 15, 1934.

7. "Mrs. Maggie Hale," (#39216), January 15, 1934.

8. Jensen, "Reclaimed Heritage," 28.

9. Jensen, "Reclaimed Heritage," 28.

10. F. Jensen interviews, April 7, 8, 2014; F. Jensen telephone conversations, July 21, September 5, October 20, 2014.

11. Eveyln B. Ruchenbach to Rebecca Butler, September 30, 1938, Box 3, CA, CCF 1907–39, RG 75, NARA-DC; Eveyln B. Reichenbach to Julia Darling, September 20, 1938, ibid. See also Riley Guthrie to Rebecca Butler, February 26, 1940, ibid.

12. Evelyn B. Reichenbach to Rebecca Butler, September 30, 1938. See also Evelyn Reichenbach to Nettie Grinnell, September 8, 1938, Box 3, CA, CCF 1907–39, RG 75, NARA-DC; and Evelyn Reichenbach to Julia Darling, September 20, 1938.

13. "Dr. Eldridge—Report of Restraints and Seclusion for November 1941," Box 67, Entry 22 (1941–42 folder), Records of St. Elizabeths Hospital, Records of Superintendents, Monthly Reports, 1907–67, RG 418, NARA-DC; "Dr. Eldridge—Report of Restraints and Seclusion for December 1941," ibid.

14. Riley Guthrie to Rebecca Butler, May 11, 1939, Box 3, CA, CCF 1907–39, RG 75, NARA-DC; "Dr. Eldridge—Report of Restraints and Seclusion for December 1941." The Potawatomi family's actions align with what Audra Simpson (Mohawk) has called "ethnographic refusal"—an everyday act of refusal to conform to settler medical and institutional norms, in a context in which unequal power relations dominate. Interpreting their actions through this lens also, hopefully, further recognizes tribal self-determination. Simpson, "On Ethnographic Refusal," 67–80. For more on refusal, see Simpson, *Mohawk Interruptus*; and Tuck and Yang, "Unbecoming Claims," 811–18.

15. Riley Guthrie to Rebecca Butler, June 28, 1940, Box 3, CA, CCF 1907–39, RG 75, NARA-DC.

16. As cited in Evelyn Reichenbach to Rebecca Butler, September 30, 1938, Box 3, CA, CCF 1907–39, RG 75, NARA-DC.

17. F. Jensen interviews, April 7, 8, 2014; F. Jensen telephone conversations, January 30, April 1, July 21, September 5, October 20, 2014. O-Zoush-Quah's daughter Julia Darling lived on the property at the time of O-Zoush-Quah's funeral. See "Obituary, Mrs. Maggie Hale," 6.

18. Jensen, "Reclaimed Heritage," 29; F. Jensen interviews, April 7, 8, 2014. For more on the Drum Religion, see, for example, Clifton, *Prairie People*, 384.

19. Rabon telephone conversations, February 18, May 7, 2014.

20. Rabon telephone conversations, January 21, February 18, May 7, June 20, 2014; Rabon email correspondence, May 20, 2013.

21. Rabon telephone conversation, February 18, 2014.

22. St. Elizabeths Hospital admissions note, George Marlow, December 30, 1933, Box 4, CA, CCF 1907–39, RG 75, NARA-DC. The author thanks Joe Rabon for sharing photos of the Marlow home from his personal collection.

23. R. H. Guthrie to Louis Marlow Sr., May 30, 1942, Box 4, CA, CCF 1907–39, RG 75, NARA-DC; Prandoni email correspondence, March 29, 2017. Very little is known about what happened to these men and even less about how they experienced this chapter of their lives. Most of what remains comes through fragmentary administrative records and across generations of family members' recollections. O-Zoush-Quah and the other women were not transferred to the Narcotic Farms. The Public Service Hospital admitted women, but for unknown reasons, the surviving Native women remained in the locked wards in Washington. Because all but one of the men were affiliated with midwestern and western reservations (and perhaps because of the long reach of Canton Asylum as an identifying marker), federal administrators initially selected the Fort Worth prison-hospital over its Kentucky counterpart to hold them. This smaller Narcotic Farm primarily held people who originally came from west of the Mississippi River. Burch, digital database; Prandoni email correspondence, July 28, 2011, March 11, April 14, August 20, 2014, January 25, February 1, 8, March 1, 8, 29, November 5, 2017; "For Board and Care of Indian Insane Patients in Saint Elizabeths Hospital for the months of July, August, and September, 1942," E. 13, RG 418, NARA-DC; "For Board and care of Indian Insane Patients in U.S. Public Health Service Hospital, Fort Worth, Texas, for the months of July, August, and September, 1942," ibid.

24. "Treat Insane Indians," 1.

25. Executive Order 9079 enabled St. Elizabeths administrators to transfer the men. Within a month of the order's issuance, Superintendent Winfred Overholser contacted J. R. McGibony, the director of health within the Office of Indian Affairs, expressing his desire that American Indians at St. Elizabeths be removed to the other facilities. In April, the hospital's medical director, Riley Guthrie, began mailing template letters to BIA superintendents and relatives of the American Indians who would be moved, including one to Louis Marlow. The executive order built on longstanding beliefs that psychiatric institutionalization benefited individuals and the broader public. Practically, the shift also served larger institutional management. In the context of global conflict, institutionalization was additionally cast as protecting the nation's especially vulnerable members—those deemed mentally ill—and providing for its especially worthy and vulnerable people—disabled soldiers—and ultimately serving as a resource in the effort to save democracy itself. Executive Order 9079, Box 3522, Folder: Insane Indians, 5-6 Health Conditions, CCF, 1937–53, RG 48, NARA-CP.

26. The Narcotic Farms were intended primarily for people incarcerated in federal prisons convicted of crimes, those whose probation in federal court cases required "treatment until cured," and veterans. See "Medicine: Drug Addicts." At the time of its opening, Fort Worth was described as one of the largest in the Treasury Department building program, with an anticipated cost of $4.5 million. "Medical Officer Assumes

Custody of New US Public Health Service Hospital Here," 8; W. L. Treadway to Henry Hutchings, March 3, 1938 (and related correspondence), Box 124, Narcotic Hospital (1930–38), Amon G. Carter Papers, Special Collections, Mary Couts Burnett Library, Texas Christian University, Fort Worth. For more background on the two federal prison farms, see Porter Narcotic Farm Act (or "Narcotic Farms"), Pub. L. No. 70-672 (1929); "Part I: The Public Health Service Narcotic Hospital in Lexington," 38; *Time Magazine*, February 15, 1937; Acker, *Creating the American Junkie*; Furman, *Profile of the United States Public Health Service*; Williams, *United States Public Health Service*, 51–52, 335; Gerstein and Harwood, *Treating Drug Problems*; and Courtwright, "A Century of American Narcotic Policy."

27. Louis telephone interview, March 23, 2014; Louis, "US Public Health Service Hospital, Fort Worth," 1; Louis correspondence, February 24, 2014.

28. Louis telephone interview, March 23, 2014; Louis, "US Public Health Service Hospital, Fort Worth," 1; Campbell, Olsen, and Walden, *Narcotic Farm*, 89–91. Likely, Louis Marlow's younger brother would have come to know the underground tunnels that linked the various structures, enabling greater management and surveillance of people's movement within the property and providing some buffer from harsh weather conditions.

29. Farm work especially dominated. Technological innovations and economic motivations contributed to workshops where institutionalized members produced materials that supported Narco and other federal carceral facilities. Campbell, Olsen, and Walden, *Narcotic Farm*; Olsen and Walden, *The Narcotic Farm* (2009), film.

30. Members of Marlow's group in 1942 ranged in age from thirty to eighty-five. Earlier Canton Asylum documents suggest that at least one individual may have been unable to walk since childhood and that several others, likely including Marlow, were unable or unwilling to provide labor.

31. Burch, digital database.

32. "Part I: The Public Health Service Narcotic Hospital at Lexington"; Campbell, Olsen, and Walden, *Narcotic Farm*, 36.

33. The Lexington facility was vast, with art deco lines, "United States Narcotic Farm" carved into the stone entryway, and a soaring iron gate facing the driveway. Often, ten people a day were processed into the facility. "Part I: The Public Health Service Narcotic Hospital at Lexington"; Campbell, Olsen, and Walden, *Narcotic Farm*, 36. For general histories of the Lexington Narcotic Farm, see Campbell, Olsen, and Walden, *Narcotic Farm*. William S. Burroughs was detained at Narco and wrote about the experience in his 1953 memoir-novel, *Junkie*. Jessica Williams, "A Look at Treatment History: The Narcotic Farm," Institute for Research, Education, and Training for Addictions, September 11, 2014, accessed January 12, 2016, https://ireta.org/resources/a-look-at-treatment-history -the-narcotic-farm/; Kosten and Gorelick, "Images in Psychiatry," 22; Lowry, "Treatment of the Drug Addict at the Lexington (Ky.) Hospital," 9–12; *Handbook for Employees, United States Public Health Service Hospital, Lexington*, 3. See also "Jobs for Every Able Patient at Lexington Narcotic Farm Provide Therapy and Training," 152.

34. Tuberculosis claimed a thirty-seven-year-old shortly after the group arrived in Fort Worth; another died of the disease several years later. Death certificates attest that at least one man from the Pueblo of Isleta died within months of arriving at Fort Worth, on September 30, 1942. The death certificate of an Oglala Lakota man from this group asserts that he entered Lexington on January 5, 1944, and died on April 13, 1945. *Kentucky*

Birth, Marriage and Death Records, Rolls 994027–58, Kentucky Department for Libraries and Archives, Frankfort, microfilm; *Kentucky Birth and Death Records: Covington, Lexington, Louisville, and Newport*, Rolls 7007125–31, 7011804–13, 7012974–7013570, 7015456–62, ibid.; *Kentucky Vital Statistics Original Death Certificates*, Rolls 7016130–7041803, ibid. One White Earth Nation member died at Lexington in September 1948.

35. On January 4, 1950, Marlow (and probably the remaining others) were relocated to St. Elizabeths again. As part of a larger restoration project at St. Elizabeths decades later, Jorges Prandoni and Frances McMillen began work to identify the graves of people previously detained at Canton. See, for example, Trinkley, Hacker, and Southerland, "Preservation Assessment of St. Elizabeths East Campus Cemetery," 32; McMillen telephone interview, April 14, 2017; and Prandoni interview, May 12, 2017. Dr. Prandoni requested that the following disclaimer be included: "The information and views represent Dr. Prandoni's understanding of events and perspectives of them. He does not represent the District of Columbia government or its Department of Behavioral Health."

36. Rabon email correspondence, May 20, 2013.

37. Prandoni email correspondence, January 25, 2017.

38. Rabon interviews, May 19, 2015, December 5, 2016.

39. Marlow's unmarked but registered grave is located at the bottom of a hill near the southern perimeter of the cemetery. According to the president of Congressional Cemetery, the row of nearby graves surrounding Marlow's are populated primarily by indigent people and those who had been incarcerated at St. Elizabeths. Williams email correspondence, May 16, 2017. The author thanks Thomas Lu for research assistance and photographic documentation of Congressional Cemetery.

40. H. R. Hummer to Commissioner, July 24, 1930, Box 11, CA, CCF 1907–39, RG 75, NARA-DC; John G. Hunter to Commissioner, August 7, 1930, ibid. Thomas Lubeck conducted an oral history interview with Clara Christopher in 1979. She did not recount her experiences with Cora Winona Faribault but offered observations of other people detained at Canton. Christopher interview, April 10, 1979.

41. H. R. Hummer to Commissioner, July 24, 1930, Box 11, CA, CCF 1907–39, RG 75, NARA-DC; C. J. Rhoads to H. R. Hummer, June 30, 1930, ibid.; John Hunter to Commissioner, August 7, 1930, ibid. The Navajo name for the Fort Defiance area is "Sa Ho-tsoi." I thank Robin and Henry Yabah for sharing background and lived history of the Good Shepherd Mission and Fort Defiance. Yabah telephone conversations, December 21, 30, 2018. For a background history of orphanages, see Hacsi, *Second Home*.

42. Indian boarding schools were, according to American Indian studies scholar K. Tsianina Lomawaima, "the most minutely surveilled and controlled federal institutions created to transform the lives of any Americans." Lomawaima, *"To Remain an Indian,"* 2–3. See also Grinde, "Taking the Indian Out of the Indian," 25–32; Jenkins, "Good Shepherd Mission to the Navajo"; and Coleman, *American Indian Children at School*, 174.

43. Janet Waring's 1929 report strongly suggests that this schedule had been and would remain the standard for Good Shepherd Mission. Jenkins's history of the mission aligns with this as well. Letter and report, Janet Waring, September 1929, Folder 6 (Ft. Defiance: Good Shepherd, 1920–42, Episcopal Diocese of Arizona Records), Box 72, ID MSS-164, Arizona State University Library and Archive, Tempe; Jenkins, "Good Shepherd Mission to the Navajo."

44. Labor assigned to boys and young men in the "outing system" also reflected settler gendered expectations. For more on the outing systems, see Paxton, "Learning Gender," 174–86; Haskins, "'Matter of Wages Does Not Seem to be Material,'" 323–46; Jacobs, *White Mothers to a Dark Race*; Jacobs, "Working on the Domestic Frontier," 165–99; Coleman, *American Indian Children at School*, 43–44, 114; Haskins, *One Bright Spot*; Hyer, *One House*; Archuleta, Child, and Lomawaima, *Away from Home*; Parker, *Phoenix Indian School*; Malehorn, *Tender Plant*; Trennert, *Phoenix Indian School*; Bailey and Bailey, *History of the Navajos*.

45. Cora Winona Faribault to Diamond Roach, July 17, 1943, personal collection of Caroline Jean Kiger-StClair; Fred Darker to Supt. C. L. Ellis, Sept. 17, 1943, ibid. Providing domestic work for white households was a typical experience for Native female students. As historian Dorothy Parker has noted: "Girls had fewer opportunities than boys: mostly how to sell, prepare meals, prepare for motherhood. Domestic service was a primary area of training." Parker, *Phoenix Indian School*, 6–7. See also Paxton, "Learning Gender," 174–86.

46. Western industrial schools' administrators, responding to chronic shortage of resources, regularly relied on student labor. As Robert Trennert has written: "Instead of receiving a full-time education, Indian pupils were pressed into service making school uniforms, doing the laundry, serving as cooks, and providing other menial labor. By the end of the 1880s this pattern had become institutionalized, and students were playing an increasingly significant role in maintaining the schools. Unfortunately, the drudgery discouraged students, many of whom ran away. Even those who remained at school acquired few usable skills and quickly returned to the ways of their people once their school days ended." Trennert, *Phoenix Indian School*, 9.

47. O'Neil interviews, June 25–26, 2012, April 6–7, 2015, March 29, 2019; Kiger-StClair interview, February 25, 2017.

48. Ruth Harmon to Preston Kieger, May 4, 1949, personal collection of Faith O'Neil.

49. As historian Marilyn Holt has explained, boarding schools and orphanages "often undermined young adults' abilities to establish family relationships and develop parenting skills. . . . They did not grow up in an environment that nurtured them emotionally, taught the behavior expected of close relatives, or transmitted the social consequences of shunning responsibilities." Holt, *Indian Orphanages*, 15. See also Berger, "After Pocahontas."

50. Cora Winna Faribault to Diamond Roach, April 11, 1945, personal collection of Faith O'Neil.

51. Winona Faribault to Diamond Roach, August 18, 1943, personal collection of Caroline Jean Kiger-StClair. Cora Winona apparently did not know and had never been in direct contact with her maternal grandmother, Mary Alexis, or other members of her extended family, including Elizabeth Faribault's sisters, Lizzie Small and Lucy Mary Greeley.

52. Winona Faribault to Diamond Roach, August 18, 1943; Diamond Roach to Cora Winona Faribault, July 30, 1943, personal collection of Caroline Jean Kiger-StClair; Cora Winona Faribault to Diamond Roach, July 17, 1943, ibid.

53. Diamond Roach to Winona Faribault, August 24, 1943, personal collection of Caroline Jean Kiger-StClair.

54. Diamond Roach to Winona Faribault, August 24, 1943.

55. In her work on the Phoenix Indian School, historian Dorothy Parker noted the enforced sex segregation between boys and girls, which she argued reflected the belief that Protestant sexual mores were one of the most important aspects of the child's indoctrination. Parker, *Phoenix Indian School*, 8–9. For more on New Deal education and the BIA, see Treglia, "A Very "Indian" Future?," 357–80. For a history of the Navajo Methodist School, see Malehorn, *Tender Plant*, 108; Jenkins, "Good Shepherd Mission to the Navajo," chap. 10.

56. Ruth Harmon to Preston Kiger, May 4, 1949, personal collection of Faith O'Neil.

57. Ruth Harmon to Preston Kiger, May 4, 1949.

58. Ruth Harmon to Preston Kiger, May 4, 1949.

59. Ruth Harmon to Elizabeth Davis, February 22, 1945, personal collection of Caroline Jean Kiger-StClair; Winona Fairbault to Mrs. Clark, March 30, 1945, ibid.

60. In her correspondence from the time, Faribault references a "Mrs. Walters," who likely had hired her for domestic work. In 1945, Faribault was listed in the Phoenix directory at 117 W. Lynwood.

61. Ruth Harmon to Elizabeth Davis, February 22, 1945, personal collection of Caroline Jean Kiger-StClair.

62. Ruth Harmon to Elizabeth Davis, February 22, 1945. Schoolteacher Gertrude Golden tells a similar story of a Native girl named Ada from Fort Defiance who became pregnant in 1914. Educator Estelle Brown tells a similar story of a young woman named Lucy. Golden and Brown cited in Adams, *Education for Extinction*, 180–81.

63. This was a prevalent outlook among social workers, educators, and much of mainstream settler society. See, for example, Holt, *Indian Orphanages*, 5; and Broder, *Tramps, Unfit Mothers, and Neglected Children*, 126, 129, 142. Margaret Jacobs described racialized attitudes toward American Indian mothers in the years after World War II that cast unwed Native mothers as "psychologically unstable and unfit." Jacobs, *Generation Removed*, 53. See also Clothier, "Psychological Implications of Unmarried Parenthood," 531–49; Solinger, "Maternity Homes," 360–62; and Solinger, *Wake Up Little Susie*, 151. Faribault and others experienced what writer-activist Talila Lewis details in a working definition of ableism: a "form of systemic oppression [that] leads to people and society determining who is valuable and worthy based on a person's appearance and/or their ability to satisfactorily [re]produce, excel, and 'behave.'" T. Lewis, "Ableism 2020."

64. Cora Winona Faribault to Mrs. Clark, March 30, 1945, personal collection of Caroline Jean Kiger-StClair.

65. National Florence Crittenton Mission, *Fourteen Years' Work among "Erring Girls"*; "Home for the Erring," 9; Wilson and Barrett, Fifty Years' Work with Girls.

66. Director Russel Cooper, cited in Kunzel, *Fallen Women, Problem Girls*, 101n59. Superintendent Corinne Dietarly to Dr. Robert Barrett, November 8, 1940, Folder 8, Phoenix, AZ, 1940–41, Box 15, Florence Crittenden Collection, Social Welfare History Archives, University of Minnesota.

67. "Coercion was inherent in incarceration of any kind, however benevolently intended," historian Regina Kunzel explains. This made it nearly impossible for Crittenton Home staff "to keep homes in which they obliged unmarried mothers to stay from becoming jails." Kunzel, *Fallen Women, Problem Girls*, 101. For more on settler custodialism, see D. K. Miller, "Spider's Web."

68. Beginning in the late 1930s, the Phoenix Crittenton Home began admitting young girls deemed delinquent by the courts.

69. Corinne Dieterly, "Annual Report to the Superintendent Florence Crittenden Home, Phoenix, Arizona," March 1, 1941–March 1, 1942, Folder 8, Phoenix, AZ, 1940–41, Box 15, Florence Crittenden Collection, Social Welfare History Archives, University of Minnesota. Dieterly resigned from the position in 1943.

70. Cora Winona Faribault to Mrs. Clark, March 30, 1945, personal collection of Caroline Jean Kiger-StClair. Institutionalization through placement in maternity homes, along with counseling and supervision by social workers and other professionals, became a common response to individuals whose pregnancies were stigmatized. By the mid-1940s, professional social workers and related secular specialists staffed Florence Crittenton Homes and other similar institutions across the nation. The Florence Crittenton Home also was closely tied to other institutions in Arizona, including penal and welfare. They coordinated with the Social Services Center, Catholic charities, and juvenile courts over all the state as well as with members of State Board of Juvenile Penal Institutions of Arizona and the convent of the Good Shepherd Work. "Arizona News," 5. For more on the institutionalization of unwed pregnant people, see Broder, *Tramps, Unfit Mothers, and Neglected Children*; Solinger, *Wake Up Little Susie*; and Solinger, "Maternity Homes," 360–62. For a photograph of the home, see Wilson and Barrett, *Fifty Years* Work with Girls, 78.

71. Faribault's letters to adults from the Good Shepherd Mission shared concerns about the cost of staying at the Phoenix Home while assuring herself and others not to worry.

72. Faribault maintained correspondence with several Navajo soldiers during their deployment, some of whom would later be honored as Code Talkers, including Timothy Notah, Jimmy Begay, and David Tsosie. Some of Faribault's former classmates contacted her to find additional news about others in their friendship group. Winona Faribault to Mrs. Davis, April 9, 1945, personal collection of Caroline Jean Kiger-StClair.

73. Cora Winna Faribault to Diamond Roach, April 11, 1945, personal collection of Faith O'Neil. Shared with permission.

74. C. L. Ellis to Cora Winona Fairbault, April 16, 1945, personal collection of Faith O'Neil.

75. Cora Winona Faribault to Diamond Roach, April 11, 1945, personal collection of Faith O'Neil. Many Native American Indigenous studies scholars have critiqued the relationships between land, selfhood, and Indigenous identity. See, for example, Teuton, *Red Land, Red Power*, 46–47, 92–93, 202–4, and passim; Tuck and McKenzie, *Place in Research*; and C. Allen, *Blood Narrative*.

76. Shortly after delivering her son, Faribault informed the BIA superintendent in Sisseton so that David would be recognized as an enrolled member of Sisseton-Wahpeton Tribe. He was listed in subsequent government documents as "David Faribault."

77. Winona Fairbault to Miss Davis, April 9, 1945 from the Florence Crittenton Home, May 7, 1945, personal collection of Caroline Jean Kiger-StClair. Residence at the Crittenton Home was finite: by early summer, 1946, the young mother had to leave.

78. Journalist Patricia Susan Hart has described a similar policy at the Washington State home, and this likely was followed nationally. Hart, *A Home for Every Child*, 41, 45.

79. Cora Winona Faribault to Mrs. Elizabeth Clark, March 30, 1945, personal collection of Caroline Jean Kiger-StClair; Cora Winona Faribault to Miss Davis, April 9, 1945, ibid.; Cora Winona Faribault to Mrs. Clark, May 7, 1945, ibid.

80. According to Faribault's daughter Caroline Jean Kiger-StClair, on June 26, 1946, Faribault went to work at the Navajo Medical Center. "She was trying to find work to establish herself and keep David," Kiger-StClair explained. Kiger-StClair interview, February 25, 2017.

81. Kiger-StClair interview, February 25, 2017. People like Faribault were especially vulnerable; poverty, limited employment opportunities, and few social connections—common outcomes of broader settler policies—constricted her chances of accessing resources to sustain herself and her child. See, for example, Jacobs, *Generation Removed*, 81; Solinger, *Wake Up Little Susie*, 15–16, 148–86.

82. Correspondence from the time refers to a "Mrs. McLean" as the adviser who oversaw Faribault's relinquishment of David.

83. It was a difficult and increasingly common decision to make. Faribault was among the tens of thousands of people between 1937 and 1945 who relinquished parental rights to their children. Scholars have noted that adoption was especially encouraged for white women, but Native women and other minoritized people were also increasingly advised to allow their children to be adopted out. Carp, *Adoption in America*, 219; Solinger, *Wake Up Little Susie*, 23–24. According to Michelle Kahan, "Adoption began to increase considerably during the World War II era, rising from 16,000 annually in 1937, to 55,000 by 1945, and then growing tremendously over the next thirty years (to 142,000 in 1965)." Kahan, "'Put Up' on Platforms," 51–72. See also Melosh, *Strangers and Kin*, 39, 159. Margaret Jacobs has noted the broad pattern of social workers and others pressuring Native women to adopt out their young children, particularly in the decades following World War II. Jacobs, *Generation Removed*, 72.

84. Abrahams, "Inquiry Answers Re. David Abrams," June 24, 2017; Kahan, "Put Up on Platforms," 102; Roth telephone interview, November 19, 2014; O'Neil interview, March 29, 2019; Kiger-StClair interview, February 25, 2017. Edward Abrahams shared with and gave to the author permission to use David Faribault Abrahams's adoption forms.

85. He was listed on adoption papers as "David Howard Tsosie." Adoption papers. David Faribault Abrahams, personal collection of Edward Abrahams. Some family members doubt that his original surname actually referred to David's other birth parent, as the form states the father's name as "John Doe." Other correspondence suggests that Cora Winona Faribault had at one time planned to marry a man named David Tsosie. Her child's name may have recognized Tsosie's important place in Faribault's life, whether or not he was biologically related to the baby. For administrators at the time, and for relatives since, David's name reflects complex belongings and adaptations, as does his broader life story.

86. Escorted back to the Crittenton Home after relinquishing David, Cora Winona was directed to retrieve her belongings. Former Good Shepherd Orphanage matron Ruth Harmon, still living in Phoenix herself, met with her that October afternoon in 1946. As Harmon recounted, "She was quite upset, having just given up her baby." Ruth Harmon to David Clark, October 7, 1946, Faribault family correspondence and photographs, personal collection of Caroline Jean Kiger-StClair. Faribault searched for options to anchor

her. Apparently, she reached out to another friend in the area and was planning to live with her "until she could secure work." Ruth Harmon to David Clark, October 7, 1946, ibid. Connections between David and his Dakota kin similarly were undermined, as extended family would have no access to him.

87. In Los Angeles, Faribault worked for a time as a maid in a downtown hotel, where she joined many other American Indians recently relocated to the city. According to her daughter Caroline Jean Kiger-StClair, Cora Winona "worked in the laundry at the orphanage. She was a laundress. She knew how to change bedding. I guess they gave her a room at the hotel." Kiger-StClair interview, February 25, 2017; Kiger-StClair correspondence, April 17, 25, 2017.

88. There are many members of Navajo Nation with the listed last name on David's adoption form—Tsosie.

89. Abrahams, "Inquiry Answers Re. David Abrams," June 24, 2017; Abrahams telephone interview, December 9, 2016. The author especially thanks Ed Abrahams, David's brother, for sharing family history.

90. Abrahams, "Inquiry Answers Re. David Abrams," June 24, 2017; Abrahams telephone interview, December 9, 2016.

91. Roth telephone interview, November 19, 2014.

92. According to his brother, David did not discuss or show interest in finding out more information about his birth family. As Edward Abrahams explained: "In fact, after our mother's death, I located his adoption papers among her papers and contacted him to discuss when to send them. He flatly stated he had no interest in seeing them and asked me to keep them. . . . I'm sure he had zero knowledge of his siblings. Had he known of them I'm sure he would have made contact." Abrahams, "Inquiry Answers re. David Abrahams," June 24, 2017; Abrahams telephone interview, December 9, 2016.

93. Cora Winona Faribault and her son had limited kinship relations and other Native communal supports. The Florence Crittenton Home and other church and state agencies filled immediate needs even as they reflected broader forces that undermined Indigenous lifeways.

94. Faribault's story in Los Angeles bears certain similarities to the story of yearning, intimacy, rage, neglect, and gentleness in the city's Urban Indian Community captured in *The Exiles*, a 1961 semidocumentary film. Yvonne Walker (San Carlos Apache) explained: "I don't remember much when a child, after my mother died or even before. But right now it isn't so bad as, as when I was a child. I always wanted to go and get away from my people there and all that. And go someplace where somebody will, maybe uh, make me feel different. Be happier. That's why I'm glad I came out to Los Angeles." Walker, who was expecting at the time, added: "I want to raise him up myself. I think I could do it." Mackenzie, *The Exiles*.

95. Kiger-StClair Oral History Interview Information Sheet, 2017. In her study of Indian adoption and fostering—primarily by white settlers—historian Margaret Jacobs has asserted, "We cannot fully understand the gravity of the fostering and adoption of Indian children outside their communities without recovering the traumatizing experiences of Indian families who lost children." Jacobs, *Generation Removed*, 71. Faribault may have faced compelling reasons to relinquish her child, and her daughters later both expressed gratitude that David grew up in a more stable home than he might have

otherwise experienced. These realities—of wounds and loss, of contingencies and diverging paths—are carried by generations of the Faribault family.

96. Faith O'Neil recalled, "My dad said my mom had gone to see 'David' one time who had come in on a ship in Long Beach." O'Neil interview, March 6, 2012.

97. O'Neil interviews, March 6, June 25, 2012; Kiger-StClair interview, February 25, 2017; "Cora W. O'Neil," *California Death Index, 1940–1997* (Sacramento: State of California Department of Health Services, Center for Health Statistics, n.d.).

98. O'Neil interview, March 6, 2012.

99. O'Neil interviews, June 25, 2012, March 29, 2019; Kiger-StClair interview, February 25, 2017; David J. Abrahams, Social Security Death Index, 1935–2014. Edward Abrahams was with his brother when David died.

100. Faribault family correspondence, all undated, personal collection of Faith O'Neil.

101. Faribault family scrapbook, personal collection of Faith O'Neil. Another undated letter reads: "David was . . . possibly born in Tucson. . . . My mom's name was 'Cora Winona Faribault' born in South Dakota 9/28/25." Faribault family correspondence, ibid.

102. The author wishes to thank Faith O'Neil for sharing her personal scrapbook and making copies of its contents available for this book.

Chapter 6

1. In 2005, the bungalow was moved to Newton Hills State Park, about seven miles outside of Canton.

2. O'Neil personal audio recording, August 14, 2012. O'Neil's pilgrimage is both distinctive and unexceptional. Dakota history scholar Collette Hyman has written extensively about ways Dakota families have honored their ancestors and tribal communities through wide-ranging practices. Hymann, *Dakota Women's Work*, 33. In her study of Canadian First Nation women's felt experiences, Dian Million contended that lived experience "rich with emotional knowledges' plays a vital role in understanding the past and present." Million, "Felt Theory," 53–76. See also Carlson, *The Power of Place, the Problem of Time*; Boyd and Thrush, *Phantom Past, Indigenous Presence*.

3. O'Neil personal audio recording, August 14, 2012; O'Neil interviews, April 6–7, 2015, March 29, 2019.

4. O'Neil interview, August 7, 2019.

5. O'Neil personal audio recording, August 14, 2012. Faribault's story is unique in many ways, but it is not exceptional. See Deer, *Beginning and End of Rape*.

6. O'Neil interviews, June 25–26, 2012.

7. Photograph of Elizabeth and Cora Winona Faribault, ca. 1928, personal collection of Faith O'Neil.

8. O'Neil personal audio recording with Pete Alcaraz, Marie Skelly, and Bill Skelly, May 18, 2015.

9. O'Neil interviews, June 25–26, 2012.

10. O'Neil personal audio recording with Pete Alcaraz, Marie Skelly, and Bill Skelly, May 18, 2015. See also photographs, ca. 1910–30s, personal collection of Gertie Hale and Bill Skelly, CPL.

11. For more on the relational dimensions of disability and institutionalization, see Kafer, *Feminist, Queer, Crip*; Clare, *Brilliant Imperfection*; Erevelles, "Thinking with

Disability Studies"; Burch, "'Dislocated Histories'"; and Rapp and Ginsburg, "Enabling Disability," 533–56.

12. O'Neil interviews, April 6–7, 2015.

13. The author thanks Professor W. J. (Sisokaduta) Bendickson and Tammy DeCouteau and Our Treasured Elders members at the AAIA Native Language Program for translating Faribault's letter.

14. O'Neil interview, March 29, 2019.

15. O'Neil personal audio recording, August 14, 2012.

16. O'Neil interviews, March 8, 2016, March 29, 2019. For more on Dakota language and kinship, and meanings of caŋté, see Wilson, *Remember This!*, 37–38, 62.

17. O'Neil personal audio recording, May 18, 2015.

18. O'Neil interview, November 24, 2014.

19. O'Neil interviews, November 24, 2014, April 6–7, 2015, March 29, 2019. O'Neil underscored this point in a newspaper interview, asserting, "I'm bound and determined to find out what happened to her." Young, "S.D. Revisits Past at Native American Indian Asylum,'" 8A.

20. Eisenman, *Blooming Patchwork*, 15–16.

21. MacDowell and Dewhurst, *To Honor and Comfort*.

22. MacDowell describes Pottawatomi people commonly using quilts for these purposes across the late nineteenth and early twentieth centuries. See Marsha L. MacDowell, "A Gathering of Cultural Expression: North American Indian and Native Hawaiian Quiltmaking," in MacDowell and Dewhurst, *To Honor and Comfort*, 3–91.

23. MacDowell, "A Gathering of Cultural Expression," 10.

24. Nettie Tork to Oscar Gifford, March 12, 1909, Box 13, CA, CCF 1907–39, RG 75, NARA-DC.

25. J. Jensen email correspondence, July 2, September, 12, 2018, January 29, 2019; J. Jensen telephone conversations, March 9, August 26, 2018.

26. Ellen Lofland, who worked with Jack Jensen on creating the current iteration of the quilt, noted that she—with an abundance of quality equipment—had spent two hundred hours on the project. She conjectured that it would have taken many more hours than that for O-Zoush-Quah and her daughter to make the various squares. Lofland telephone interview, August 4, 2019; Lofland email correspondence, August 3, 2019; "Ancestral Quilt," 53–55.

27. Historian Jacki Rand (Choctaw Nation of Oklahoma) offers a cogent critique of artifacts' biographies as a way to "recover the histories of people who are not to appear in conventional sources." Jacki Thompson Rand, "Primary Sources: Indian Goods and the History of American Colonialism and the 19th-Century Reservation," in Shoemaker, *Clearing a Path*, 142. In her scholarship on blankets, American studies scholar Kara Thompson has written that "so many others use blankets to intervene in dominant discourse, and to create their own narratives with materials available and familiar. . . . To quilt is to make a memory, a proxy to fill the absence." Thompson, *Blanket*, 115. Social anthropologist Max Carocci observed that quilts and blankets can also be healing tools. Carocci, "Textiles of Healing," 68–84.

28. Disability and public historian Katherine Ott has argued that "objects edit who we are." Ott, Comment to Disability History Panel at the OAH Conference.

29. J. Jensen email correspondence, March 26, 2018, January 29, 2019, March 20, 21, 2020; J. Jensen interviews, October 3–5, 2019; Lofland email correspondence, March 20–21, 2020.

30. F. Jensen interviews, April 7, 8, 2014; J. Jensen interviews, April 22, 23, 2017; J. Jensen telephone conversation, February 17, 2017.

31. A particularly important part of this experience occurred when Jensen reread a family Bible that he had inherited. On the family tree drawn on its pages, kin had documented O-Zoush-Quah's forced removal. Family Bible, ca. 1880s–, personal collection of Jack Jensen; J. Jensen interviews, April 22, 23, 2017; J. Jensen telephone conversations, February 17, 2017, August 26, 2018.

32. Anthropologist and Indigenous studies scholar Audra Simpson details the concept of refusal in Simpson, "On Ethnographic Refusal," 67–80.

33. J. Jensen interviews, April 22, 23, 2017.

34. J. Jensen interviews, April 22, 23, 2017; J. Jensen telephone conversations, August 26, 2018, January 19, 2020. For a broad study of the dynamic relationships between Indigenous kin across generations, the fluidity of time, and the porous boundaries between natural and supernatural worlds, see Boyd and Thrush, *Phantom Past, Indigenous Presence*; Stevenson, *Life Beside Itself*.

35. J. Jensen interviews, October 3–5, 2019; J. Jensen email correspondence, September 12, 2018; J. Jensen telephone conversation, January 19, 2020.

36. Family quilt, Ancestry Project, ca. 1900–2019, personal collection of Jack Jensen.

37. For more on Potawatomi history, see Mitchell, "Stories of the Potawatomi People"; and Edmunds, *Potawatomis*.

38. J. Jensen interview, October 3, 2019; J. Jensen, unpublished remarks, October 5, 2019.

39. Among the initial motivations for Iron Shield's public gathering was South Dakota's proclaimed Year of Reconciliation (1987), which commemorated the 125th anniversary of the U.S.–Dakota Wars. National movements for American Indian repatriation had gained significant momentum during the 1980s as well, and Iron Shield explicitly tied the commemorations at Canton to these larger repatriation and tribal-sovereignty campaigns. For example, he had founded the Native American Reburial Restoration Committee, which sponsored the ceremonies at the Indian Asylum. Iron Shield, "South Dakota Should Protect Remains in Sacred Burial Grounds of Indians," 12A; Linck, "Indians Ask for Respect at Burials at Golf Course," A4; Iron Shield, "Research Indicates Asylum Wasn't in Indians' Best Interest," 10A; "Ceremony to Memorialize Those Buried at Old Asylum," C3; Hascall, "Spiritual Walk Honors Indians Who Lived in Insane Asylum," 27D; Jordan, "Golfcourse Graves a Painful Legacy," B5; Jordan, "National Indian Asylum's Legacy"; Miller, "Sad Legacy at Quiet Cemetery," 1B; Tollefson, "Program to Honor Indians Who Died in Asylum," C1; "Winter Memorial," C3. See also Butler, "Proper Burial"; Bolding, "Journalist: Canton Golf Course No Place for Graveyard," 1C; and LaDuke, *Recovering the Sacred*. For more on Indigenous self-determination work, see Barker, *Native Acts*; Barker, *Sovereignty Matters*; Mallon, *Decolonizing Native Histories*; Churchill, *Struggle for the Land*; Biolsi, "Imagined Geographies"; Simpson and Smith, *Theorizing Native Studies*; D. Cobb and Fowler, *Beyond Red Power*; and Champagne, "Self-Determination and Activism among American Indians." I thank Yvonne Stretches

for sharing memories of her relative, Harold Iron Shield. Stretches telephone interview, February 17, 2017.

40. The superintendent of the golf course at the time explained that "the graves were caving in. . . . It had been neglected for too long." "Indian Reburial Movement Spurs Interest in Asylum Graves," H6.

41. "This Plaque Marks Burial of 120 Indians at Canton," cover, 3; Hiawatha National Register of Historical Places Registration Form, Section 7, May 5, 1998, 1, SDSA. Archival sources and an archaeological study in 2015 confirmed that there are at least six additional people buried in the cemetery.

42. One eighty-nine-year-old Santee Sioux Tribe member said at the time: "As a child I remember when I was a student at Pipestone Indian school in Minnesota. They (school officials) threatened to send us to the insane asylum if we didn't behave in school or the dorms." Cited in Iron Shield, "Legacy of an Infamous Institution," 3. The witness may have been classmates with Nellie Kampeska, who was forcibly removed to Canton from the Pipestone School in 1917. Other elders have described similar memories to the author, including during a public meeting about the research for this book with members of the Oglala Lakota College community at Pine Ridge on November 7, 2019.

43. Quoted in Steen, "Walkers Honor 121 Indians Who Died at Asylum," 1D; Iron Shield, "Letter to the Editor," 10A; Steen, "Ceremony Dignifies Memory of Hiawatha Asylum Inmates,"1C, 4C; Yellow Bird, "Wild Indians," 7, accessed December 17, 2014. Pemina Yellow Bird observed: "Something sacred started moving, and a gentle breeze started blowing the dust off these stories. . . . *Tell the story. Look what happened.*" Yellow Bird, interview, July 22, 2019. Iron Shield's relative Yvonne Stretches explained that he had "started by thinking it was about graves and a golf course, and it became how people got treated and how they got sent there. . . . Some were taken from their families and never seen again." Stretches telephone interview, February 17, 2017.

44. Congress conveyed the property to the city of Canton in 1946. Deed Record No. 53, Lincoln County, SD. Before that, the grounds had been used as a farm and state penitentiary. "Will Put Canton Asylum into Use," 11; "Canton Asylum May be Given to State," 2; Hillgreen, "Institution Now Leased for $1 for Prisoners," 4; "Tale of Two Cities," 4E, 6E; "Dakota Given Canton," 10; "South Dakota Executive Also Takes Up Seed Loan," 1; "Berry Signs Asylum for Pen Use."

45. Butler, "Final Place of Rest," 3A; "Canton Asylum Lease Extended," 4; "Idle Buildings Available for Use," 6; "Indian Activists Want 119 Bodies Reburied," A1; "Buried between Fairways," 1A, 3A; "Vermillion Man Wants Indians Reburied," A2; Bolding, "Journalist: Canton Golf Course No Place for Graveyard," 1C; "Forgotten Cemetery to Be Remembered by Canton Indians," 1A; Limoges, "Hiawatha Memorial Service Source of Mixed Emotions," 5; Limoges, "Memorial Ceremony Held at Hiawatha Cemetery," 1A; Native American Reburial Restoration Committee, "Call for Action." See also Daniels, "Cultural Identities among the Oglala Sioux," 198–245. Drawing on field research in the 1960s, Daniels noted that his "informants claimed that the Public Health Service hospital offered no services for people with 'illnesses of the mind,' but that sometimes hopeless cases were taken 'East River' (to Eastern South Dakota) and 'locked up in a crazy house.'" I believe the "crazy house" refers to Canton. Ibid., 209n10.

46. Yellow Bird, "Wild Indians," 5, accessed December 17, 2014. See also Iron Shield, "Ceremony Planned for S.D. Native Cemetery." Leonard Bruguier (Yankton Sioux), director of the Institute of American Indian Studies at the University of South Dakota in the 1990s, echoed Iron Shield's interpretation. He noted that all BIA officials had to do was claim that "'this person's insane,' and have him shipped to Canton to be administered by a whole different set of rules. Basically you'd just be able to get rid of 'em." Bruguier quoted in Stawicki, "Haunting Legacy." For more on settler colonialism and resistance in South Dakota, see P. Hall, *To Have This Land*.

47. Quoted in Butler, "Unfit Resting Place," 1A, 3A.

48. "Pipe Ceremony Held Oct. 4 at Cemetery"; Limoges, "Memorial Ceremony Held at Hiawatha Cemetery," 1A; Limoges, "Hiawatha Memorial Service Source of Mixed Emotions," 5. Horrific conditions and experiences have been common in many North American psychiatric and other disability-related institutions. See Ben-Moshe, Chapman, and Carey, *Disability Incarcerated*; Burch and Joyner, *Unspeakable*; Malacrida, *Special Hell*; Rossiter and Clarkson, "Opening Ontario's 'Saddest Chapter'"; Daly, dir., *Where's Molly?*; and Parsons, *From Asylum to Prison*.

49. Yellow Bird, "Wild Indians," accessed December 17, 2014. See also Harriman, "Memories Honored at Asylum Site," 1B.

50. Quoted in Harriman, "Memories Honored at Asylum Site," B1, B9.

51. Harold Iron Shield to President William Clinton, July 7, 1997, CA File, CPL; Iron Shield, "Legacy of an Infamous Institution," 3, 6; B. Davis, "Journalist Talks about Indian Asylum," 4; Stretches telephone interview, February 17, 2017; Kills Small telephone conversation, July 21, 2019.

52. According to Pemina Yellow Bird, Iron Shield had reached out to her in the 1990s in part because they were active in repatriation organizational work. Yellow Bird interview, March 8, 2015. A brief reference to Deegan's attendance at the 2000 ceremony can be found in Harriman, "Memories Honored at Asylum Site," 1B, 9B. For more on Yellow Bird's work in preservation and repatriation, see, for example, "New Agreement Meant to Help Preserve Tribal Culture," 4C; Worthington, "Where Archaeologists See Discovery, Indians See Only Lost Souls," A6; and Yellow Bird, "Indian Healers Were Spiritually Revered," 12.

53. Iron Shield's engagement with Canton Asylum history also sprang from long-established repatriation and sovereignty-movement work. For more on this broader history, see Fine-Dare, *Grave Injustice*. See also Trope and Echo-Hawk, "Native American Graves Protection and Repatriation Act"; Lonetree, *Decolonizing Museums*; Echo-Hawk, *In the Light of Justice*; and Krech and Hail, *Collecting Native America*. For more on the overlaps of disability and Indigenous North American histories, see Teuton, "Disability in Indigenous North America"; Lovern and Locust, *Native American Communities on Health and Disability*; Chapman, "Colonialism, Disability, and Possible Lives"; and Cowing, "Obesity and (Un)fit Homes"; Cowing, "Settler States of Ability."

54. Deegan interview, February 20, 2017. For more on Deegan's disability rights activism and recovery work, see Deegan, "Spirit Breaking," 194–209; Deegan, "Independent Living Movement and People with Psychiatric Disabilities," 3–19; Deegan, "Remember My Name"; and Danvers State Memorial Committee, "A Grave Injustice." For more on mad people's histories and histories of disability and institutionalization, see Ben-Moshe,

Chapman, and Carey, *Disability Incarcerated*; Rembis, *Defining Deviance*; LeFrançois, Menzies, and Reaume, *Mad Matters*; Reaume, "Mad People's History"; Menzies and Palys, "Turbulent Spirits," 149–75; Jackson, "In Our Own Voice"; and B. Lewis, "Mad Fight."

55. Yellow Bird, "Wild Indians," 3, accessed December 17, 2014. This aligns also with Quechua anthropologist Guillermo Delgado-P's description of "re-membering" as a process of recovering, coalition, Indigenous self-determination, and decolonization. See Delgado-P, "Makings of a Transnational Movement," 36–38.

56. This resembles in some ways what American studies scholar Renya K. Ramirez (Winnebago Tribe of Nebraska) described as a Native hub-making activity. These activities "bridge tribal differences so that Native Americans can unify to struggle for social change. The meeting offers a microcosm of the variety of differences—tribal, gender, and otherwise—across which Native Americans must work to communicate." Ramirez, *Native Hubs*, 8.

57. Judah interviews, June 24, 2011, February 12, 2017; Judah correspondence, January 15, 2013; photographs, ca. 2011–15, personal collection of Lavanah Judah; Young, "Insane Asylum," A1, A9.

58. Judah interviews, February 12, May 12, 2012, May 10–11, June 17, 2013, April 27, 2014, November 7, 2015, February 12, 2017, September 19, 2019; Judah correspondence, January 15, February 12, April 7, May 3, 18, July 12, 2013, August 6, November 14, 2015, April 8, 2016, January 18, 2017.

59. Judah interviews, February 12, May 12, 2012, May 10–11, June 17, 2013, April 27, 2014, November 7, 2015, February 12, 2017, September 19, 2019; Judah correspondence, January 15, February 12, April 7, May 3, 18, July 12, 2013, August 6, November 14, 2015, April 8, 2016, January 18, 2017; Davis, "Hiawatha Insane Asylum for Indians Canton," 9.

60. English professor Deborah Miranda (Ohlone Costanoan Esselen Nation of California, and of Chumash and Jewish ancestry) has described similar experience with Indigenous inheritances: "Along the way, I've learned a lot about stories, their power to rebuild or silence," and "sometimes our bodies are the bridges over which our descendants cross, spanning unimaginable landscapes of loss." Miranda, *Bad Indians*, xiv, 74.

61. Anne Gregory quoted in Young, "S.D. Revisits Past at Native American Insane Asylum."

62. Young, "Shameful Past," 5. For more on the historical entanglement of institutionalization, kinship, and tribal sovereignty, see Burch, "'Dislocated Histories'"; and Burch, "Disorderly Pasts," 362–85. Disability studies scholar Julie Minich offers a cogent critique of structural and social conditions that propel injustice and ways that a critical disability studies analysis can identify and contribute to dismantling these structures and practices. Minich, "Enabling Whom?."

63. Davis worked in the BIA's Branch of Acknowledgment and Research for several years and participated in numerous tribal efforts to gain federal recognition. Davis interviews, June 8–10, 2014; Davis, Oral History Interview Information Sheet, July 7, 2017. For more on her work as tribal historian, see Davis, "Christmastime Blessings," 7; and Davis, "Hiawatha Insane Asylum for Indians Canton," 9.

64. Describing another history project of Bois Forte people, Davis had noted, "As a Historian, I had collected numerous documents to enable our Tribe to know its history, but I collected mostly information about people: where they were, how they were living,

etc." Davis, "Trygg Files." In her study of enslaved women, professor of women's and gender studies and history Marisa J. Fuentes details how structural forms of oppression and violence saturate the archive. See Fuentes, *Dispossessed Lives*.

65. Historian Donald Fixico described the power of story and of adaptation this way: "The survival of Indian people has enabled them to rebuild and adapt their communities and cultures. This ability might be called transformation of cultural adaptive systems." Fixico, *Call for Change*, 6.

66. Gregory had added, "I realized I could do that—learning the history well and right." Meeting Davis had "lit the fire to go to school and pursue this." Gregory interview, July 3, 2017.

67. The ceremony that year was on Mother's Day—May 13, 2012—which was also Kay Davis's seventy-sixth birthday. Many Native American Indigenous studies scholars have detailed adaptations and transformations as part of Indigenous survivance. Native American literature scholar Scott Richard Lyons has pointed out that adaptations can travel in multiple directions—toward and away from traditional forms. Gregory and Davis described their kin connection as doing both of these things. See Lyons, *X-Marks*, 33.

68. Gregory interviews, May 9, 2012, February 23, 2015, July 3, 2017, December 28, 2018, July 19, 2019. Gregory also specifically credited Iron Shield with introducing her to ceremonies through his writings. Keith Thor Carlson detailed the power of story and complex Indigenous identities in *The Power of Place, the Problem of Time*. For more on the centrality of oral history and storytelling, see Underwood, *Walking People*.

69. For more on natural, supernatural, and interpersonal connections in American Indian worlds, see P. Allen, *Sacred Hoop*; and Johnson, "American Indians, Manifest Destiny, and Indian Activism."

70. Vizenor, "Aesthetics of Survivance," in *Survivance*, 1.

71. Davis, "Insight into a Bit of Nett Lakes' History," 2.

72. Gregory interview, July 19, 2019. This image or variations of it cover numerous books and anchor numerous popular and scholarly articles. Conspicuously absent from the image is any indication of the Native people detained within it. See, for example, Joinson, *Vanished in Hiawatha*; Young, "S.D. Revisits Past"; and Gevik, "Canton's Hiawatha Indian Asylum." See also "Indian Insane Asylum, Canton, S.D.," postcard; "Indian Insane Asylum, Canton, S.D.," postcards; and *Nice Place to Visit* (blog).

73. Gregory interview, July 19, 2019. Geographer David Delany has offered useful critiques of pervasive whiteness in most U.S. universities, illustrating classrooms as highly racialized spaces. Delaney, "Space That Race Makes," 6–14.

74. Gregory interview, July 19, 2019.

75. Gregory interview, July 19, 2019.

Epilogue

1. Garcia added: "And the one who gave me the ability to understand the gift of medicine started in the 1960s and he died in 2008 . . . his name was Danny Lopez. Along with my father. He told me who I was, who to trust." Garcia went on to say: "I was healed by my grandpa, my dad, my uncles . . . the men in my community. . . . I was shielded by them and told every time that things happened *why* they happened and I was taken to other medicine. So I grew up with the older medicine until I got a chance to choose what

I was gonna be." Garcia telephone interviews, January 3, 28, 2020. A delegation from Gila River Indian Community had invited Garcia to join them at Canton, where they offered additional tributes to their ancestors buried at the cemetery and to the others who had been detained at the institution. For documented examples of Garcia's work, see "SANE Program Development and Operation Guide," video; Belcourt, Facebook post, August 18, 2019; "Green Forests Work—UNEP in the Field"; Denby, "Keeping the Salt in the Earth"; and "Young Women's Gathering," 2.

2. Garcia had been part of a delegation sponsored by Gila River Indian Community to attend the ceremony.

3. O'Neil interviews, March 29, 2019, January 28, 2020; O'Neil conversation, December 9, 2019; Garcia telephone interview, January 28, 2020.

4. Garcia telephone interviews, June 30, August 22, November 20, 2015, January 21, July 6, November 1, 2016, September 11, 2019, January 3, 2020.

5. Garcia telephone interviews, July 6, 2016, January 3, 28, 2020; O'Neil interviews, March 29, 2019, January 28, 2020.

6. O'Neil interviews, June 22, 2017, March 29, 2019; Garcia telephone interviews, July 6, November 1, 2016, September 11, 2019, January 3, 2020.

7. Garcia telephone interviews, September 11, 2019, January 28, 2020; O'Neil interview, January 28, 2020.

8. O'Neil interviews, March 12, October 29, November 11, 24, 2014, April 6–7, 2015, March 8, 2016, March 29, 2019; O'Neil conversation, December 9, 2019.

9. O'Neil interviews, March 8, 2016, March 29, 2019, January 28, 2020.

10. Garcia telephone interviews, January 3, 28, 2020.

11. K. Anderson, Campbell, and Belcourt, *Keetsahnak*; A. Anderson, Kubik, and Hampton, *Torn from Our Midst*; Deer, *Beginning and End of Rape*; Adams, *Education for Extinction*; P. Allen, *Sacred Hoop*; Jacobs, *Generation Removed*; O'Brien, *Firsting and Lasting*; Child, *Boarding School Seasons*; L. Hall, "Strategies of Erasure"; Weaver, "Colonial Context of Violence"; Hernández, *City of Inmates*. For more on Indigenous activism and feminists of color coalitional work, see, for example, Seeding Sovereignty, website and blog; Coalition to Stop Violence against Native Women, "MMIW"; and Moraga and Anzaldúa, *This Bridge Called My Back*.

12. Garcia telephone interviews, August 22, November 20, 2015, January 21, July 6, November 1, 2016, September 11, 2019, January 3, 2020.

13. Garcia telephone interviews, July 6, November 1, 2016, September 11, 2019, January 3, 28, 2020. Garcia added: "How are we suppose to know who we are? If we don't acknowledge what has been done to us . . . to deny this . . . Is the Genocide & Historical Trauma we carry forth to the new generations! Our Language, Songs, & Ceremonies can heal us . . . likewise others too." Garcia correspondence, February 8, 2020. For more on stories and the universe of medicine, see P. Allen, *Grandmothers of the Light*.

14. See, for example, Thomas King, *Truth about Stories*; Mitchell, *Stories of the Potawatomi People*; Bruchac, *Our Stories Remember*; Sium and Ritskes, "Speaking Truth to Power"; Stromberg, *American Indian Rhetorics of Survivance*; Wilson, "Grandmother to Granddaughter," 27–36; Weaver, Womack, and Warrior, *American Indian Literary Nationalism*; P. Deloria et al., "Unfolding Futures,"; and LaDuke, Recovering the Sacred.

See also Anishinaabe writer Leanne Simpson's reflections on storytelling in "RBC Taylor Emerging Writer Award Leanne Simpson."

15. Yellow Bird, "Wild Indians," 9, accessed December 17, 2014; Yellow Bird, interviews, October 14, 2013, November 12–13, 2019.

16. Yellow Bird, "Wild Indians," accessed December 17, 2014; J. Jensen interviews, April 22, 23, 2017, October 3–5, 2019; J. Jensen telephone conversations, February 17, 2017, March 9, August 26, 2018, January 19, 2020; J. Jensen email correspondence, September 12, 2018, January 19, 2020; Mitchell interview, April 8, 2014; O'Neil interview, March 29, 2019; Garcia telephone interviews, July 6, November 1, 2016, September 11, 2019, January 3, 28, 2020; Gregory interviews, December 28, 2018, July 19, 2019; Gregory email correspondence, May 5, 2012–April 6, 2020; F. Jensen interviews, April 7, 8, 2014; Judah interviews, February 12, 2012, September 19, 2019; Davis interviews, June 8–10, 2014.

BIBLIOGRAPHY

Archival Sources
CANTON, SOUTH DAKOTA
  Canton Public Library
    Canton Insane Asylum File
COLLEGE PARK, MARYLAND
  National Archives and Records Administration
    Record Group 48: Department of the Interior, Office of the Secretary
      James McLaughlin to Secretary of the Interior, July 21, 1910,
        Box 1078, 5-1 (California–Canton Asylum) Central Classified Files, 1907–36
    Record Group 411: Records of the General Accounting Office
      Indian Office Files, 1907–39
        Canton Asylum, UD Entry 11, Boxes 25–27
DENVER, COLORADO
  National Archives and Records Administration
    Record Group 75: Records of the Bureau of Indian Affairs
      Records of the Consolidated Ute Agency
        Series 723, Asylums, Insane
          723-000 through 723-006, Correspondence,
          Utes, Asylums: Deaf and Blind
        Decimal Files, 1879–1952, Box 4
FORT WORTH, TEXAS
  National Archives and Records Administration
    Record Group 75: Records of the Bureau of Indian Affairs
      Central Classified Files, 1907–39
      Canton Asylum for Insane Indians, case files
      "Enrollment Cards for the Five Civilized Tribes, 1898–1914," NAI 251747
    Record Group 511: Records of the Alcohol, Drug Abuse,
      and Mental Health Administration
      Fort Worth Clinical Research Center
  Mary Couts Burnett Library, Texas Christian University
    Special Collections
      Amon G. Carter Papers, Box 124, Narcotic Hospital, 1930–38
KANSAS CITY, MISSOURI
  National Archives and Records Administration
    Record Group 75: Records of the Bureau of Indian Affairs
      Agency Buildings Survey 1915–20
      Canton Asylum for Insane Indians. Box 1–end
      Correspondence Relating to Individuals, 1895–1936
      Letters Received from the Commissioner
      Letters Sent to Commissioner
      Program Mission Correspondence, Boxes 1–9
      Record of Employees, 1901–17

MAYETTA, KANSAS
  Potawatomi Agency
    Folder M, Box 221, Series 8, Correspondence Relating
      to Individuals, 1895–1936, M–N
MINNEAPOLIS, MINNESOTA
  Social Welfare History Archives, University of Minnesota
    Florence Crittenton Collection, Box 15, Folder 7, Phoenix, AZ, 1933–37
PIERRE, SOUTH DAKOTA
  South Dakota State Archives
    Canton Asylum for Insane Indians
    Asylum for Insane Indians, Annual Reports and Census, 1910–18, 1920–29
    Weekly Reports, May 1928
      H83-1: Canton Indian Asylum
        Correspondence, 1929–33, Box 3600B, Folder 2
        Memoranda, 1929–33, Box 3600B, Folder 1
    Photographs of Canton, South Dakota, H2000-068, Boxes 8534A and B
    Postcards of Canton, South Dakota, Box 8535B
    Vertical Files: Canton Asylum for Insane Indians (Hiawatha)
  South Dakota Department of Health
    Index to South Dakota Death Records, 1905–1955. Pierre,
      SD: South Dakota Department of Health.
  South Dakota State Historical Society
    South Dakota, State Census, 1905
    South Dakota, State Census, 1925
    South Dakota, State Census, 1935
TEMPE, ARIZONA
  Distinctive Collections, Arizona State University Library
    Box 72, Folder 6, MSS-164, "Ft. Defiance: Good Shepard Letters"
RIVERSIDE, CALIFORNIA
  National Archives and Records Administration
    Record Group 75: Records of the Bureau of Indian Affairs
      Student Case Files, 1902–1990, Box 28, Folder: Cora
        Winona Fairbaut [sic], Phoenix Indian School
SEATTLE, WASHINGTON
  National Archives and Records Administration
    Record Group 75: Records of the Bureau of Indian Affairs
      Warm Springs Agency, Insanity Files
      Warm Springs Agency, Lunacy Files
WASHINGTON, DC
  National Archives and Records Administration
    Record Group 29: Records of the Bureau of the Census
      Ninth Census of the United States, 1870
      Tenth Census of the United States, 1880
      Twelfth Census of the United States, 1900
      Thirteenth Census of the United States, 1910

Fourteenth Census of the United States, 1920
Fifteenth Census of the United States, 1930
Sixteenth Census of the United States, 1940
Record Group 75: Records of the Bureau of Indian Affairs
Indian Census Rolls, 1885–1940, M595, microfilm
Consolidated Ute Agency, 1935, Roll 78
Devil's Lake Agency, 1889, Roll 94
Green Bay Agency, 1895–96, 1899, 1906, 1908, Rolls 173–74
Keshena Agency, 1923, 1924, 1927, 1932, 1934,
1937, 1942, Rolls 202–3, 205, 207–9
Kiowa Agency, 1917, 1924, 1929, 1931, Rolls 216–17, 219
Pine Ridge Agency, 1901–2, 1920, 1923, 1931,
1933, Rolls 368, 371–72, 377, 380
Potawatomi Agency, 1891, 1898, 1908–12, 1916, 1918, 1928, Rolls 392–93
Rosebud Agency, 1919–21, Roll 435
Sisseton Agency, 1890, 1899, 1903–4, 1907, 1910–19,
1921–23, 1926–28, Rolls 507–13
Southern Ute Agency, 1894–1923, Rolls 544–45
Central Classified Files, 1907–39
Canton Asylum for Insane Indians, Boxes 1–20
Cheyenne and Arapaho Agency
Choctaw Agency
Keshena Agency
Navajo Agency
Phoenix Agency
Pima Agency
Pine Ridge Agency
Pipestone School Agency
Red Lake Agency
Rosebud Agency
Sisseton Agency
Tongue River Agency
Western Navajo Agency
White Earth Agency
Record Group 418: Records of St. Elizabeths Hospital
Entry 13, Department of the Interior: Indian Insane

Interviews and Correspondence

Abrahams, Edward, III. "Inquiry Answers Re. David Abrams." Unpublished interview by the author, June 24, 2017.
———. Telephone interview by the author, December 9, 2016.
BigFoot, Dee. Telephone interview by the author, April 29, 2014.
Brings Plenty, Trevino. Email correspondence with the author, September 30, 2014.
———. Telephone interviews by the author, September 8, 29, 2014.
Caldwell, Frank, Jr. Telephone interview by the author, April 14, 2014.

Christopher, Clara. Interview by Thomas Lubeck, April 10, 1979. South Dakota Oral History Center, University of South Dakota, Vermillion.

Davis, J. Kay. Email correspondence with the author, May 20, 2013–June 17, 2015.

———. Interviews by the author, June 8, 9, 10, 2014, Nett Lake, MN.

———. Oral History Interview Information Sheet, July 7, 2017.

Deegan, Pat. Interview by the author, February 20, 2017.

Dexter, Donna. Interview by the author, April 5, 2017.

Garcia, Mary. Correspondence with author, February 8, 2020.

———. Telephone interviews by the author, June 30, August 22, November 20, 2015; January 21, July 6, November 1, 2016; September 11, 2019; January 3, 28, 2020.

Gregory, Anne. Email correspondence with the author, May 5, 2012–April 6, 2020.

———. Interviews by the author, May 9, 2012; February 23, 2015; July 3, 2017; December 28, 2018; July 19, 2019.

Hill, Manfred. Interview by Donna Dexter, July 26, 2013, Augustana College, Canton, SD.

———. Interviews by the author, May 15, 2012; May 18, 2013; May 14, 2015; February 13, 2017.

———. Telephone conversations with the author, September 12, 2014; December 4, 2016; July 18, 2017.

Iron Cloud, Richard. Email correspondence with the author, May 20, 2015.

———. Telephone interviews by the author, May 19, 2015; March 27, 2018.

Jensen, Francis. Interviews by the author, April 7, 8, 2014, Holton, KS.

———. Telephone conversations with the author, January 30, April 1, July 21, September 5, October 20, 2014.

Jensen, Jack. Email correspondence with the author, March 26, July 2, September, 12, 2018; January 29, June 6, 2019; January 19, March 20, 21, 2020.

———. Interviews by the author, April 22, 23, 2017; October 3, 4, 5, 2019.

———. Telephone conversations with the author, February 17, 2017; March 9, August 26, 2018; January 19, 2020.

———. Unpublished remarks at Deer Dancer Ranch, TX, October 5, 2019.

Jerz, Fawn. Interviews by the author, January 27, April 1, 2017; January 9, 2020.

Judah, Lavanah Smith. Correspondence with the author, June 29, July 2, 7, 13, 2011; January 15, February 12, April 7, May 3, 18, July 12, 2013; August 6, November 14, 2015; April 8, 2016; January 18, 2017.

———. Interviews by the author, June 24, December 28, 2011; February 12, May 12, 2012; May 10–11, June 17, 2013; April 27, 2014; November 7, 2015; February 12, 2017; September 19, 2019.

Juel, Mildred S. Email correspondence with author, October 9, 11, 16, 2013.

———. Informal interview by the author, May 18, 2015, Brookings, SD.

———. Telephone conversations with author, October 6, 2013; April 4, 2020.

Kiger-StClair, Caroline Jean. Correspondence with author, April 17, 25, 2017; July 29, 30, 2019; February 20, 2020.

———. Interview by the author, February 25, 2017.

———. Oral History Interview Information Sheet, 2017.

Kills Small, Jerome. Telephone conversation with author, July 21, 2019.

Lofland, Ellen. Email correspondence with author, August 3, 2019, March 20–21, 2020.
———. Telephone interview by the author, August 4, 2019.
Longhat, Franklin James. Telephone interviews by the author, May 3, August 1, 2014.
Louis, Sidney. Correspondence with author, February 24, 2014.
———. Telephone interview by the author, March 23, 2014.
McMillen, Frances. Telephone interview by author, April 14, 2017.
Mitchell, Gary. Email correspondence with author, December 18, 2013; April 14, 2014.
———. Interview by the author, April 8, 2014, Potawatomi Reservation, KS.
O'Neil, Faith. Conversation with the author, December 9, 2019.
———. Interviews by the author, March 6, June 25, 26, 2012, Denver, CO; March 12, October 29, November 11, 24, 2014, May 17, 2015, Canton, SD; April 6, 7, 2015, Los Angeles, CA; March 8, 2016, June 22, 2017, March 29, 2019, Buena Park, CA; August 7, 2019; January 28, 2020.
———. Personal audio recordings, with author, August 14, 2012; with author, May 18, 2015, and with Pete Alcaraz, Marie Skelly, and Bill Skelly, May 18, 2015, Canton Public Library, SD.
Napos (David Turney Sr.). Interviews by the author, July 18–19, 2015, Keshena, WI.
———. Telephone interviews by the author, June 16, July 5, 16, October 25, 2015; January 6, February 23, March 6, 13, December 18, 2016; May 5, 2017.
Peterson, Omar. Telephone interviews by the author, July 29, 2017; August 3, 2019.
Prandoni, Jogues. Email correspondence with author, July 28, 2011; March 11, April 14, August 20, 2014; January 25, February 1, 8, March 1, 8, 29, November 5, 2017.
———. Interview by the author, May 12, 2017.
Rabon, Joe. Email correspondence with author, May 20, 2013; January 15, February 18, April 28, 30, 2014; November 26, December 6, 2016; May 18, 2017; February 8, 2018.
———. Interviews by the author, August 28, 2013; May 19, 2015, Sioux Falls, SD; December 5, 2016.
———. Telephone conversations with the author, January 21, February 18, May 7, June 20, 2014.
Rhodd, Ben. Conversations with the author, August 17, 2017, Rosebud, SD; November 9, 2019, Hill City, SD.
Roth, Steven. Telephone interview by the author, November 19, 2014.
Stretches, Yvonne. Telephone interview by the author, February 17, 2017.
Teeman, Diane. Email correspondence with the author, March 12, April 5, May 19, July 16, 18, 2014.
Williams, Paul. Email correspondence with the author, May 16, 2017.
Yabah, Robin. Telephone conversations with the author, December 21, 30, 2018.
Yellow Bird, Pemina. Interviews by the author, October 14, 2013; March 8, 2015; July 22, 2019; November 12–13, 2019, Plaza, ND.

Artifacts/Material Objects

Bandolier, ca. 1890s, by O-Zoush-Quah (Prairie Band Potawatomi). Photograph only, personal collection of Jensen family.
Canton, SD, photographs. Personal collection of Manfred Hill, Canton, SD.

Canton, SD, photographs. Personal collection of Omar F. Peterson, Canton, SD.

Family Bible, ca. 1880s. Personal collection of Jack Jensen, Houston, TX.

Family quilt, Ancestry Project, ca. 1900–2019. Personal collection of Jack Jensen, Houston, TX.

Faribault family correspondence. Personal collection of Faith O'Neil, Buena Park, CA.

Faribault family correspondence and photographs. Personal collection of Caroline Kiger-StClair, Seattle, WA.

Faribault family scrapbook, 1960s–2019. Personal collection of Faith O'Neil, Buena Park, CA.

Gregory family photographs. Personal collection of Anne Gregory, Eugene, OR.

Handmade map, ca. 2010–14. Personal collection of Kay Davis, Nett Lake, MN.

"Indian Insane Asylum, Canton, S.D." Postcard, September 25, 1918, Robert Bogdan Collection, Disability History Museum. https://www.disabilitymuseum.org/dhm/lib/catcard.html?id=268.

"Indian Insane Asylum, Canton, S.D." Postcards. US GenWeb Archives, Lincoln, SD. Accessed December 1, 2019. http://usgwarchives.net/sd/lincoln/postcards/indasy.jpg.

Marlow family photographs, 1890s–1940s. Personal collection of Joe Rabon, Sioux Falls, SD.

O-Zoush-Quah and Jensen family photographs, 1890s–2019. Personal collection of Jack Jensen, Houston, TX.

Photographs, ca. 2011–15. Personal collection of Lavanah Judah, Yankton, SD.

Photographs, ca. 1910–30s. Personal collection of Gertie Hale and Bill Skelly, Canton Public Library, Canton, SD.

Published Primary Sources

"Apparently an Expensive Move." *Argus Leader* (Sioux Falls, SD), December 20, 1933, 6.

"Appointed Asylum Superintendent." *Washington Post*, October 17, 1901, 11.

"Arizona News." *Los Angeles Times*, October 22, 1897, 5.

"Ask Senators to Investigate Conditions at Asylum; Immediate Closing Unlikely." *Sioux Valley (SD) News*, September 28, 1933.

"Asylum for Insane Indians." *Boston Daily Globe*, July 30, 1899, 35.

"An Asylum for Insane Indians." *New York Daily Tribune*, January 19, 1902, 4.

"Asylum for Insane Indians." *Norfolk (NE) News*, October 18, 1901, 5.

"Asylum for Insane Indians: Federal Institution at Canton, S.D., Now Completed." *New York Times*, December 22, 1901, 10.

"Asylum for Insane Indians: Now Completed and the Keys Given to the Government Agent Wednesday." *Sioux Valley (SD) News*, October 4, 1901, 1.

"Asylum Is Abolished." *Santa Cruz (CA) News*, March 30, 1934, 1.

"Asylum Needs Larger Quarters." *Sioux Valley (SD) News*, February 5, 1925, 17.

"Asylum Story Listed as Most Important." *Sioux Valley (SD) News*, December 28, 1933, 1.

Belcourt, Christi. Facebook post, August 18, 2019. Accessed April 17, 2020. https://www.facebook.com/christibelcourt/posts/10157156091230272.

"Berry Signs Asylum for Pen Use." *Sioux Valley (SD) News*, April 12, 1934.

"Bidding for Construction of Asylum." *Omaha Daily Bee*, October 25, 1899, 1.

"Birds-eye View of Canton, the Gate City of Dakota." *Canton Advocate*, February 18, 1883, 2.

Bolding, Julie. "Journalist: Canton Golf Course No Place for Graveyard." *Argus Leader* (Sioux Falls, SD), October 6, 1989, 1C.

"Brief Filed in Asylum Action: Collier Says Court Here Has No Jurisdiction; Type of Case Called Improper." *Sioux Valley (SD) News*, November 2, 1933, 10.

"Buried between Fairways: Vermillion Man Wants Indians' Remains Returned." *Argus Leader* (Sioux Falls, SD), November 10, 1991, 1A, 3A.

Butler, Pat. "A Final Place of Rest: Writer Wants Bodies Sent to Reservations." *Argus Leader* (Sioux Falls, SD), November 10, 1991, 3A.

———. "A Proper Burial: Writer Wants Bodies Sent to Reservations." *Argus Leader* (Sioux Falls, SD), n.d. Canton Asylum for Insane Indians file, Canton Public Library, SD.

———. "An Unfit Resting Place." *Argus Leader* (Sioux Falls, SD), November 10, 1991, 1A, 3A.

"Canton Asylum Conditions 'Sickening,' Director Says; Indians 'Chained to Pipes.'" *Argus Leader* (Sioux Falls, SD), October 15, 1933, 1.

"Canton Asylum Lease Extended." *Argus Leader* (Sioux Falls, SD), April 12, 1935, 4.

"Canton Asylum May Be Given to State." *Argus Leader* (Sioux Falls, SD), January 11, 1935, 2.

"Canton Indians Entrain for Capitol." *Argus Leader* (Sioux Falls, SD), December 21, 1933, 1.

"Canton's New Asylum." *St. Paul (MN) Globe*, September 13, 1901, 3.

"Ceremony to Memorialize Those Buried at Old Asylum." *Rapid City (IA) Journal*, May 28, 1997, C3.

"Chief Flying Iron Makes Plea for Indian's Citizenship Rights." *Star-Gazette* (Elmira, NY), April 30, 1926, 15.

"Christopher Estate Sold to United States for Indian Asylum." *Sioux Valley (SD) News*, January 20, 1927.

"Collier Postpones Visit: Senators to Be Here to Determine Whether Asylum Is as Obsolete as Collier Has Stated." *Sioux Valley (SD) News*, October 5, 1933, 6.

"Collier Visits in So. Dakota: Washington Indian Commission Are Not Expected to Stop at Canton." *Sioux Valley (SD) News*, December 7, 1933, n.p. Canton Asylum for Insane Indians file, Canton Public Library, SD.

"Dakota Given Canton." *Independent* (Hawarden, IA), Apr 12, 1934, 10.

Davis, Brad. "Journalist Talks about Indian Asylum." *Minnesota Daily*, May 20, 1994, 4.

Davis, J. Kay. "Christmastime Blessings." *Bois Forte News* (Nett Lake, MN), December 2012, 7. http://www.boisforte.com/pdf/BFeNwsltrDec2012final.pdf.

———. "An Insight into a Bit of Nett Lakes' History." *Bois Forte News* (Nett Lake, MN), January 2001, 2. http://www.boisforte.com/pdf/BFN_JANUARY_2001.pdf.

———. "Hiawatha Insane Asylum for Indians Canton, South Dakota." *Bois Forte News* (Nett Lake, MN), August 2012, 9. http://www.boisforte.com/documents/BFNwsltrAug2012final.pdf.

———. "The Trygg Files and Their Link to Indian Land Claims." *Bois Forte News* (Nett Lake, MN), April 2010. https://www.boisforte.com/documents/April_000.pdf.

Deegan, Patricia E. "The Independent Living Movement and People with Psychiatric Disabilities: Taking Control Back over Our Own Lives." *Psychosocial Rehabilitation Journal* 15 (1992): 3–19.

———. "Remember My Name: Reflections on Spirituality in Individual and Collective Recovery." October 2004. https://www.patdeegan.com/pat-deegan/lectures/remember-my-name.

———. "Spirit Breaking: When the Helping Professions Hurt." *Humanistic Psychologist* 28, no. 1–3 (Spring-Summer-Fall 2000): 194–209.

Denby, Samantha. "Keeping the Salt in the Earth." *Border Wars* (blog). NACLA (North American Congress on Latin America), July 5, 2018. Accessed April 17, 2020. https://nacla.org/blog/2018/07/05/keeping-salt-earth.

"Dr. Culp, Physician, Will Take Charge: Supt. of Pipestone Indian School Here Checking Equipment, Supplies." *Sioux Valley (SD) News*, October 19, 1933, 12.

Dutcher, Rodney, "End of Misrule Is Heralded for Indians." *Santa Cruz (CA) News*, March 30, 1934, 9–10.

Eagle, Kathleen. *Sunrise Song*. Memphis: Bell Bridge Books, 2013.

Egan, Jodie. "Historians Revive Stories of Dakota Territory." *Argus Leader* (Sioux Falls, SD), April 9, 1983, 4B.

"Forgotten Cemetery to Be Remembered by Canton Indians." *Sioux City (IA) Journal*, October 7, 1989, 1A.

Fourteen Years' Work among "Erring Girls" as Conducted by the National Florence Crittenton Mission with Practical Suggestions for the Same. Washington, DC: National Florence Crittenton Mission, 1897. https://babel.hathitrust.org/cgi/pt?id=mdp.39015009024061;view=1up;seq=7.

"Gain in Indian Insanity: Chief Cause Attributed to Forced Civilization." *Chicago Daily Tribune*, January 3, 1904, 44.

"Gov. Official Here to Make Report to US: No Information Available at Hiawatha Asylum; Dr. Silk Here from Washington." *Sioux Valley (SD) News*, September 9, 1933, 3.

"Green Forests Work—UNEP in the Field." Planting Trees on Legacy Mines, Appalachian Regional Reforestation Initiative, Office of Surface Mining Reclamation and Enforcement, November 2011. Accessed April 17, 2020. https://arri.osmre.gov/Legacy/GFW%20UNEP%20Field%20November%202011.pdf.

Handbook for Employees, United States Public Health Service Hospital, Lexington, Kentucky. N.p., ca. 1940s. Van Horn Narcotics Farm Collection, Kentucky Historical Society, Frankfort.

Harriman, Peter. "Memories Honored at Asylum Site." *Argus Leader* (Sioux Falls, SD), May 28, 2000, 1B, 9B.

Hascall, Randy. "Spiritual Walk Honors Indians Who Lived in Insane Asylum." *Argus Leader* (Sioux Falls, SD), May 26, 1997, 27D.

"Head of Indian Asylum Fired by Ickes." *Washington Post*, October 17, 1933, 4.

"Hiawatha Asylum for Insane Indians." *USA Today* online, May 5, 2013. Video, 4:22. https://www.usatoday.com/videos/news/nation/2013/05/05/2137133/.

"Hiawatha Asylum for Insane Indians Was Only of Its Kind in the World, 1902–1933." *Doon (IA) Press*, February 19, 1970, 5.

"Hiawatha Asylum's Dark Past Featured in Romantic Novel." *Sioux Valley (SD) News*, March 14, 1996, 5.

"Hiawatha Warhoops." *Sioux Valley (SD) News*, December 21, 1933, 14.

Hillgreen, Ralph O. "Institution Now Leased for $1 for Prisoners." *Argus Leader* (Sioux Falls, SD), February 15, 1935, 4.

"Home for Insane Red Men." *Holt County Sentinel* (Oregon, MO), December 29, 1905, 8.

"Home for Insane Red Men." *Portsmouth (NH) Herald*, January 3, 1906.

"Home for the Erring: National Florence Crittenton Mission Incorporated in This City." *Washington Post*, January 19, 1897, 9.

Hummer, Harry R. "Insanity among the Indians." *American Journal of Insanity* 69 (January 1913): 613–23.

"Hummer Asked to Disregard Closing Order: Immediate Hearing on Injunction Refused Silk; Left for Wash. Tuesday." *Sioux Valley (SD) News*, September 28, 1933, 1.

"Hummer Denies All Charges." *Lead (SD) Daily Call*, October 17, 1933, 1.

"Idle Buildings Available for Use." *Argus-Leader* (Sioux Falls, SD), August 22, 1945, 6.

"Indian Activists Want 119 Bodies Reburied." *Sioux City (IA) Journal*, November 11, 1991, 1A.

"'Indian Hunters' Impressed at Civilization Fund Out Here." *Sioux Valley (SD) News*, September 28, 1933, 1.

"Indian Mental Patients Reach Hospital Here: Group of 69 Freed from Asylum Received at St. Elizabeths." *Washington Post*, December 23, 1933, 4.

"Indian Reburial Movement Spurs Interest in Asylum Graves." *Albuquerque Journal*, October 7, 1989, H6.

"Indians' 'Inhuman' Asylum Is Closed." *Baltimore Sun*, December 23, 1933, 2.

"Insane Asylum for Indians: No Mental Maladies among Them until Intermarriage with White Race." *New York Daily Tribune*, May 24, 1899, 5.

"Insane Indians Are Gathered in an Asylum from All Over the Country." *Pittsburgh Post-Gazette*, August 25, 1905.

"Insane Indians Left at Canton." *Evening Huronite* (Huron, SD), September 27, 1933, 8.

"Insane Patients Reach Washington." *Evening Huronite* (Huron, SD), December 22, 1933, 1.

Iron Cloud, Richard. *From the Badlands to Alcatraz*. Documentary. Directed by Nancy Iverson. San Francisco: Pathstar, 2009.

Iron Shield, Harold. "Ceremony Planned for S.D. Native Cemetery." *American Indian Press* (Bemidji, MN), June 12, 1992. http://cdm16022.contentdm.oclc.org/cdm/ref /collection/p16022coll2/id/18598 (page removed).

———. "The Legacy of an Infamous Institution: Hiawatha Insane Asylum for American Indians." *Native American Press*, November 13, 1997, 3.

———. "Letter to the Editor: Ceremony Will Honor Indian Leaders." July 5, 1997. *Sioux Valley (SD) News*, July 2, 1997, 10A.

———. "Research Indicates Asylum Wasn't in Indians' Best Interest." *Argus Leader: Different Voices*, August 4, 1988, 10A.

———. "South Dakota Should Protect Remains in Sacred Burial Grounds of Indians." *Argus Leader: Different Voices*, September 6, 1989, 12A.

Jensen, Francis, and Pauline Jensen. "Reclaimed Heritage." *Heritage of the Great Plains* 12, no. 4 (1979): 28–41.

"Jobs for Every Able Patient at Lexington Narcotic Farm Provide Therapy and Training." *Louisville Courier-Journal*, November 26, 1950, 152.

Jordan, Melissa. "Golfcourse Graves a Painful Legacy." *Rapid City (SD) Journal*, October 6, 1989, B5.

———. "National Indian Asylum's Legacy: Graces amid a Golf Course." AP News, October 6, 1989. http://www.apnewsarchive.com/1989/National-Indian-Asylum -s-Legacy-Graves-Amid-a-Golf-Course/id-b8ae6d100becfb98afe2554cefb90577.

"Kay Davis, Part 2." Audio interview. Bois Forte Tribal Community Radio. https://beta .prx.org/stories/137628/details.

"The Leader." *Dakota Farmers' Leader* (Canton, SD), December 27, 1901, 4.

Limoges, Jeanne. "Hiawatha Memorial Service Source of Mixed Emotions." *Sioux Valley (SD) News*, July 2, 1997, 5.

———. "Memorial Ceremony Held at Hiawatha Cemetery." *Sioux Valley (SD) News*, June 5, 1997, 1A.

Linck, Michelle. "Indians Ask for Respect at Burials at Golf Course: Canton Cemetery Is Located at Site of Former Asylum." *Sioux City (IA) Journal*, May 29, 1998, A4.

"Local." *Dakota Farmers Leader*, November 5, 1915, 5.

"Medical Officer Assumes Custody of New US Public Health Service Hospital Here." *Fort Worth Star Telegram*, July 2, 1938, 8.

"Medicine: Drug Addicts." *Time*, November 14, 1938. Accessed November 5, 2013, https://drugs-forum.com/forum/showthread.php?t=70212. Registration required.

Meriam, Lewis, and Hubert Work. *The Problem of Indian Administration: Summary of Findings and Recommendations*. Washington, DC: Institute for Government Research, 1928.

Middleton, Arthur E. "Supplanting the Medicine Man." *Modern Hospital* 19, no. 2 (August 1922): 139–42.

Miller, Steve. "Sad Legacy at Quiet Cemetery." *Rapid City Journal*, February 11, 1992, 1B.

Mitchell, Gary. "Boarding Schools and the Potawatomi." Native American Bode'wadmi, *Pokagon Times*, February 11, 2010. http://pokagon.blogspot.com/2010/02/indian -boarding-school.html?m=0.

———. *The Native Blog: Gary Mitchell's Column*. http://nativeblog.typepad.com /the_potawatomitracks_blog/gary_mitchells_column/.

———. Stories of the Potawatomi People. http://www.kansasheritage.org/PBP/books /mitch/mitch_toc.html.

———. *Stories of the Potawatomi People: From the Early Days to Modern Times*. Mayetta, KS: G. E. Mitchell, 1996.

"Moen, Judge Daugherty Offer Argument: Many High Government Officials Enlisted in Move to Keep Institution." *Sioux Valley (SD) News*, September 14, 1933, 3.

"Moving the Insane Indians." *Daily Argus Leader* (Sioux Falls, SD), September 12, 1933, 6.

"The National Hospital for Insane Indians." *Daily Republican* (Monongahela, PA), March 25, 1904, 3.

Native American Reburial Restoration Committee. "Call for Action." 1998. Accessed March 23, 2017. http://web.archive.org/web/20010606184952/http://home .earthlink.net/~clendaniel/page4.html.

"Near-By News Notes." *Hawarden (IA) Independent*, December 28, 1933, 3.

"Nephew Pres. Taft Counsel for Asylum; Injunction Contends That Indians Are Not Admissible in Wash. Hospital." *Sioux Valley (SD) News*, September 21, 1933, 21.

"New Agreement Meant to Help Preserve Tribal Culture." *Bismarck Tribune*, December 15, 2004, 4C.

"New Hospital Building at Indian Insane Asylum." *Sioux Valley (SD) News*, September 19, 1913, 1.

"News and Gossip from Washington Departments." *Atlanta Constitution*, August 9, 1899, 4.

"No Indian Lunatics." *Los Angeles Times*, June 25, 1899, 19.

"North Dakota Interests." *Omaha Daily Bee*, December 8, 1901, 1.

"Obituary, Mrs. Maggie Hale." *Topeka State Journal*, July 23, 1943, 6.

"Only Asylum for Insane Indians in US." *Minneapolis Journal*, October 19, 1901, 18.

"Only 125 of 225,000 Indians Insane, Says Government Report." *Washington Post*, June 12, 1923, 1.

"Orders Davis to an Asylum." *Chicago Daily Tribune*, December 26, 1899, 5.

"O. S. Gifford Gets It!" *Sioux Valley (SD) News*, October 18, 1901, 1.

"Ousted Asylum Head to Fight Charges." *Daily Argus Leader* (Sioux Falls, SD), October 17, 1933, 1.

"Part I: The Public Health Service Narcotic Hospital in Lexington." *What's New Anniversary Issue* 220, n.d., 38.

"Pettigrew Hard to Please." *Omaha Daily Bee*, May 25, 1900, 3.

"Pipe Ceremony Held Oct. 4 at Cemetery." *Winnebago Indian News* (NE), October 11, 1997, NP.

"Plan Removal Canton Indians." *Lead (SD) Daily Call*, December 20, 1933, 1.

"Prairie Band Potawatomi: Preserving Language & Culture." YouTube, January 25, 2015. Video, 8:43. https://www.youtube.com/watch?v=oZYHVeKIVtE.

"Prosperity at Canton." *Dakota Farmers Leader* (Canton, SD), August 9, 1901, 1.

"RBC Taylor Emerging Writer Award Leanne Simpson on the Significance of Storytelling." CBC Radio-Canada. http://www.cbc.ca/books/canadawrites/2014/06/rbc-taylor-emerging-writer-award-leanne-simpson-on-the-significance-of-storytelling.html (page removed).

"Real Estate." *Denison (IA) Review*, April 15, 1902, 4.

Report of the Commissioner of Indian Affairs. Annual Reports of the Department of the Interior for the Fiscal Year Ended June 30, 1897. Washington, DC: Government Printing Office, 1897.

"'Sane' Indians Held in Dakota Asylum: Dr. S. A. Silk in Report to Ickes Charges 'Sickening' Conditions at Canton. Patients Kept Shackled 'Imprisoned' over Trifles, with 'Greed' Preventing Their Release—Action Begun to Free Score." *New York Times*, October 15, 1933, N2.

"SANE Program Development and Operation Guide: Community Uniqueness." YouTube, August 31, 2016. Video, 5:55. https://www.youtube.com/watch?v=b95szNKovqE.

"Sane Reds Confined in Asylum." *Helena (MT) Independent*, October 15, 1933, 1.

"Says Indians Have Fewer Rights Than Newly Arrived Immigrants." *Niagara Falls (NY) Gazette*, March 28, 1933, 4.

"Says U.S. Court Has Power." *Daily Argus Leader* (Sioux Falls, SD), November 21, 1933, 5.

Shattuck, George B., F. B. Lund, and E. W. Taylor, eds. "Asylum for Insane Indians." *Boston Medical and Surgical Journal* 141 (July–December 1899): 121.

"Sioux Chief Asks Fair Play from U.S. for Indians." *Warren (PA) Tribune*, March 14, 1928, 2.

"South Dakota Executive Also Takes Up Seed Loan, Canton Asylum Matters." *Argus Leader* (Sioux Falls, SD), April 12, 1935, 1.

Steen, Jomay. "Ceremony Dignifies Memory of Hiawatha Asylum Inmates." *Argus Leader* (Sioux Falls, SD), May 31, 1998, 1C, 4C.

———. "Walkers Honor 121 Indians Who Died at Asylum." *Argus Leader* (Sioux Falls, SD), June 1, 1997, 1D.

"Surprise Move Came without Warning Here: First Inkling Came Wednesday; Indians Loaded, Gone by Evening." *Sioux Valley (SD) News*, December 21, 1933, 1.

"A Tale of Two Cities: Share Hospital since 1949." *Sioux Valley (SD) News*, July 28, 1966, 4E, 6E.

"30,000 Indians Petition to Retain Asylum." *Sioux Valley (SD) News*, October 26, 1933, 1.

"This Plaque Marks Burial of 120 Indians at Canton." *Doon (IA) Press* 6, no. 35 (February 19, 1970): cover, 3.

Tollefson, Chris. "Program to Honor Indians Who Died in Asylum." *Argus Leader* (Sioux Falls, SD), April 4, 1992, C1.

"Transfers at Asylum Here Being Made: Eight Indians Remain; Four Nurses Transferred to New Positions." *Sioux Valley (SD) News*, January 11, 1934, 1.

"Transferring of Patients from St. Elizabeth's to Canton." *Omaha Daily Bee*, October 29, 1901, 2.

"Treat Insane Indians." *Waco (TX) News-Tribune*, June 6, 1942, 1.

Turner, John F. "Insane Indians." *New Albany Medical Herald* 25 (August 1907): 147–48.

"20 Sane Indians Held in Asylum, Ickes Charges." *St. Louis Post-Dispatch*, October 15, 1933, 1.

"Two More Indian Patients Are Taken to Washington: Work Bill Last Week That They Could Not Be Moved; Two Others Return Home." *Sioux Valley (SD) News*, December 28, 1933, 23.

Valandra, Clement. "Naming a Committee." *Argus Leader* (Sioux Falls, SD), November 6, 1933, 6.

"Vermillion Man Wants Indians Reburied." *Rapid City (SD) Journal*, November 11, 1991, A2.

"Washington, Instructions Issued." *Minneapolis Journal*, November 28, 1901, 9.

"Weather." *Aberdeen (SD) Weekly News*, June 3, 1915, 7.

"Wheeler Gets Results." *Helena (MT) Daily Independent*, October 23, 1933, 4.

"Will Put Canton Asylum into Use." *Daily Plainsman* (Huron, SD), April 11, 1934, 11.

Willis, Frank N., Larry M. Dean, and Larry Larsen. "The First Mental Hospital for American Indians, 1900–1934." *Bulletin of the Menninger Clinic* 45, no. 2 (March 1981): 149–54.

"Winter Memorial." *Rapid City (SD) Journal*, February 22, 1998, C3.

Worthington, Rogers. "Where Archaeologists See Discovery, Indians See Only Lost Souls." *Chicago Tribune*, July 24, 1988, A6.

Yellow Bird, Pemina. "Indian Healers Were Spiritually Revered." *Capital Times* (Madison, WI), December 8, 1986, editorial section, 12.

———. "Wild Indians: Native Perspectives on the Hiawatha Asylum for Insane Indians." National Empowerment Center. http://www.power2u.org/downloads /NativePerspectivesPeminaYellowBird.pdf.

Young, Steve. "Hiawatha Remembered." *On the Beat* (blog). *Argus Leader* (Sioux Falls, SD), May 14, 2013. https://steveyoungonthebeat-blog-blog.tumblr.com /post/50424914871/hiawatha-remembered.

———. "Insane Asylum: Place of Solemnity Is among Ideas for Preservation." *Argus Leader* (Sioux Falls, SD), May 5, 2013, A1, A9.

———. "Keepers of Canton Native American Asylum Don't Want People to Forget." *Argus Leader* (Sioux Falls, SD), May 30, 2014. https://www.argusleader.com/story /news/2014/05/30/keepers-canton-native-american-asylum-want-people -forget/9778783/.

———. "S.D. Revisits Past at Native American Insane Asylum." *USA Today*, May 5, 2013. https://www.usatoday.com/story/news/nation/2013/05/05 /sd-native-american-insane-asylum/2137011/.

———. "A Shameful Past: Indian Insane Asylum." *Argus Leader* (Sioux Falls, SD), May 5, 2013, 5.

"Young Women's Gathering." *Wa:k Newsletter* 27, no. 7 (July 2017): 2. Accessed April 17, 2020. http://www.waknet.org/Newsletters/2017-07-NL.pdf.

Published Secondary Sources

A Nice Place to Visit (blog). Accessed December 1, 2019. http:// cantonasylumforinsaneindians.com/history_blog/tag/chautauqua/.

Achebe, Chinua. *Home and Exile*. Oxford: Oxford University Press, 2000.

Acker, Caroline J. *Creating the American Junkie: Addiction Research in the Classic Era of Narcotic Control*. Baltimore, MD: Johns Hopkins University Press, 2002.

Adams, David Wallace. *Education for Extinction: American Indians and the Boarding School Experience, 1875–1928*. Lawrence: University Press of Kansas, 1995.

Adams, David Wallace, and Christa DeLuzio, eds. *On the Borders of Love and Power: Families and Kinship in the Intercultural American Southwest*. Berkeley: University of California Press, 2012.

Alabama Department of Archives and History. "Indian Removal Era." Alabama Moments in American History. http://www.alabamamoments.alabama.gov/seco8qs.html.

Allen, Chadwick. *Blood Narrative: Indigenous Identity in American Indian and Maori Literary and Activist Texts*. Durham, NC: Duke University Press, 2002.

Allen, Paula Gunn. *Grandmothers of the Light: A Medicine Woman's Sourcebook*. Boston: Beacon, 1991.

———. *Off the Reservation: Reflections on Boundary-Busting, Border-Crossing, Loose Cannons*. Boston: Beacon, 1998.

———. *The Sacred Hoop: Recovering the Feminine in American Indian Traditions*. Boston: Beacon, 1992.

"An Ancestral Quilt, Completed." *Love of Quilting* (January–February 2020): 53–55.

Andersen, Chris, and Jean M. O'Brien. "Feminism, Gender, and Sexuality." In *Sources and Methods in Indigenous Studies*, 183–226. New York: Routledge, 2016.

Anderson, A. Brenda, Wendee Kubik, and Mary Rucklos Hampton, eds. *Torn from Our Midst: Voices of Grief, Healing, and Action from the Missing Indigenous Women Conference, 2008*. Regina, SK: Canadian Plains Research Center, 2010.

Anderson, Kim, Maria Campbell, and Christi Belcourt, eds. *Keetsahnak: Our Missing and Murdered Indigenous Sisters*. Edmonton: University of Alberta Press, 2018.

Anderson, Terry L., Bruce L. Benson, and Thomas Flanagan, eds. *Self-Determination: The Other Path for Native Americans*. Stanford, CA: Stanford University Press, 2006.

Anderson, Warwick. *Colonial Pathologies: American Tropical Medicine, Race, and Hygiene in the Philippines*. Durham, NC: Duke University Press, 2006.

Angel, Michael. *Preserving the Sacred: Historical Perspectives on the Ojibwa Midewiwin*. Winnipeg: University of Manitoba Press, 2002.

Appleman, Laura I. "Deviancy, Dependency, and Disability: The Forgotten History of Eugenics and Mass Incarceration." *Duke Law Journal* 68, no. 3 (December 2018): 417–78.

Archuleta, Margaret L., Brenda J. Child, and K. Tsianina Lomawaima, eds. *Away from Home: American Indian Boarding School Experiences, 1879–2000*. Phoenix: Heard Museum, 2000.

Arnold, David, ed. *Imperial Medicine and Indigenous Societies*. Manchester, UK: Manchester University Press, 1988.

Bailey, Garrick, and Roberta Glenn Bailey. *A History of the Navajos: The Reservation Years*. Santa Fe, NM: School of American Research Press, 1986.

Barkanp, Elliott Robert, ed. *Immigrants in American History: Arrival, Adaptation, and Integration*. Santa Barbara, CA: ABC Clio, 2012.

Barker, Joanne. *Native Acts: Law, Recognition, and Cultural Authenticity*. Durham, NC: Duke University Press, 2011.

Barker, Joanne, ed. *Sovereignty Matters: Locations of Contestation and Possibility in Indigenous Struggles for Self-Determination*. Lincoln: University of Nebraska Press, 2005.

Bashford, Alison. *Imperial Hygiene: A Critical History of Colonialism, Nationalism, and Public Health*. New York: Springer, 2003.

Beck, David R. M. *The Struggle for Self-Determination: History of the Menominee Indians since 1854*. Lincoln: University of Nebraska Press, 2005.

———. *Siege and Survival: History of the Menominee Indians, 1634–1856*. Lincoln: University of Nebraska Press, 2002.

Ben-Moshe, Liat, Chris Chapman, and Allison C. Carey, eds. *Disability Incarcerated: Imprisonment and Disability in the United States and Canada*. New York: Macmillan, 2014.

Benson, Heather. "Keepers of the Canton Indian Asylum Share History." South Dakota Public Broadcasting, June 7, 2018. https://www.sdpb.org/blogs/arts-and-culture /keepers-of-the-canton-indian-asylum-share-history/.

Benson, Todd. "Blinded with Science: American Indians, the Office of Indian Affairs, and the Federal Campaign against Trachoma, 1924–1927." In Trafzer and Weiner, *Medicine Ways*, 52–75.

Berger, Bethany Ruth. "After Pocahontas: Indian Women in the Law, 1830 to 1934." *American Indian Law Review* 21, no. 1 (1997): 1–62.

Berger, Thomas R. *A Long and Terrible Shadow: White Values, Native Rights in the Americas, 1492–1992*. Seattle: University of Washington Press, 1992.

Bergland, Renee. *The National Uncanny: Indian Ghosts and American Subjects*. Lebanon, NH: University Press of New England, 2000.

Berkhofer, Robert F. *The White Man's Indian: Images of the American Indian from Columbus to the Present*. Random House Digital, Inc., 2011.

Berthrong, Donald J. "Legacies of the Dawes Act: Bureaucrats and Land Thieves at the Cheyenne-Arapaho Agencies of Oklahoma." In *The Plains Indians of the Twentieth Century*, edited by Peter Iverson. Norman: University of Oklahoma Press, 1985, 32–54.

Bhatara, Vinod S., Sanjay Gupta, and Martin Brokenleg. "Images in Psychiatry—The Hiawatha Asylum for Insane Indians: The First Federal Mental Hospital for an Ethnic Group." *American Journal of Psychiatry* 156, no. 5 (May 1999): 767.

Bieder, Robert E. *Native American Communities in Wisconsin, 1600–1960*. Madison: University of Wisconsin Press, 1995.

———. *Science Encounters the Indian, 1820–1880: The Early Years of American Ethnology*. Norman: University of Oklahoma Press, 2003.

Biolsi, Thomas. "The Birth of the Reservation: Making the Modern Individual among the Lakota." *American Ethnologist* 22, no.1 (1995): 28–53.

———. "Imagined Geographies: Sovereignty, Indigenous Space, and American Indian Struggle." *American Ethnologist* 32, no. 2 (2005): 239–59.

Birnbaum, M. "Eugenic Sterilization: A Discussion of Certain Legal, Medical, and Moral Aspects of Present Practices in Our Public Mental Institutions." *JAMA* 175, no. 11 (1961): 951–58.

Blackhawk, Ned. *Violence over the Land: Indians and Empires in the Early American West*. Cambridge, MA: Harvard University Press, 2006.

Blegen, Theodore C. *Norwegian Migration to America, 1825–1860*. New York: Arno, 1969.

Boyd, Colleen E., and Coll Thrush, eds. *Phantom Past, Indigenous Presence: Native Ghosts in North American Culture and History*. Lincoln: University of Nebraska Press, 2011.

Braman, Donald. *Doing Time on the Outside: Incarceration and Family Life in Urban America*. Ann Arbor: University of Michigan Press, 2004.

Braslow, Joel. *Mental Ills and Bodily Cures: Psychiatric Treatment in the First Half of the Twentieth Century*. Berkeley: University of California Press, 1997.

Briggs, Laura. "The Race of Hysteria: 'Overcivilization' and the 'Savage' Woman in Late-Nineteenth-Century Obstretrics and Gynecology." *American Quarterly* 52, no. 2 (June 2000): 246–73.

———. *Somebody's Children: The Politics of Transnational and Transracial Adoption*. Durham, NC: Duke University Press, 2012.

Broder, Sherri. *Tramps, Unfit Mothers, and Neglected Children: Negotiating the Family in Nineteenth-Century Philadelphia*. Philadelphia: University of Pennsylvania Press, 2002.

Brown, Samuel J. Biographical sketch of the author. In *A Sioux Narrative of the Outbreak in 1862, and of Sibley's Expedition in 1863*, by Gabriel Renville. St. Paul, Minn.: Minnesota Historical Society, 1905. Collections of the Minnesota Historical Society, vol. 10, part 2, 595–618, Library of Congress, F601 .M66 vol. 10, pt. 2, https://lccn .loc.gov/18011007.

Brown, Wendy. *States of Injury: Power and Freedom in Late Modernity*. Princeton, NJ: Princeton University Press, 1995.

Bruchac, Joseph. *Our Stories Remember: American Indian History, Culture, and Values Through Storytelling*. Vol. 1. Golden, CO: Fulcrum, 2003.

Bruinius, Harry. *Better for All the World: The Secret History of Forced Sterilization and America's Quest for Racial Purity*. New York: Alfred Knopf, 2006.

Burch, Susan. "'Dislocated Histories': The Canton Asylum for Insane Indians." *Women, Gender, and Families of Color* 2, no. 2 (2014): 141–62.

———. "Disorderly Pasts: Kinship, Diagnoses, and Remembering in American Indian–U.S. Histories." *Journal of Social History* 50, no. 2 (2016): 362–85.

Burch, Susan, ed. *Encyclopedia of American Disability History*. 3 vols. New York: Facts on File, 2009.

Burch, Susan, and Hannah Joyner. *Unspeakable: The Story of Junius Wilson*. Chapel Hill: University of North Carolina Press, 2007.

———. "The Disremembered Past." In *Civil Disabilities: Citizenship, Membership, Belonging*, edited by Nancy J. Hirschmann and Beth Linker, 65–82. Philadelphia: University of Pennsylvania Press, 2015.

Burch, Susan, and Penny Richards. "Methodology." In *Oxford University Press Handbook for Disability History*, edited by Michael Rembis, Kim Nielsen, and Catherine Kudlick. Oxford: Oxford University Press, 2018.

Burghardt, Madeline C. *Broken: Institutions, Families, and the Construction of Intellectual Disability*. Montreal: McGill-Queen's University Press, 2018.

Burroughs, William S. *Junkie: Confessions of an Unredeemed Drug Addict*. New York: Ace Books, 1953.

Cahill, Cathleen D. *Federal Fathers and Mothers: A Social History of the United States Indian Service, 1869–1933*. Chapel Hill: University of North Carolina Press, 2011.

———. "'Seeking the Incalculable Benefit of a Faithful, Patient Man and Wife': Families in the Federal Indian Service, 1880–1925." In Adams and DeLuzio, *On the Borders of Love and Power*, 71–92.

Cahn, Susan. "Border Disorders: Mental Illness, Feminist Metaphor, and the Disordered Female Psyche in the Twentieth-Century United States." In *Disability Histories*, edited by Susan Burch and Michael Rembis, 258–83. Urbana: University of Illinois Press, 2014.

Cameron, Catherine M., Paul Kelton, and Alan C. Swedlund, eds. *Beyond Germs: Native Depopulation in North America*. Tucson: University of Arizona Press, 2015.

Campbell, Fiona A. K. *Contours of Ableism: The Production of Disability and Abledness*. New York: Palgrave Macmillan, 2009.

Campbell, Nancy D., J. P. Olsen, and Luke C. Walden. *The Narcotic Farm*. New York: Abrams, 2008.

Carey, Alison C. *On the Margins of Citizenship: Intellectual Disability and Civil Rights in Twentieth-Century America*. Philadelphia: Temple University Press, 2009.

Carlson, Keith Thor. *The Power of Place, the Problem of Time: Aboriginal Identity and Historical Consciousness in the Cauldron of Colonialism*. Toronto: University of Toronto Press, 2010.

Carocci, Max. "Sodomy, Ambiguity, and Feminization: Homosexual Meanings and the Male Native American Body." In Fear-Segal and Tillet, *Indigenous Bodies: Reviewing, Relocating, Reclaiming*, 68–84.

———. "Textiles of Healing: Native American AIDS Quilts." *Textile* 8, no.1 (2010): 68–84.

Carp, E. Wayne, ed. *Adoption in America: Historical Perspectives*. Ann Arbor: University of Michigan Press, 2004.

Chamberlain, Ava. *The Notorious Elizabeth Tuttle: Marriage, Murder, and Madness in the Family of Jonathan Edwards*. New York: New York University Press, 2012.

Champagne, Duane. "Self-Determination and Activism among American Indians in the United States, 1972–1997." *Cultural Survival Quarterly* 21, no. 2 (July 1997): 32–35.

Chang, David A. *The Color of the Land: Race, Nation, and the Politics of Landownership in Oklahoma, 1832–1929*. Chapel Hill: University of North Carolina Press, 2010.

———. "Enclosures of Land and Sovereignty the Allotment of American Indian Lands." In "New Approaches to Enclosures" issue, edited by Amy Chazkel and David Serlin, *Radical History Review* 2011, no. 109 (Winter 2011): 108–19.

Chapman, Chris. "Colonialism, Disability, and Possible Lives: The Residential Treatment of Children Whose Parents Survived Indian Residential Schools." *Journal of Progressive Human Services* 23, no. 2 (2012): 127–58.

Chase, Robert T., ed. *Caging Borders and Carceral States: Incarceration, Immigration Detention, and Resistance*. Chapel Hill: University of North Carolina Press, 2019.

Child, Brenda J. *Boarding School Seasons: American Indian Families, 1900–1945*. Lincoln: University of Nebraska Press, 1998.

———. *Holding Our World Together: Ojibwe Women in the Survival of Community*. New York: Penguin Books, 2013.

Chow, Winnie S., and Stefan Priebe. "Understanding Psychiatric Institutionalization: A Conceptual Review." *BMC Psychiatry* 13, no. 169 (2013). http://www.biomedcentral.com/1471-244X/13/16.

Christianson, Scott. *With Liberty for Some: 500 Years of Imprisonment in America*. Boston: Northeastern University Press, 2001.

Churchill, Ward. *Struggle for the Land: Indigenous Resistance to Genocide, Ecocide, and Appropriation in Contemporary North America*. Monroe, ME: Common Courage, 1993.

Clare, Eli. *Brilliant Imperfection: Grappling with Cure*. Durham, NC: Duke University Press, 2017.

———. *Exile and Pride: Disability, Queerness, and Liberation*. Durham, NC: Duke University Press, 2015.

Clark, Frank. *St. Elizabeths Hospital for the Insane*. Washington, DC, 1906.

Clifton, James A. *The Invented Indian: Cultural Fictions and Government Policies.* New Brunswick, NJ: Transaction, 1990.

———. *The Prairie People: Continuity and Change in Potawatomi Indian Culture, 1665–1965.* Lawrence: Regents Press of Kansas, 1977.

Clothier, Florence. "Psychological Implications of Unmarried Parenthood." *American Journal of Orthopsychiatry* 13, no. 3 (July 1943): 531–49.

Coalition to Stop Violence against Native Women. "MMIWG2S." https://www.csvanw .org/mmiw/.

Cobb, Amanda J. *Listening to Our Grandmothers' Stories: The Bloomfield Academy for Chickasaw Females, 1852–1949.* Lincoln: University of Nebraska Press, 2007.

———. "Understanding Tribal Sovereignty: Definitions, Conceptualizations, and Interpretations." *American Studies* 46, no. 3/4 (Fall–Winter 2005): 115–32.

Cobb, Daniel M. *Native Activism in Cold War America: The Struggle for Sovereignty.* Lawrence: University Press of Kansas, 2008.

Cobb, Daniel M., and Loretta Fowler, eds. *Beyond Red Power: American Indian Politics and Activism since 1900.* Santa Fe: School for Advanced Research, 2007.

Cobb, Daniel M., and Helen Sheumaker, eds. *Memory Matters: Proceedings from the 2010 Conference Hosted by the Humanities Center, Miami University of Ohio.* Albany: State University of New York Press, 2011.

Coleman, Michael C. *American Indian Children at School, 1850–1930.* Jackson: University Press of Mississippi, 1993.

Collier, John. "Introduction." In *The Changing Indian*, edited by Oliver La Farge, 3–8. Norman: University of Oklahoma Press, 1942.

Collins, Patricia Hill. "It's All in the Family: Intersections of Gender, Race, and Nation." *Hypatia* 13 (1998): 62–82.

Comaroff, Jean, and John L. Comaroff. *Of Revelation and Revolution.* Vol. 2, *The Dialectics of Modernity on a South African Frontier.* Chicago: University of Chicago Press, 1991.

Comfort, Megan. *Doing Time Together: Love and Family in the Shadow of the Prison.* Chicago: University of Chicago Press, 2009.

Courtwright, David. "A Century of American Narcotic Policy." In Gerstein and Harwood, *Treating Drug Problems*, 2:1–65.

Crawford O'Brien, Suzanne. *Coming Full Circle: Spirituality and Wellness among Native Communities in the Pacific Northwest.* Lincoln: University of Nebraska Press, 2013.

Currell, Susan, and Christina Cogdell. *Popular Eugenics: National Efficiency and American Mass Culture in the 1930s.* Athens: Ohio University Press, 2006.

D'Amore, Arcangelo R. T., and A. Louise Eckburg. *William Alanson White: The Washington Years, 1903–1937: The Contributions to Psychiatry, Psychoanalysis, and Mental Health by Dr. White While Superintendent of Saint Elizabeths Hospital.* Public Health Service, Alcohol, Drug Abuse, and Mental Health Administration, Department of Health, Education, and Welfare. Washington, DC: US Government Printing Office, 1976.

Daley, Jeff, dir. *Where's Molly?.* New York: Sproutflix, 2007.

Daniels, Robert E. "Cultural Identities among the Oglala Sioux." In Nurge, *Modern Sioux*, 198–245.

Danvers State Memorial Committee. "A Grave Injustice." Accessed February 15, 2017. http://dsmc.info/index.shtml.

Davis, Lennard, ed. *The Disability Studies Reader*. 3rd ed. New York: Routledge, 2011.

Davis, Rose M. "How Indian Is Hiawatha?" *Midwest Folklore* 7, no. 1 (Spring 1957): 5–25.

Deer, Sarah. *The Beginning and End of Rape: Confronting Sexual Violence in Native America*. Minneapolis: University of Minnesota Press, 2015.

———. "Decolonizing Rape Law: A Native Feminist Synthesis of Safety and Sovereignty." *Wicazo Sa Review* 24, no. 2 (2009): 149–67.

de Finney, Sandrina. "Indigenous Girls' Resilience in Settler States: Honouring Body and Land Sovereignty." *Agenda* 31, no.2 (2017): 10–21.

DeJong, David H. *"If You Knew the Conditions": A Chronicle of the Indian Medical Service and American Indian Health Care, 1908–1955*. Boston: Lexington Books, 2008.

Delaney, David. "The Space That Race Makes." *Professional Geographer* 54, no.1 (2002): 6–14.

Delgado-P, Guillermo. "The Makings of a Transnational Movement." *NACLA Report on the Americas* 35, no. 6 (2002): 36–38.

Deloria, Ella. *Speaking of Indians*. Lincoln: University of Nebraska Press, 1998.

Deloria, Philip J. "From Nation to Neighborhood: Land, Policy, Culture, Colonialism, and Empire in U.S.–Indian Relations." In *The Cultural Turn in U.S. History: Past, Present, and Future*, edited by James W. Cook, Lawrence B. Glickman, and Michael O'Malley, 343–82. Chicago: University of Chicago Press, 2008.

———. *Playing Indian*. New Haven, CT: Yale University Press, 1998)

Deloria, Philip J., K. Tsianina Lomawaima, Bryan McKinley Jones Brayboy, Mark Neil Trahant, Loren Ghiglione, Douglas L. Medin, and Ned Blackhawk, eds. "Unfolding Futures: Indigenous Ways of Knowing for the Twenty-First Century." *Daedalus* (Spring 2018): 6–172.

Deloria, Philip J., and Neal Salisbury, eds. *A Companion to American Indian History*. Malden, MA: Blackwell, 2002.

Deloria, Vine, Jr., ed. *American Indian Policy in the Twentieth Century*. Norman: University of Oklahoma Press, 1985.

Deloria, Vine, Jr., and Clifford Lytle. *American Indians, American Justice*. Austin: University of Texas Press, 1983.

———. *The Nations Within: The Past and Future of American Indian Sovereignty*. Pantheon, 1984.

DeMallie, Raymond. "Kinship: The Foundation for Native American Society." In Thornton, *Studying Native America*, 306–56.

Denevan, William M., ed. *The Native Population of the Americas in 1492*. Madison: University of Wisconsin Press, 1992.

Den Ouden, Amy E., and Jean M. O'Brien, eds. *Recognition, Sovereignty Struggles, and Indigenous Rights in the United States: A Sourcebook*. Chapel Hill: University of North Carolina Press, 2013.

Deutsch, Albert. *The Mentally Ill in America: A History of Their Care and Treatment from Colonial Times*. 2nd ed. New York: Columbia University Press, 1967.

Devens, Carol. "'If We Get the Girls, We Get the Race': Missionary Education of Native American Girls." In Hoxie, Mancall, and Merrill, *American Nations*, 156–71.

Dilenschneider, Anne. "An Invitation to Restorative Justice: The Canton Asylum for Insane Indians." *Northern Plains Ethics Journal* (2013): 105–28.

Dolmage, Jay. *Academic Ableism: Disability and Higher Education*. Ann Arbor: University of Michigan Press, 2017.

Dowbiggin, Ian Robert. *Keeping America Sane: Psychiatry and Eugenics in the United States and Canada, 1880–1940*. Ithaca, NY: Cornell University Press, 1997.

Driskill, Qwo-Li. *Asegi Stories: Cherokee Queer and Two-Spirit Memory*. Tucson: University of Arizona Press, 2016.

Driskill, Qwo-Li, Chris Finley, Brian Joseph Gilley, and Scott Lauria Morgensen, eds. *Queer Indigenous Studies: Critical Interventions in Theory, Politics, and Literature*. Tucson: University of Arizona Press, 2011.

Dwyer, Ellen. *Homes for the Mad: Life inside Two Nineteenth-Century Asylums*. New Brunswick, NJ: Rutgers University Press, 1987.

Dunbar-Ortiz, Roxanne. *An Indigenous Peoples' History of the United States*. Boston: Beacon, 2014.

Echo-Hawk, Walter R. *In the Light of Justice: The Rise of Human Rights in Native America and the UN Declaration on the Rights of Indigenous Peoples*. Golden, CO: Fulcrum, 2013.

Edmunds, R. D. *The Potawatomis, Keepers of the Fire*. Norman: University of Oklahoma Press, 1978.

Edney, Matthew H. "Mapping Empires, Mapping Bodies: Reflections on the Use and Abuse of Cartography." *Treballs de la Societat Catalana de Geografia* 63 (2007): 83–104.

Eisenman, Deanne. *Blooming Patchwork: A Celebration of Applique in Quilts*. Kansas City: Kansas City Star Books, 2014.

Emmerich, Lisa E. "'Save the Babies!': American Indian Women, Assimilation Policy, and Scientific Motherhood, 1912–1918." In *Writing the Range: Race Class and Culture in the Women's West*, edited by Elizabeth Jameson and Susan Armitage, 393–409. Norman: University of Oklahoma Press, 1997.

Erdrich, Louise. *The Bingo Palace*. New York: HarperCollins, 1994.

Erevelles, Nirmala. "(Im)Material Citizens: Cognitive Disability, Race, and the Politics of Citizenship." In *Foundations of Disability Studies*, edited by Matthew Wappett and Katrina Arndt, 145–76. New York: Palgrave Macmillan, 2013.

———. "Thinking with Disability Studies." *Disability Studies Quarterly* 34, no. 2 (2014). http://dsq-sds.org/article/view/4248/3587.

Ernst, Waltraud, ed. *Work, Psychiatry, and Society, c.1750–2015*. Oxford: Oxford University Press, 2016.

Farmer, Paul. "The House of the Dead: Tuberculosis and Incarceration." In *Invisible Punishment: The Collateral Consequences of Mass Imprisonment*, edited by Marc Mauer and Meda Chesney-Lind, 239–57. New York: New Press, 2002.

Farr, William E. *Blackfoot Redemption: A Blood Indian's Story of Murder, Confinement, and Imperfect Justice*. Norman: University of Oklahoma Press, 2014.

Feagin, Joe R. *The White Racial Frame: Centuries of Racial Framing and Counter-Framing*. New York: Routledge, 2013.

Fear-Seagal, Jacqueline. *White Man's Club: Schools, Race, and the Struggle of Indian Acculturation*. Lincoln: University of Nebraska Press, 2007.

Fear-Seagal, Jacqueline, and Rebecca Tillett, eds. *Indigenous Bodies: Reviewing, Relocating, Reclaiming.* Albany: State University of New York Press, 2013.

Fine-Dare, Kathleen S. *Grave Injustice: The American Indian Repatriation Movement and NAGPRA.* Lincoln: University of Nebraska Press, 2002.

Fixico, Donald Lee. *American Indians in a Modern World.* New York: Rowman Altamira, 2006.

———. *Call for Change: The Medicine Way of American Indian History, Ethos, and Reality.* Lincoln: University of Nebraska Press, 2013.

———. "Ethics and Responsibilities in Writing American Indian History." In Mihesuah, *Natives and Academics,* 84–99.

———. *Termination and Relocation: Federal Indian Policy, 1945–1960.* Albuquerque: University of New Mexico Press, 1986.

Forbes, Jack D. *Africans and Native Americans: The Language of Race and the Evolution of Red-Black Peoples.* 2nd ed. University of Illinois Press, 1993.

Freedman, Estelle B. *Redefining Rape: Sexual Violence in the Era of Suffrage and Segregation.* Cambridge, MA: Harvard University Press, 2013.

Freeman, Victoria. "Indigenous Haunting in Settler-Colonial Spaces: The Activism of Indigenous Ancestors in Toronto." In Boyd and Thrush, *Phantom Pasts, Indigenous Presence,* 209–44.

Frost, Linda. *Never One Nation: Freaks, Savages, and Whiteness in Popular Culture, 1850–1877.* Minneapolis: University of Minnesota Press, 2005.

Fuentes, Marisa J. *Dispossessed Lives: Enslaved Women, Violence, and the Archive.* Philadelphia: University of Pennsylvania Press, 2016.

Furman, Bess. *A Profile of the United States Public Health Service, 1789–1948.* Washington, DC: Department of Health, Education, and Welfare, 1973.

Galloway, Patricia. "'The Chief Who Is Your Father': Choctaw and French Views of the Diplomatic Relation." In *Powhatan's Mantle: Indians in the Colonial Southeast,* edited by Peter H. Wood, Gregory A. Waselkov, and M. Thomas Hatley, 254–78. Lincoln: University of Nebraska Press, 1989.

Gamwell, Lynn, and Nancy Tomes. *Madness in America: Cultural and Medical Perceptions of Mental Illness before 1914.* Ithaca, NY: Cornell University Press, 1995.

Gerstein, D. R., and H. J. Harwood, eds. *Treating Drug Problems.* 2 vols. Committee for the Substance Abuse Coverage Study, Division of Health Care Services, Institute of Medicine. Washington, D.C.: National Academies Press, 1990–92.

Gevik, Brian. "Canton's Hiawatha Indian Asylum." South Dakota Public Broadcasting, September 21, 2018. Accessed December 1, 2019. http://www.sdpb.org/blogs /images-of-the-past/the-hiawatha-asylum-for-insane-indians/.

Gibbon, Guy. *The Sioux: The Dakota and Lakota Nations.* Oxford: Blackwell, 2003.

"Gifford, Oscar S." In *Doane Robinson's Encyclopedia of South Dakota,* 323. Pierre, SD: The author, 1925.

"Gifford, Oscar Sherman (1842–1913)." *Biographical Directory of the United States Congress, 1774–Present.* https://bioguideretro.congress.gov/Home /MemberDetails?memIndex=G000170.

Gilmore, Ruth. "Fatal Couplings of Power and Difference: Notes on Racism and Geography." *Professional Geographer* 54, no.1 (February 2002): 15–24.

Gish Hill, Christina. *Webs of Kinship: Family in Northern Cheyenne Nationhood*. Norman: University of Oklahoma Press, 2017.

Glenn, Evelyn Nakano, Grace Chang, and Linda Rennie Force, eds. *Mothering: Ideology, Experience, and Agency*. New York: Routledge, 1994.

Goeman, Mishuana R., and Jennifer Nez Denetdale. "Guest Editors' Introduction. Native Feminisms: Legacies, Interventions, and Indigenous Sovereignties." *Wicazo Sa Review* 24, no. 2 (2009): 9–13.

Goffman, Erving. *Asylums: Essays on the Social Situation of Mental Patients and Other Inmates*. Garden City, NY Anchor Books, 1961.

———. "The Characteristics of Total Institutions." In *Symposium on Preventative and Social Psychiatry*, April 15–17, 1957. Washington, DC: Walter Reed Army Institute of Research, 1957.

Gonzales, Angela, Judy Kertész, and Gabrielle Tayac. "Eugenics as Indian Removal: Sociohistorical Processes and the De(con)struction of American Indians in the Southeast." *Public Historian* 29, no. 3 (Summer 2007): 53–67.

Gonzales, Patrisia. *Red Medicine: Traditional Indigenous Rites of Birthing and Healing*. Tucson: University of Arizona Press, 2012.

Gooding, Erik. "'We Come to You as the Dead': Ethnomusicology, Colonialism, and the Standing Rock Reservation, 1868–1934." *ReSOUND* 16, nos. 1–2 (1997): 1–14.

Goodkind, Jessica R., Julia M Hess, Beverly Gorman, and Danielle Parker. "'We're Still in a Struggle': Diné Resilience, Survival, Historical Trauma, and Healing." In "Mental Health." Special issue, *Qualitative Health Research* 22, no. 8 (2012): 1019–36.

Gordon, Avery F. *Ghostly Matters: Haunting and the Sociological Imagination*. Minneapolis: University of Minnesota Press, 1997.

Gray, Susan E. "Limits and Possibilities: White-Indian Relations in Western Michigan in the Era of Removal." *Michigan Historical Review* 20 (Fall 1994): 71–92.

Grech, Shaun. "Decolonising Eurocentric Disability Studies: Why Colonialism Matters in the Disability and Global South Debate." *Social Identities* 21, no. 1 (2015): 6–21.

Grinde, Jr., Donald A. "Taking the Indian Out of the Indian: U.S. Policies of Ethnocide through Education." *Wicazo Sa Review* 19, no. 2 (Fall 2004): 25–32.

Grob, Gerald N. *The Mad among Us: A History of the Care of America's Mentally Ill*. New York: Free Press, 1994.

———. *Mental Illness and American Society, 1875–1940*. Princeton, NJ: Princeton University Press, 1983.

———. "Public Policy and Mental Illnesses: Jimmy Carter's Presidential Commission on Mental Health." *Milbank Quarterly* 83, no. 3 (2005): 425–56.

Hall, Kim Q., ed. *Feminist Disability Studies*. Bloomington: Indiana University Press, 2011.

Hall, Lisa Kahaleole. "Strategies of Erasure: U.S. Colonialism and Native Hawaiian Feminism." *American Quarterly* 60, no. 2 (June 2008): 273–80.

Hall, Philip S. *To Have This Land: The Nature of Indian/White Relations, South Dakota, 1888–1891*. Vermillion: University of South Dakota Press, 1991.

Haller, John S., Jr. *Outcasts from Evolution: Scientific Attitudes of Racial Inferiority, 1859–1900*. Carbondale: Southern Illinois University Press, 1995.

Hamill, James, and John Cinnamon. "This Strange Journey: Stories of Trails of Tears from Indian Families in Eastern Oklahoma." In Porter, *Place and Native American Indian History and Culture*, 93–111.

Hansen, Karen V. *Encounter on the Great Plains: Scandinavian Settlers and the Dispossession of Dakota Indians, 1890–1930*. New York: Oxford University Press, 2013.

Hansen, Randall, and Desmond S. King. *Sterilized by the State: Eugenics, Race, and the Population Scare in Twentieth-Century North America*. New York: Cambridge University Press, 2013.

Harley, J. B. "Deconstructing the Map." *Cartographica* 26, no. 2 (Summer 1989): 1–20.

Hart, Patricia Susan. *A Home for Every Child: The Washington Children's Home Society in the Progressive Era*. Seattle: University of Washington Press, 2010.

Hacsi, Timothy A. *Second Home: Orphan Asylums and Poor Families in America*. Cambridge, MA: Harvard University Press, 1997.

Haskins, Victoria K. "'The Matter of Wages Does Not Seem to Be Material': Native American Workers' Wages under the Outing System in the United States, 1880s–1930s." In *Towards a Global History of Domestic and Caregiving Workers*, edited by Dirk Hoerder, Elise van Nederveen Meerkerk, and Silke Neunsinger, 323–46. Leiden, Netherlands: Brill, 2015.

———. *One Bright Spot*. New York: Palgrave Macmillan, 2005.

Hechler, Andreas. "Diagnoses That Matter: My Great-Grandmother's Murder as One Deemed 'Unworthy of Living' and Its Impact on Our Family." *Disability Studies Quarterly* 37, no. 2 (2017). http://dsq-sds.org/article/view/5573.

Herman, Ellen. *Kinship by Design: A History of Adoption in the Modern United States*. Chicago: University of Chicago Press, 2009.

Hernández, Kelly L. *City of Inmates: Conquest, Rebellion, and the Rise of Human Caging in Los Angeles, 1771–1965*. Chapel Hill: University of North Carolina Press, 2017.

Hewitt, B. N. "Hiawatha." In Hodge, *Handbook of American Indians*, 1:546.

———. "Nanabozho." In Hodge, *Handbook of American Indians*, 2:19.

History of Lincoln County, South Dakota. Canton, SD: Lincoln County History Committee, 1985.

Hixson, Walter L. *American Settler Colonialism: A History*. New York: Palgrave Macmillan, 2013.

Hodge, Frederick Webb. *Handbook of American Indians North of Mexico*. 2 vols. Smithsonian Institution Bureau of American Ethnology Bulletin 30. Washington, DC: Government Printing Office, 1907–10.

Holt, Marilyn Irvin. *Indian Orphanages*. Lawrence: University Press of Kansas, 2001.

Horwitz, Allan V. *Creating Mental Illness*. Chicago: University of Chicago Press, 2002.

Hoxie, Frederick E. *A Final Promise: The Campaign to Assimilate the Indians, 1880–1920*. Lincoln: University of Nebraska Press, 1984.

———. "Retrieving the Red Continent: Settler Colonialism and the History of American Indians in the US, Ethnic and Racial Studies." *Ethnic and Racial Studies* 31, no. 6 (2008): 1153–67.

Hoxie, Frederick E., Peter C. Mancall, and James H. Merrell, eds. *American Nations, 1850 to the Present*. New York: Routledge, 2001.

Huhndorf, Shari Michelle. *Going Native: Indians in the American Cultural Imagination.* Ithaca, NY: Cornell University Press, 2001.

Hunt-Kennedy, Stephanie. *Between Fitness and Death: Disability and Slavery in the Caribbean.* Champaign: University of Illinois Press, 2020.

Hyde, Anne. *Empires, Nations, and Families: A History of the North American West, 1800–1860.* Lincoln: University of Nebraska Press, 2011.

Hyde, George E. *Red Cloud's Folk: A History of the Oglala Sioux Indians.* 1937. Reprint, Norman: University of Oklahoma Press, 1975.

Hyer, Sally. *One House, One Voice, One Heart: Native American Education at the Santa Fe Indian School.* Santa Fe: Museum of New Mexico Press, 1990.

Hyman, Collette A. *Dakota Women's Work: Creativity, Culture, and Exile.* St. Paul: Minnesota Historical Society, 2012.

Imada, Adria. "A Decolonial Disability Studies?" *Disability Studies Quarterly* 37, no. 3 (2019). http://dsq-sds.org/article/view/5984/4694.

Inglis, Kerri A. "Disease and the 'Other': The Role of Medical Imperialism in Oceana." In Smithers and Newman, *Native Diasporas,* 385–406.

Iverson, Peter. *Diné: A History of the Navajos.* Albuquerque: University of New Mexico Press, 2002.

Iverson, Peter, ed. *The Plains Indians of the Twentieth Century.* Norman: University of Oklahoma Press, 1985.

Jackson, Vanessa. "In Our Own Voice: African-American Stories of Oppression, Survival, and Recovery." *Off Our Backs* 33, no. 7/8 (2003): 19–21.

Jacobs, Margaret D. "Diverted Mothering among American Indian Domestic Servants." In *Indigenous Women at Work: From Labor to Activism,* edited by Carol Williams, 179–92. Urbana: University of Illinois Press, 2012.

———. *A Generation Removed: The Fostering and Adoption of Indigenous Children in the Postwar World.* Lincoln: University of Nebraska Press, 2014.

———. *White Mothers to a Dark Race: Settler Colonialism, Maternalism, and the Removal of Indigenous Children in the American West and Australia, 1880–1940.* Lincoln: University of Nebraska Press, 2009.

———. "Working on the Domestic Frontier: American Indian Domestic Servants in White Women's Households in the San Francisco Bay Area, 1920–1940." *Frontiers* 28, no. 1/2 (2007): 165–99.

Jarman, Michelle. "Coming up from Underground: Uneasy Dialogues at the Intersections of Race, Mental Illness, and Disability Studies." In *Blackness and Disability: Critical Examinations and Cultural Interventions,* edited by Christopher M. Bell, 9–29. East Lansing: Michigan State University Press, 2011.

Jenkins, J. Rockwood. *"The Good Shepherd Mission to the Navajo."* Manuscript, 1956. Transcribed by Wayne Kempton, 2008. Project Canterbury. http://anglicanhistory .org/indigenous/jenkins_navajo1956/.

Jimenez, Mary Anne. *Changing Faces of Madness: Early American Attitudes and Treatment of the Insane.* Hanover, NH: University Press of New England, 1987.

Johnson, Basil. *Crazy Dave.* Toronto: Key Porter Books, 1999.

———. *Indian School Days.* Norman: University of Oklahoma Press, 1988.

Johnson, Troy. "American Indians, Manifest Destiny, and Indian Activism: A Cosmology of Sense of Place." In Porter, *Place and Native American Indian History and Culture*, 71–92.

Johnston, Susan L. "Native American Traditional and Alternative Medicine." *Annals of the American Academy of Political and Social Science* 583, no. 1 (September 2002): 195–213.

Joinson, Carla. *Vanished in Hiawatha: The Story of the Canton Asylum for Insane Indians.* Lincoln, NE: Bison Books, 2016.

Justice, Daniel Heath. "Go Away, Water! Kinship Criticism and the Decolonization Imperative." In Womack, Justice, and Teuton, *Reasoning Together*, 147–68.

———. *Our Fire Survives the Storm: A Cherokee Literary History.* Minneapolis: University of Minnesota Press, 2006.

Jutel, Annemarie. "Sociology of Diagnosis: A Pulmonary Review." *Sociology of Health and Illness* 31, no. 2 (2009): 278–99.

Kaelber, Lutz. "Eugenics: Compulsory Sterilization in 50 American States." Paper presented at the Social Science History Association meeting, 2012. "Eugenics" and Nazi "Euthanasia" Crimes. http://www.uvm.edu/%7Elkaelber/eugenics/.

Kafer, Alison. *Feminist, Queer, Crip.* Bloomington: Indiana University Press, 2013.

Kahan, Michelle. "'Put Up' on Platforms: A History of Twentieth Century Adoption Policy in the United States." *Journal of Sociology and Social Welfare* 33, no. 3 (2006): 51–72.

Kanani, Nadia. "Race and Madness: Locating the Experiences of Racialized People with Psychiatric Histories in Canada and the United States." *Critical Disability Discourses /Discours critiques dans le champ du handicap* 3 (2011): 1–14.

Kauanui, J. Kēhaulani. "Precarious Positions: Native Hawaiians and US Federal Recognition." *Contemporary Pacific* 17, no. 1 (2005): 1–27.

———. "'A Structure, Not an Event': Settler Colonialism and Enduring Indigeneity." *Lateral* 5, no. 1 (2016). https://doi.org/10.25158/L5.1.7.

———. "Tracing Historical Specificity: Race and the Colonial Politics of (In)capacity." *American Quarterly* 69, no. 2 (2017): 257–65.

Kauanui, J. Kēhaulani, and Patrick Wolfe. "Settler Colonialism Then and Now." *Politica and Societá* 2 (2012): 235–58.

Keller, Jean A. *Empty Beds: Indian Student Health at Sherman Institute, 1902–1922.* East Lansing: Michigan State University Press, 2002.

Kaufman, Ned. *Place, Race, and Story: Essays on the Past and Future of Historic Preservation.* New York: Routledge, 2009.

Kelly, Lawrence C. *The Assault on Assimilation: John Collier and the Origins of Indian Policy Reform.* Albuquerque: University of New Mexico Press, 1983.

Kelman, Ari. *A Misplaced Massacre: Struggling over Memory of Sand Creek.* Cambridge, MA: Harvard University Press, 2013.

Kelton, Paul. *Cherokee Medicine, Colonial Germs: An Indigenous Nation's Fight against Smallpox, 1518–1824.* Norman: University of Oklahoma Press, 2015.

Kern, Emily. "Sugarcane and Lepers: Health Policy and the Colonization of Hawaii (1860–1900)." *Penn History Review* 17, no. 2 (2010): 78–100.

Kevles, Daniel J. *In the Name of Eugenics: Genetics and the Uses of Human Heredity.* New York: Knopf, 1985.

Kills Small, Jerome. "Lakota." YouTube, May 5, 2010. Video, 4:01. https://www.youtube.com/watch?v=oijAiJQFacM.

Kilpatrick, Alan. "A Spirit Descending: A Perspective on Native American Health: 1880–1940." In *Proceedings of the Third and Fourth Native American Symposiums: "Stealing/Steeling the Spirit: American Indian Identities" and "Smoke Screens/Smoke Signals: Looking through Two Worlds,"* edited by Lucretia Scoufos, Mark Spencer, and Chad Litton, 92–98. Southeastern Oklahoma State University, 2003–2004, 92–98.

Kilty, Jennifer M., and Erin Dej, eds. *Containing Madness: Gender and 'Psy' in Institutional Contexts.* Cham, Switzerland: Springer International, 2018.

Kimmerer, Robin Wall. *Braiding Sweetgrass.* Minneapolis: Milkweed, 2013.

King, C. Richard. "The Good, the Bad, and the Mad: Making Up (Abnormal) People in Indian Country, 1900–30." *European Journal of American Culture* 22, no.1 (2003): 37–47.

King, Thomas. *The Truth about Stories: A Native Narrative.* Minneapolis: University of Minnesota Press, 2008.

Kirwan, Padraig. "'Mind the Gap': Journeys in Indigenous Sovereignty and Nationhood." *Comparative American Studies* 13, no. 1–2 (June 2015): 42–57.

Kluchin, Rebecca M. *Fit to Be Tied: Sterilization and Reproductive Rights in America, 1950–1980.* New Brunswick, NJ: Rutgers University Press, 2009.

Koithan, M., and C. Farrell. "Indigenous Native American Healing Traditions." *Journal for Nurse Practitioners* 6, no. 6 (2010): 477–78.

Kosek, Jake. *Understories: The Political Life of Forests in New Mexico.* Durham, NC: Duke University Press, 2006.

Kosten, Thomas R., and David A. Gorelick. "Images in Psychiatry: The Lexington Narcotic Farm." *American Journal of Psychiatry* 159, no. 1 (January 2002): 22.

Krech, Shepard, III, and Barbara A. Hail, eds. *Collecting Native America: 1870–1960.* Washington, DC: Smithsonian Institution Press, 1999.

Kudlick, Catherine Jean. "Comment: On the Borderland of Medical and Disability History." *Bulletin of the History of Medicine* 87, no. 4 (2013): 540–59.

———. "Social History of Medicine and Disability History." In Rembis, Kudlick, and Nielsen, *Oxford Handbook of Disability History,* 105–24.

Kunzel, Regina G. *Fallen Women, Problem Girls: Unmarried Mothers and the Professionalization of Social Work, 1890–1945.* New Haven, CT: Yale University Press, 2010.

Kvasnicka, Robert M., and Herman J. Viola, eds. *The Commissioners of Indian Affairs, 1824–1977.* Lincoln: University of Nebraska Press, 1979.

LaDuke, Winona. *Recovering the Sacred: The Power of Naming and Claiming.* Cambridge, MA: South End Press, 2005.

Larson, Edward. *Sex, Race, and Science: Eugenics in the Deep South.* Baltimore: Johns Hopkins University Press, 1995.

Lasch, Christopher. *The World of Nations: Reflections on American History, Politics, and Culture.* New York: Alfred A. Knopf, 1973.

Lawrence, Jane. "The Indian Health Service and the Sterilization of Native American Women." *American Indian Quarterly* 24, no. 3 (Summer 2000): 400–419.

Lawson, Michael L. "Indian Heirship Lands: The Lake Traverse Experience." *South Dakota History* (1983): 217–18.

Leahy, Todd E. *They Called It Madness: The Canton Asylum for Insane Indians, 1899–1934.* Baltimore: PublishAmerica, 2009.

LeFrançois, Brenda A., Peter Beresford, and Jasna Russo. "Destination Mad Studies." *Intersectionalities* 5, no. 3 (2016): 1–10.

LeFrançois, Brenda A., Robert Menzies, and Geoffrey Reaume, eds. *Mad Matters: A Critical Reader in Canadian Mad Studies*. Toronto: Canadian Scholars' Press, 2013.

Lenz, Mary Jane. *The Stuff of Dreams: Native American Dolls*. New York: Museum of the American Indian, 1986.

Lenz, Mary J., and Clara Sue Kidwell. *Small Spirits: Native American Dolls from the National Museum of the American Indian*. Washington, DC: Smithsonian National Museum of the American Indian in association with University of Washington Press, 2004.

Leonard, Thomas C. *Illiberal Reformers: Race, Eugenics, and American Economics in the Progressive Era*. Princeton, NJ: Princeton University Press, 2016.

Leong, Karen J., and Myla Vicenti Carpio. "Carceral States." *Amerasia Journal* 42, no. 1 (2016): vii–xviii.

Lerma, Michael. "Indigeneity and Homeland: Land, History, Ceremony, and Language." *American Indian Culture and Research Journal* 36, no. 3 (2012): 75–98.

Lesser, Alexander. "Caddoan Kinship Systems." *Nebraska History* 60 (1979): 260–71.

Levene, Mark. "The Chittagong Hill Tracts: A Case Study in the Political Economy of 'Creeping' Genocide." *Third World Quarterly* 20, no. 2 (1999): 339–69.

———. *Genocide in the Age of the Nation State*. New York: Bloomsbury, 2005.

Lewis, Bradley. "A Mad Fight: Psychiatry and Disability Activism." In Davis, *Disability Studies Reader*, 339–55.

Lewis, David Rich. *Neither Wolf nor Dog: American Indians, Environment, and Agrarian Change*. Oxford: Oxford University Press, 1994.

Lewis, Talila A. "Ableism 2020: An Updated Definition." Blog, January 25, 2020. https://www.talilalewis.com/blog/ableism-2020-an-updated-definition.

Lipsitz, George. *The Possessive Investment in Whiteness: How White People Profit from Identity Politics*. Philadelphia: Temple University Press, 2006.

Lockard, Joe. "The Universal Hiawatha." *American Indian Quarterly* 24, no. 1 (2000): 110–25.

Locust, Carol. *American Indian Beliefs Concerning Health and Unwellness*. Native American Research and Training Center Monograph Series. Tucson: University of Arizona, 1985.

Lomawaima, K. Tsianina. *"Federalism: Native, Federal, and State Sovereignty."* In *Why You Can't Teach United States History without American Indians*, edited by Susan Sleeper Smith, Julianna Barr, Jean M. O'Brien, Nancy Shoemaker, and Scott Manning Stevens, 273–86. Chapel Hill: University of North Carolina Press, 2015.

———. *They Called It Prairie Light: The Story of Chilocco Indian School*. Lincoln: University of Nebraska Press, 1995.

———. *"To Remain an Indian": Lessons in Democracy from a Century of Native American Education*. New York: Teachers College Press, 2006.

Lombardo, Paul. *Three Generations, No Imbeciles: Eugenics, the Supreme Court, and Buck v. Bell*. Baltimore: Johns Hopkins University Press, 2008.

Lonetree, Amy. *Decolonizing Museums: Representing Native America in National and Tribal Museums*. Chapel Hill: University of North Carolina Press, 2012.

Lovern, Lavonna L., and Carol Locust. *Native American Communities on Health and Disability: A Borderland Dialogues*. New York: Palgrave, 2013.

Lovett, Laura L. *Conceiving the Future: Pronatalism, Reproduction, and the Family in the United States, 1890–1938*. Chapel Hill: University of North Carolina Press, 2007.

Lovoll, Odd S. *Norwegians on the Prairie: Ethnicity and the Development of the Country Town*. Minneapolis: Minnesota Historical Society Press, 2010.

Lowry, James V. "Treatment of the Drug Addict at the Lexington (Ky.) Hospital." *Bulletin on Narcotics* 10, no. 2 (January–March 1958): 9–12.

Lugones, María. "Heterosexualism and the Colonial/Modern Gender System." *Hypatia* 22, no. 1 (Winter 2007): 186–209.

Lunbeck, Elizabeth. *The Psychiatric Persuasion: Knowledge, Gender, and Power in Modern America*. Princeton, N.J.: Princeton University Press, 1994.

Lyons, Scott Richard. *X-Marks: Native Signatures of Assent*. Minneapolis: University of Minnesota Press, 2010.

MacDowell, Marsha L., and Kurt C. Dewhurst, eds. *To Honor and Comfort: Native Quilting Traditions*. Santa Fe: Museum of New Mexico Press, 1997.

Mackenzie, Kent, dir. *The Exiles*. 1961; Harrington Park, NJ: Milestone Film & Video, 2008. DVD.

Maddox, Lucy. *Citizen Indians: Native American Intellectuals, Race, and Reform*. Ithaca, NY: Cornell University Press, 2005.

Mad in America: Science, Psychiatry, and Social Justice (blog). Mad in America Foundation. https://www.madinamerica.com/.

Mahuika, Nēpia. "Re-storying Māori Legal Histories: Indigenous Articulations in Nineteenth-Century New Zealand." *NAIS* 2, no. 1 (Spring 2015): 40–66.

Malacrida, Claudia. *A Special Hell: Institutional Life in Alberta's Eugenic Years*. Toronto: University of Toronto Press, 2015.

Malehorn, Pauline G. *The Tender Plant: The History of the Navajo Methodist Mission, Farmington, New Mexico, 1891–1948*. N.p., 1948.

Mallon, Florencia E., ed. *Decolonizing Native Histories: Collaboration, Knowledge, and Language in the Americas*. Durham, NC: Duke University Press, 2012.

Manitowabi, Darrel, and Marion Maar. "Coping with Colonization: Aboriginal Diabetes on Manitoulin Island." In Fear-Segal and Tillet, *Indigenous Bodies*, 145–59.

Marks, Shula. "Every Facility That Modern Science and Enlightened Humanity Have Devised." In Melling and Forsythe, *Insanity, Institutions, and Society*, 268–92.

McCandless, Peter. *Moonlight, Magnolias, and Madness: Insanity in South Carolina from the Colonial to the Progressive Eras*. Chapel Hill: University of North Carolina Press, 1996.

McLennan, Rebecca M. *The Crisis of Imprisonment: Protest, Politics, and the Making of the American Penal State, 1776–1941*. Cambridge: Cambridge University Press, 2008.

McDonnell, Janet A. *The Dispossession of the American Indian, 1887–1934*. Bloomington: Indiana University Press, 1991.

McMillen, Christian W. "'The Red Man and the White Plague': Rethinking Tuberculosis and American Indians, ca. 1890–1950." *Bulletin of Medical History* 82 (2008): 608–45.

Melling, Joseph, and Bill Forsythe, eds. *Insanity, Institutions, and Society, 1800–1914.* London: Routledge, 1999.

Melosh, Barbara. *Strangers and Kin: The American Way of Adoption.* Cambridge, MA: Harvard University Press, 2006.

Mendoza, Mary E. "Caging Out, Caging In: Building a Carceral State at the U.S.–Mexico Divide." *Pacific Historical Review* 88, no. 1 (Winter 2019): 86–109.

Menzies, Robert, and Ted Palys. "Turbulent Spirits: Aboriginal Patients in the British Columbia Psychiatric System, 1879–1950." In *Mental Health and Canadian Society: Historical Perspectives,* edited by J. Moran and D. Wright, 149–75. Montreal: McGill-Queen's University Press, 2006.

Merrell, James Hart. *The Indians' New World: Catawbas and Their Neighbors from European Contact.* New York: W. W. Norton, 1991.

Metzl, Jonathan. *The Protest Psychosis: How Schizophrenia Became a Black Disease.* Boston: Beacon, 2010.

Meyer, Roy W. *History of the Santee Sioux: United States Indian Policy on Trial.* Lincoln: University of Nebraska Press, 1967.

Michalko, Rod, and Tanya Titchkovsky. *Rethinking Normalcy: A Disability Studies Reader.* Toronto: Canadian Scholars' Press, 2009.

Mihesuah, Devon A. *American Indians: Stereotypes and Realities.* Atlanta: Clarity Press, 1998.

Mihesuah, Devon A., ed. *Natives and Academics: Researching and Writing about American Indians.* Lincoln: University of Nebraska Press, 1998.

Mihesuah, Devon A. *Ned Christie: The Creation of an Outlaw and Cherokee Hero.* Norman: University of Oklahoma Press, 2018.

Milk, Theresa. *Haskell Institute: 19th Century Stories of Sacrifice and Survival.* Lawrence, KS: Mammoth, 2007.

Miller, David R. "The Mossman Administration, 1917–1921." In *The History of the Fort Peck Assiniboine and Sioux Tribes, 1800–2000,* edited by David R. Miller, Dennis J. Smith, Joseph R. McGeshick, James Shanley, and Caleb Shields, 233–49. Fort Peck, MT: Fort Peck Community College, 2008. https://archive.org/stream/64CC2DD6-94F0-432F-A419-5266F7AE0743/64CC2DD6-94F0-432F-A419-5266F7AE0743_djvu.txt.

Miller, Douglas K. "The Spider's Web: Mass Incarceration and Settler Custodialism in Indian Country." In Chase, *Caging Borders and Carceral States,* 385–408.

Miller, Jay. "Kinship, Family Kindreds, and Community." In Deloria and Salisbury, *Companion to American Indian History,* 139–51.

Million, Dian. "Felt Theory: An Indigenous Feminist Approach to Affect and History." *Wicazo Sa Review* 24, no. 2 (Fall 2009): 53–76.

Milwaukee Public Museum, "Kinship." Accessed December 8, 2017. http://www.mpm.edu/content/wirp/ICW-48.

Mingus, Mia. *Leaving Evidence* (blog). https://leavingevidence.wordpress.com/.

Minich, Julie Avril. "Enabling Whom? Critical Disability Studies Now." *Lateral* 5, no. 1 (2016). http://csalateral.org/issue/5-1/forum-alt-humanities-critical-disability-studies-now-minich/.

Mintz, Steven, and Susan Kellogg. *Domestic Revolutions: A Social History of American Family Life.* New York: Simon and Schuster, 1989.

Miranda, Deborah A. *Bad Indians: A Tribal Memoir.* Berkeley, CA: Heydey, 2013.

Miron, Janet. *Prisons, Asylums, and the Public: Institutional Visiting in the Nineteenth Century.* Toronto: University of Toronto Press, 2011.

Mohatt, Gerald, and Joseph Eagle Elk. *The Price of a Gift: A Lakota Healer's Story.* Lincoln: University of Nebraska Press, 2000.

Moraga, Cherríe, and Gloria Anzaldúa, eds. *This Bridge Called My Back: Writings by Radical Women of Color.* 4th ed. Albany: State University of New York Press, 2015.

Morgensen, Scott Lauria. *Spaces between Us: Queer Settler Colonialism and Indigenous Decolonization.* Minneapolis: University of Minnesota Press, 2011.

———. "Theorising Gender, Sexuality, and Settler Colonialism: An Introduction." *Settler Colonial Studies* 2, no.2 (2012): 2–22.

Morrison, Toni. "Unspeakable Things Unspoken: The Afro-American Presence in American Literature." Lecture delivered at the University of Michigan, 1988, Tanner Lectures on Human Values. https://tannerlectures.utah.edu/_documents/a-to-z/m /morrison90.pdf.

Napos (David Turney Sr.). "Faces and Places of Northern Wisconsin." YouTube, October 30, 2013. Video, 4:17. https://www.youtube.com/watch?v=DQpe18wzVMs.

Nario-Redmond, Michelle R. *Ableism: The Causes and Consequence of Disability Prejudice.* Hoboken, NJ: Wiley-Blackwell, 2020.

Nichols, Joshua, and Amy Swiffen, eds. *Legal Violence and the Limits of the Law.* New York: Routledge, 2018.

Nichols, Roger L. *The American Indian: Past and Present.* 6th ed. Norman: University of Oklahoma Press, 2008.

Nielsen, Kim E. *A Disability History of the United States.* Boston: Beacon, 2013.

Nielsen, Kim E., and Susan Burch. "Disability History." In *Keywords in Disability Studies,* edited by Benjamin Reiss, David Serlin, and Rachel Adams, 95–98. New York: New York University Press, 2015.

Nixon, Rob. *Slow Violence and the Environmentalism of the Poor.* Cambridge, MA: Harvard University Press, 2011.

Nurge, Ethel. *The Modern Sioux: Social Systems and Reservation Culture.* Lincoln: University of Nebraska Press, 1970.

O'Brien, Jean M. *Firsting and Lasting: Writing Indians Out of Existence in New England.* Minneapolis: University of Minnesota Press, 2010.

Olsen, J. P., and Luke Walden, dirs. *The Narcotic Farm.* Hollywood, CA: PBS, 2009. Film, 55 minutes.

Olson, Gary. "Yankee and European Settlement." In *A New South Dakota History,* 2nd ed., edited by Harry F. Thompson, 117–42. Sioux Falls, SD: Center for Western Studies, 2009.

Olson, Kay Melchisedech. *Norwegian, Swedish, and Danish Immigrants, 1820–1920.* Mankato, MN: Blue Earth Books, 2002.

Omi, Michael, and Howard Winant. *Racial Formation in the United States.* New York: Routledge, 2015.

Oneroad, Amos E., and Alanson B. Skinner. *Being Dakota: Tales and Traditions of the Sisseton and Wahpeton*. Edited by Laura L. Anderson. St. Paul: Minnesota Historical Society Press, 2003.

Ortiz, Simon J. "Towards a National Indian Literature: Cultural Authenticity in Nationalism." *MELUS* 8, no. 2 (1981): 7–13.

Osburn, Katherine Marie Birmingham. *Southern Ute Women: Autonomy and Assimilation on the Reservation, 1887–1934*. Lincoln: University of Nebraska Press, 2009.

———. "'To Build Up the Morals of the Tribe': Southern Ute Women's Sexual Behavior and the Office of Indian Affairs, 1895–1932." *Journal of Women's History* 9, no. 3 (Autumn 1997): 10–27.

Ostler, Jeffrey. "'Just and Lawful War' as Genocidal War in the (United States) Northwest Ordinance and Northwest Territory, 1787–1832." *Journal of Genocide Research* 18, no. 1 (2016): 1–20.

———. *The Plains Sioux and U.S. Colonialism from Lewis and Clark to Wounded Knee*. New York: Cambridge University Press, 2004.

Otto, Thomas. *St. Elizabeths Hospital: A History*. Washington, DC: GSA, 2013.

Ourada, Patricia K. *The Menominee Indians: A History*. Norman: University of Oklahoma Press, 1979.

Painter, Nell Irvin. *The History of White People*. New York: W. W. Norton, 2010.

Parker, Dorothy R. *Phoenix Indian School: The Second Half-Century*. Tucson: University of Arizona Press, 1996.

Parsons, Anne E. *From Asylum to Prison: Deinstitutionalization and the Rise of Mass Incarceration after 1945*. Chapel Hill: University of North Carolina Press, 2018.

Paxton, Katrina A. "Learning Gender: Female Students at the Sherman Institute, 1907–1925." In *Boarding School Blues: Revisiting American Indian Educational Experiences*, edited by Clifford E. Trifler, Jean A. Keller, and Lorene Sisquoc, 174–86. Lincoln: University of Nebraska Press, 2006.

Peers, Laura, and Jennifer S. H Brown. "There Is No End to Relationship among the Indians." *History of the Family* 4, no. 4 (1999): 529–55.

Pengra, Lilah Morton. "Lakota Quality of Life: Mitakuye Oyasin." In *Cross-Cultural Perspectives on Quality of Life*, edited by Kenneth D. Keith and Robert L. Schalock, 191–204. Washington, DC: American Association on Mental Retardation, 2000.

Pengra, Lilah Morton, and Joyzelle Gingway Godfrey. "Different Boundaries, Different Barriers: Disability Studies and Lakota Culture." *Disability Studies Quarterly* 21, no. 3 (Summer 2001): 36–53.

Perreira, Christopher. "Unsettling Archives: Cultures of Carceral States and Settler Logics." *American Quarterly* 70, no. 2 (2018): 327–34.

Philp, Kenneth R. *John Collier's Crusade for Indian Reform, 1920–1954*. Tucson: University of Arizona Press, 1977.

Piatote, Beth H. *Domestic Subjects: Gender, Citizenship, and Law in Native American Literature*. New Haven, CT: Yale University Press, 2013.

———. "The Indian/Agent Aporia." *American Indian Quarterly* 37, no. 3 (Spring 2013): 45–62.

Pickering, Kathleen Ann. *Lakota Culture, World Economy*. Lincoln: University of Nebraska Press, 2004.

Porter, Joy, ed. *Place and Native American Indian History and Culture*. Oxford: Peter Lang, 2007.

Porter, Roy, and David Wright, eds. *The Confinement of the Insane: International Perspectives, 1800–1965*. Cambridge: Cambridge University Press, 2003.

Portman, Tarrell A. A., and Michael T. Garrett. "Native American Healing Traditions." *International Journal of Disability, Development, and Education* 53, no. 4 (December 1, 2006): 453–69.

Price, Margaret. *Mad at School: Rhetorics of Mental Disability and Academic Life*. Ann Arbor: University of Michigan Press, 2011.

Prucha, Francis Paul. *American Indian Policy in Crisis: Christian Reformers and the Indian, 1865–1900*. Norman: University of Oklahoma Press, 1976.

———. *The Great Father: The United States Government and the American Indian*. Lincoln: University of Nebraska Press, 1986.

Putney, Diane T. "The Canton Asylum for Insane Indians, 1902–1934." *South Dakota History* 14, no. 1 (1984): 1–30.

Radford, John P., and Denise C. Park. "'A Convenient Means of Riddance': Institutionalization of People Diagnosed as 'Mentally Deficient' in Ontario, 1876–1934." *Health and Canadian Society* 1, no. 2 (1993): 369–92.

Ramírez, Dixa. *Colonial Phantoms: Belonging and Refusal in the Dominican Americas, from the 19th Century to the Present*. New York: New York University Press, 2018.

Ramirez, Renya K. *Native Hubs: Culture, Community, and Belonging in Silicon Valley and Beyond*. Durham, NC: Duke University Press, 2007.

Rapp, Rayna Reiter, and Faye D. Ginsburg. "Enabling Disability: Rewriting Kinship, Reimagining Citizenship." *Public Culture* 13, no. 3 (2001): 533–56.

Rasmussen, Birgit Brander, Eric Klinenberg, Irene J. Nexica, and Matt Wray, eds. *The Making and Unmaking of Whiteness*. Durham, NC: Duke University Press, 2001.

Raup, Ruth M. *The Indian Health Program from 1800 to 1955*. Washington, DC: Department of Health, Education, and Welfare, 1959.

Reaume, Geoffrey. "Mad People's History." In "Disability and History" issue, edited by Teresa Meade and David Serlin, *Radical History Review* 2006, no. 94 (Winter 2006): 170–82.

———. "Patients at Work: Insane Asylum Inmates' Labour in Ontario, 1841–1900." In *Mental Health in Canadian Society: Historical Perspectives*, edited by James Moran and David Wright, 69–96. Montreal: McGill-Queen's University Press, 2006.

———. "Posthumous Exploitation?: The Ethics of Researching, Writing, and Being Accountable as a Disability Historian." In *Untold Stories: A Canadian Disability History Reader*, edited by Nancy Hansen, Roy Hanes, and Diane Driedger, 26–39. Toronto: Canadian Scholars' Press, 2018.

Reis, Benjamin. *Theaters of Madness: Insane Asylums and Nineteenth-Century American Culture*. Chicago: University of Chicago Press, 2008.

Rembis, Michael A. *Defining Deviance: Sex, Science, and Delinquent Girls, 1890–1960*. Urbana-Champaign: University of Illinois Press, 2011.

Rembis, Michael A., Catherine Jean Kudlick, and Kim E. Nielsen, eds. *The Oxford Handbook of Disability History*. Oxford: Oxford University Press, 2018.

Richards, Penny, and Susan Burch. "Dreamscapes for Public Disability History: How (and Why, and Where, and with Whom) We Collaborate." *Public Disability History* 1 (2016). https://www.public-disabilityhistory.org/2016/12/dreamscapes-for-public -disability.html.

Rifkin, Mark. *When Did Indians Become Straight?: Kinship, the History of Sexuality, and Native Sovereignty*. Oxford: Oxford University Press, 2010.

Rimke, Heidi. "Sickening Institutions: A Feminist Sociological Analysis and Critique of Religion, Medicine, and Psychiatry." In Kilty and Dej, *Containing Madness*, 15–39.

Riney, Scott. "Power and Powerlessness: The People of the Canton Asylum for Insane Indians." *South Dakota History* 27, nos. 1/2 (Summer 1997): 41–64.

Risjord, Norman K. *Dakota: The Story of the Northern Plains*. Lincoln: University of Nebraska Press, 2012.

Rohrer, Judy. "Ableism." In *Encyclopedia of American Disability History*, edited by Susan Burch, vol. 1, 1–3. New York: Facts on File, 2009.

Rølvaag, Ole Edvart. *Giants of the Earth: A Saga of the Prairie*. Norway: Aschehoug, 1924.

Roman, Leslie, Sheena Brown, Steven Noble, Rafael Wainer, and Alannah Earl Young. "No Time for Nostalgia!: Asylum-making, Medicalized Colonialism in British Columbia (1859–97), and Artistic Praxis for Social Transformation." *International Journal of Qualitative Studies in Education* 22, no. 1 (2009): 17–63.

Rose, Deborah Bird. *Hidden Histories: Black Stories from Victoria River Downs, Humbert River, and Wave Hill Stations*. Canberra: Aboriginal Studies Press, 1991.

Ross, Luana. *Inventing the Savage: The Social Construction of Native American Criminality*. University of Texas Press, 2010.

Rossiter, Kate, and Annalise Clarkson. "Opening Ontario's 'Saddest Chapter': A Social History of Huronia Regional Centre." *Canadian Journal of Disability Studies* 2, no. 3 (September 2013): 1–30.

Rothman, David. *Conscience and Convenience: The Asylum and Its Alternatives in Progressive America*. Rev. ed. New York: Aldine, 2002.

———. *The Discovery of the Asylum: Social Order and Disorder in the New Republic*. Boston: Little, Brown, 1971.

Rumi, Mark. "Mitákuye Owás'į (All My Relatives): Dakota Wiconi (Way of Life) and Wicozani Waste (Well-Being)." *Aboriginal Policy Research Consortium International*. Paper 81 (2010). http://ir.lib.uwo.ca/aprci/81.

Samuels, Ellen. *Fantasies of Identification: Disability, Gender, Race*. New York: New York University Press, 2014.

Saxman, Michelle C. "The Canton Asylum for Insane Indians (South Dakota)." *CRM [Bulletin]* 22, no. 9 (1999): 40–42.

Schalk, Sami. *Bodyminds Reimagined: (Dis)ability, Race, and Gender in Black Women's Speculative Fiction*. Durham, NC: Duke University Press, 2018.

Schoolcraft, Henry R. *The Myth of Hiawatha: And Other Oral Legends, Mythologic and Allegoric, of the North American Indians*. New York: Kraus Reprint, 1971.

Schwartz, Maureen Trudelle. *"I Choose Life": Contemporary Medical and Religious Practices in the Navajo World*. Norman: University of Oklahoma Press, 2008.

Schweik, Susan. "Disability and the Normal Body of the (Native) Citizen." *Social Research* 78, no. 2 (2011): 417–42.

Scotch, Richard K. "Medical Model of Disability." In *Encyclopedia of American Disability History*, edited by Susan Burch. New York: Facts on File, 2009.

Scull, Andrew, ed. *Madhouses, Mad-Doctors, and Madmen: The Social History of Psychiatry in the Victorian Era*. Philadelphia: University of Pennsylvania Press, 1981.

———. *Madness in Civilization: A Cultural History of Insanity, from the Bible to Freud, from the Madhouse to Modern Medicine*. Princeton, NJ: Princeton University Press, 2015.

Scuro, Jennifer. *Addressing Ableism: Philosophical Questions via Disability Studies*. New York: Lexington Books, 2019.

Seeding Sovereignty (website and blog). https://seedingsovereignty.org.

Senier, Siobhan. "Rehabilitation Reservations: Native Narrations of Disability and Community." *Disability Studies Quarterly* 32, no. 4 (2012). http://dsq-sds.org/article/view/1641.

Shanley, Kathryn W. "Talking to the Animals and Taking Out the Trash: The Functions of American Indian Literature." *Wicazo Sa Review* 14, no. 2 (1999): 32–45.

Shoemaker, Nancy, ed. *Clearing a Path: Theorizing the Past in Native American Studies*. New York: Routledge, 2002.

Simpson, Audra. *Mohawk Interruptus: Political Life across the Borders of Settler States*. Durham, NC: Duke University Press, 2014.

———. "On Ethnographic Refusal: Indigeneity, 'Voice,' and Colonial Citizenship." *Junctures* 9 (December 2007): 67–80.

Simpson, Audra, and Andrea Smith, eds. *Theorizing Native Studies*. Durham, NC: Duke University Press, 2014.

Sins Invalid. *Skin, Tooth, and Bone: The Basis of Movement Is Our People*. Berkeley, CA: Sins Invalid, 2016.

Sium, Aman, and Eric Ritskes. "Speaking Truth to Power: Indigenous Storytelling as an Act of Living Resistance." *Decolonization: Indigeneity, Education, and Society* 2, no. 1 (2013): i–x.

Smith, Andrea. "Queer Studies and Native Studies: The Heteronormativity of Settler Colonialism." In Driskill et al., *Queer Indigenous Studies*, 43–65.

Smith, J. David. *The Eugenic Assault on America: Scenes in Red, White, and Black*. Fairfax, VA: George Mason University Press, 1993.

Smith, Linda Tuhiwai. *Decolonizing Methodologies: Research and Indigenous Peoples*. London: Zed Books, 2005.

Smith, Linda Tuhiwai, Te Kahautu Maxwell, Haupai Puke, and Pou Temara. "Indigenous Knowledge, Methodology, and Mayhem: What Is the Role of Methodology in Producing Indigenous Insights? A Discussion from Matauranga Maori." *Knowledge Cultures* 4, no. 3 (2016): 131–56.

Smith, Paul Chaat, and Robert Allen Warrior. *Like a Hurricane: The Indian Movement from Alcatraz to Wounded Knee*. New York: New Press, 1996.

Smithers, Gregory D. "The 'Pursuits of the Civilized Man': Race and the Meaning of Civilization in the United States and Australia, 1790s–1850s." *Journal of World History* 20, no. 2 (June 2009): 245–72.

Smithers, Gregory D., ed. *Science, Sexuality, and Race in the United States and Australia, 1780–1940*. Rev. ed. Lincoln: University of Nebraska Press, 2017.

Smithers, Gregory D., and Brooke N. Newman, eds. *Native Diasporas: Indigenous Identities and Settler Colonialism in the Americas*. Lincoln: University of Nebraska Press, 2014.

Sneve, Virginia D. H. *That They May Have Life: The Episcopal Church in South Dakota, 1859–1976*. New York: Seabury, 1977.

Snyder, Christina. *Great Crossings: Indians, Settlers, and Slaves in the Age of Jackson*. Oxford: Oxford University Press, 2017.

Spens, Iona, ed. *Architecture of Incarceration*. London: Academy Editions, 1994.

Solinger, Rickie. "Maternity Homes." In *The Reader's Companion to U.S. Women's History*, edited by Wilma Mankiller, Gwendolyn Mink, Marysa Navarro, Barbara Smith, and Gloria Steinem, 360–62. Boston: Houghton Mifflin, 1998.

———. *Wake Up Little Susie: Single Pregnancy and Race before Roe v. Wade*. New York: Routledge, 1992.

Soule, Bradley, and Jennifer Soule. "Death at the Hiawatha Asylum for Insane Indians." *South Dakota Journal of Medicine* 56, no. 1 (January 2003): 15–18.

Soule, Jennifer. "Hiawatha Asylum for Insane Indians." *South Dakota Review* 47, no. 2 (Summer 2009): 34.

———. "How to Get Committed to the Hiawatha Asylum for Insane Indians." *South Dakota Review* 47, no. 2 (June 2009): 35–36.

Spaulding, John M. "The Canton Asylum for Insane Indians: An Example of Institutional Neglect." *Hospital and Community Psychiatry* 37, no. 10 (October 1986): 1007–11.

Spindler, George, and Louise S. Spindler. *Dreamers without Power: The Menomini Indians*. New York: Holt, Rinehart, and Winston, 1971.

Spindler, Louise S. *Menomini Women and Culture Change*. Menasha, WI: American Anthropological Association, 1962.

Stawicki, Elizabeth. "A Haunting Legacy: Canton Insane Asylum for American Indians." Minnesota Public Radio, December 9, 1997. Audio recording.

Stern, Alexandra Minna. *Eugenic Nation: Faults and Frontiers of Better Breeding in Modern America*. Berkeley: University of California Press, 2005.

Stevenson, Lisa. *Life Beside Itself: Imagining Care in the Canadian Artic*. Berkeley: University of California Press, 2014.

Stiker, Henri-Jacques. *A History of Disability*. Ann Arbor: University of Michigan Press, 1999.

Stoler, Ann Laura. *Carnal Knowledge and Imperial Power: Race and the Intimate in Colonial Rule*. Berkeley: University of California Press, 2002.

Stoler, Ann Laura, ed. *Haunted by Empire: Geographies of Intimacy in North American History*. Durham, NC: Duke University Press, 2006.

Stratton, Ray. "The Cherokee National Insane Asylum." *Bulletin of the Menninger Clinic* 47, no. 3 (May 1983): 266–68.

Stromberg, Ernest, ed. *American Indian Rhetorics of Survivance: Word Medicine, Word Magic*. Pittsburgh: University of Pittsburgh Press, 2006.

Swartz, Sally. "The Black Insane in the Cape, 1891–1920." *Journal of Southern African Studies* 21, no. 3 (1995): 399–415.

Szasz, Thomas S. *Coercion as Cure: A Critical History of Psychiatry*. New Brunswick: Transaction, 2007.

———. *Insanity: The Idea and Its Consequences*. New York: Wiley, 1987.

———. *The Manufacture of Madness: A Comparative Study of the Inquisition and the Mental Health Movement*. 1970. Reprint, Syracuse, NY: Syracuse University Press, 1997.

Takaki, Ronald T. *Iron Cages: Race and Culture in 19th-Century America*. Oxford: Oxford University Press, 1979.

Taliman, Valerie, and Susan Zwinger. "Sacred Landscapes." *Sierra* (November–December 2002): 36–43, 73.

TallBear, Kim. "Dossier: Theorizing Queer Inhumanisms: An Indigenous Reflection on Working beyond the Human/Not Human." *GLQ* 21, no. 2–3 (2015): 230–35.

Taylor, Sunaura. *Beasts of Burden: Animal and Disability Liberation*. New York: New Press, 2017.

Teuton, Sean Kicummah. "Disability in Indigenous North America: In Memory of William Sherman Fox." In *The World of the Indigenous Americas*, edited by Robert Warrior, 569–93. Hoboken, NJ: Taylor and Francis, 2014.

———. *Red Land, Red Power: Grounding Knowledge in the American Indian Novel*. Durham, NC: Duke University Press, 2008.

Thompson, Kara. *Blanket*. New York: Bloomsbury Academic, 2018.

Thompson, Stith. "The Indian Legend of Hiawatha." *PMLA* 37, no. 1 (March 1922): 128–40.

Thornton, Russell. *American Indian Holocaust and Survival: A Population History since 1492*. Norman: Oklahoma University Press, 1987.

———. "Population History of Native North Americans." In *A Population History of North America*, edited by Michael R. Haines and Richard H. Steckel. Cambridge: Cambridge University Press, 2000, 9–50.

Thornton, Russell, ed. *Studying Native America: Problems and Prospects*. Madison: University of Wisconsin Press, 1998.

Tiro, Karim M. *The People of the Standing Stone: The Oneida Nation from the Revolution through the Era of Removal*. Amherst: University of Massachusetts Press, 2011.

Tomes, Nancy. "Germ Theory, Public Health Education, and the Moralization of Behavior in the Antituberculosis Crusade." In *Major Problems in the History of American Medicine and Public Health: Documents and Essays*, edited by John Harley Warner and Janet A. Tighe, 257–64. Boston: Houghton Mifflin, 2001.

Topp, Leslie, James E. Moran, and Jonathan Andrews, eds. *Madness, Architecture, and the Built Environment: Psychiatric Spaces in Historical Context*. New York: Routledge, 2007.

Trachtenberg, Alan. *Shades of Hiawatha: Staging Indians, Making Americans, 1880–1930*. New York: Hill & Wang, 2004.

Trafzer, Clifford E. *Fighting Invisible Enemies: Health and Medical Transitions among Southern California Indians*. Norman: University of Oklahoma Press, 2019.

Trafzer Clifford E., and Diane Weiner, eds. *Medicine Ways: Disease, Health, and Survival among Native Americans*. New York: Altamira, 2001.

Treglia, Gabriella. "A Very 'Indian' Future? The Place of Native Cultures and Communities in BIA and Native Thought in the New Deal Era." In Porter, *Place and Native American Indian History and Culture*, 357–80.

Trennert, Robert A., Jr. *The Phoenix Indian School: Forced Assimilation in Arizona, 1891–1935*. Norman: University of Oklahoma Press, 1988.

Trent, James. *Inventing the Feeble Mind: A History of Mental Retardation in the United States*. Berkeley: University of California Press, 1994.

Treuer, David. *Rez Life: An Indian's Journey through Reservation Life*. New York: Atlantic Monthly Press, 2012.

Trinkley, Michael, Debi Hacker, and Nicole Southerland. *Preservation Assessment of St. Elizabeths East Campus Cemetery, Washington, DC*. Chicora Research Contribution 514. Columbia, SC: Chicora Foundation, 2009.

Trope, Jack F,. and Walter R. Echo-Hawk. "The Native American Graves Protection and Repatriation Act: Background and Legislative History." *Arizona State Law Journal* 35, no. 36 (1992): 35–77.

Trouillot, Michel-Rolph. *Silencing the Past: Power and the Production of History*. Boston: Beacon, 1995.

Troutman, John. *Indian Blues: American Indians and the Politics of Music, 1879–1934*. Norman: University of Oklahoma Press, 2013.

Tuck, Eve. "Suspending Damage: A Letter to Communities." *Harvard Educational Review* 79, no. 3 (2009): 409–28.

Tuck, Eve, and Marcia McKenzie. *Place in Research: Theory, Methodology, and Methods*. New York: Routledge, 2014.

Tuck, Eve, and K. Wayne Yang. "Unbecoming Claims: Pedagogies of Refusal in Qualitative Research." *Qualitative Inquiry* 20 (2014): 811–18.

Underwood, Paula. *The Walking People: A Native American Oral History*. Bayfield, CO: Tribe of Two Press, 1993.

Unger, Steven, ed. *The Destruction of American Indian Families*. New York: Association on American Indian Affairs, 1977.

Unsettling America: Decolonization in Theory and Practice (website and blog). https://unsettlingamerica.wordpress.com/.

Utley, Robert M. *The Last Days of the Sioux Nation*. New Haven, CT: Yale University Press, 2004.

Valandra, Edward C. *Not without Our Consent: Lakota Resistance to Termination, 1950–59*. Urbana: University of Illinois Press, 2006.

Vizenor, Gerald. *Manifest Manners: Narratives on Postindian Survivance*. Lincoln: University of Nebraska Press, 1999.

Vizenor, Gerald, ed. *Survivance: Narratives of Native Presence*. Lincoln: University of Nebraska Press, 2008.

Voyles, Traci Brynne. *Wastelanding: Legacies of Uranium Mining in Navajo Country*. Minneapolis: University of Minnesota Press, 2015.

Waldram, James. *Revenge of the Windigo: The Construction of the Mind and Mental Health of North American Aboriginal Peoples*. Toronto: University of Toronto Press, 2004.

Walker, James R., Raymond J. DeMallie, and Elaine Jahner, eds. *Lakota Belief and Ritual*. Lincoln: University of Nebraska Press, 1980.

Weaver, Hilary N. "The Colonial Context of Violence: Reflections on Violence in the Lives of Native American Women." *Journal of Interpersonal Violence* 24, no. 9 (September 2009): 1552–63.

———. "Perspectives on Wellness: Journeys on the Red Road." *Journal of Sociology and Social Welfare* 29, no. 1 (March 2002): 5–17.

Weaver, Jace, Craig S. Womack, and Robert A. Warrior. *American Indian Literary Nationalism*. Albuquerque: University of New Mexico Press, 2006.

Westerman, Gwen, and Bruce M. White. *Mni Sota Makoce: The Land of the Dakota*. Minneapolis: Minnesota Historical Society, 2012.

Whitaker, Robert. *Mad in America: Bad Science, Bad Medicine, and the Enduring Mistreatment of the Mentally Ill*. New York: Perseus Books, 2002.

Williams, Ralph C. *The United States Public Health Service, 1798–1950*. Washington, DC: Commissioned Officers Association of the United States Public Health Service, 1951.

Wilkinson, Charles. *Blood Struggle: The Rise of Modern Indian Nations*. New York: W. W. Norton, 2005.

Willie, Charles V., Bernard M. Kramer, and Bertram S. Brown. *Racism and Mental Health: Essays*. Pittsburgh: University of Pittsburgh Press, 1973.

Wilson, Angela Cavender. "Grandmother to Granddaughter: Generations of Oral History in a Dakota Family." In Mihesuah, *Natives and Academics*, 27–36.

Wilson, Otto, and Robert S. Barrett. *Fifty Years' Work with Girls, 1883–1933: A Story of the Florence Crittenton Homes*. Alexandria, VA: National Florence Crittenton Mission, 1933.

Wilson, Waziyatawin Angela. *Remember This!: Dakota Decolonization and the Eli Taylor Narratives*. Lincoln: University of Lincoln Press, 2005.

Wolfe, Patrick. "Settler Colonialism and the Elimination of the Native." *Journal of Genocidal Research* 8, no. 4 (December 2006): 387–409.

Wolframe, PhebeAnn Marjory. "The Madwoman in the Academy, or, Revealing the Invisible Straightjacket: Theorizing and Teaching Saneism and Sane Privilege." *Disability Studies Quarterly* 33, no. 1 (2013). https://dsq-sds.org/article/view/3425.

Womack, Craig S., Daniel Heath Justice, and Christopher B. Teuton, eds. *Reasoning Together: The Native Critics Collective*. Norman: University of Oklahoma Press, 2008.

Wong, Sau-ling C. "Diverted Mothering: Representations of Caregivers of Color in the Age of 'Multiculturalism.'" In Glenn, Chang, and Force, *Mothering*, 67–91.

Woolford, Andrew. *This Benevolent Experiment: Indigenous Boarding Schools, Genocide, and Redress in Canada and the United States*. Lincoln: University of Nebraska Press, 2015.

Yanni, Carla. *The Architecture of Madness: Insane Asylums in the United States*. Minneapolis: University of Minnesota Press, 2007.

Young, Richard Keith. *The Ute Indians of Colorado in the Twentieth Century*. Norman: University of Oklahoma Press, 1997.

Young Bear, Severt, and R. D. Theisz. *Standing in the Light: A Lakota Way of Seeing*. Lincoln: University of Nebraska Press, c1994.

Unpublished Secondary Sources

Arms, E. Clyde. "Asylum for Insane Indians." Manuscript, June 30, 1937. Canton Asylum for Insane Indians file, Canton Public Library, SD.

Burch, Susan. Digital database for *Committed*.

Cowing, Jessica. "Obesity and (Un)fit Homes: Health and Belonging in a Settler Nation." Talk delivered at the American Studies Association Conference, Denver, CO, November 18, 2016.

———. "Settler States of Ability: Assimilation, Incarceration, and Native Women's Crip Interventions." PhD diss., College of William and Mary, 2020.

Gambino, Matthew. "Mental Health and Ideals of Citizenship: Patient Care at St. Elizabeths Hospital in Washington, D.C., 1903–1962." PhD diss., University of Illinois at Urbana-Champaign, 2010.

Gough, Heather Robyn. "Colonization and Madness: Involuntary Psychiatric Commitment Law and Policy Frameworks as Applied to American Indians." PhD diss., Arizona State University, 2013.

Laudenschlager, David D. "An Infamous Institution: The Hiawatha Asylum." Research paper, 1983, Canton Asylum for Insane Indians file, Canton Public Library, SD.

Leahy, Todd E. "The Canton Asylum: Indians, Psychiatrists, and Government Policy, 1899–1934." PhD diss., Oklahoma State University, 2004.

Lieffers, Caroline. "Imperial Ableism: Disability and American Expansion, c. 1850–1930." PhD diss., Yale University, 2020.

Louis, Sidney S. "US Public Health Service Hospital, Fort Worth, Texas, 1959–1962." Fort Worth: printed by the author, 1962.

McMillen, Frances Margaret. "Ministering to a Mind Diseased: Landscape, Architecture, and Moral Treatment at St. Elizabeths Hospital, 1852–1905." Master's thesis, University of Virginia School of Architecture, 2008.

Meader, Ben. Canton Asylum for Insane Indians: GIS Visualizations. 2013–14. Material generated from archival database for *Committed*, in the author's possession.

Millikan, Frank Rives. "Wards of the Nation: The Making of St. Elizabeths Hospital, 1852–1920." PhD diss., George Washington University, 1990.

Osburn, Katherine Marie Birmingham. "'And as the Squaws Are a Secondary Consideration': Southern Ute Women under Directed Culture Change, 1887–1934." PhD diss., University of Denver, 1993.

Ott, Katherine. Comment to Disability History Panel at the OAH Conference, April 6, 2019, Philadelphia.

Swartz, Sally. "Colonialism and the Production of Psychiatric Knowledge at the Cape, 1891–1920." PhD diss., University of Cape Town, 1996.

Sweet, Kelli K. "Controversial Care: The Canton Indian Insane Asylum: 1902–1934." Master's thesis, University of Nebraska at Omaha, 2000.

Whitt, Sarah. "False Promises: Race, Power, and the Chimera of Indian Assimilation, 1879–1934." PhD diss., University of California–Berkeley, 2020.

INDEX

Page numbers in italics refer to illustrations or their captions.

Buntin, John A., 31, 45, 125nn46–47, 141n32. *See also* staff, institutional
Burch, Cora, 42, 47, 132n22
Burch, Jane, 12, 41–44, 47, 77, 131n12, 133n24
Burch, Ruth Bent, 41
Burch, Steve, 41, 133n24
Burch, Susan, 12, 41–44, 47, 77, 131n12, 133n24
burden, 31, 42, 47
Bureau of Indian Affairs, 5, 23, 68, 89–90, 92, 97, 99, 100, 103, 134n32, 136n67, 137n74, 140n27, 143n66, 148n47, 149n59, 150n65, 152n84, 155n25, 160n76; diagnosis and, 1–2, 8, 10, 11, 27–28, 56–58, 71, 76, 78, 125n47, 137–38n75, 150n73, 167n46; sustaining institutionalization, 3, 6, 8, 11, 35, 36, 48–52, 56–58, 69–70, 74–76, 79–80, 87, 151n79, 152n85; targeting families, 3, 12, 27–31, 39–48, 53, 60–64, 133n24
Burke, Charles, 8, 48, 63, 69. *See also* staff, institutional

Caddo Nation, 30, 38, 45, 126n50
Caddo Reservation, 30, 126n50
Caldwell, Agnes Bear, 39–41, 46–47, 48–52, 68, 74–75, 133n29, 136n57
Caldwell, George, 39–40, 46–47
Caldwell, Luke, 39–41, 49
Caldwell, Madeline, 39–41, 49
Canton, South Dakota, 1, 17, 18, 22, 29, 32–34, 36, 50, 62, 76–77, 80, 97, 98, 102, 127n61
Canton Asylum, 1–3, 4–7, 11–3, 17–20, 22–25, 30–31, 32–35, 38, 42–44, 45–48, 53–59, 68, 79–81, 87–88, 102–5; conditions inside, 3, 17, 35, 48–52, 59, 64, 68–70, 71–75, 76, 79–80, 103, 136–37n67, 137n74, 145n5, 146n28, 152n85; inspections of, 51, 57–58, 71, 77–78, 79, 145n5, 147n32, 147–48n39, 152n85; as site of settler colonialism, 3–7, 8–10, 12, 16–17, 23, 25, 28–29, 32–35, 38, 40–41, 43–44, 47, 50, 63, 76, 78, 98, 106,

108–12. *See also* asylums; cemeteries: at Canton Asylum; escapes; incarceration; institutionalization; labor; staff, institutional; transinstitutionalization; violence; *and names of institutionalized people and their kin*
carceral institutions. *See* incarceration; *and names of individual institutions*
caregiving, 4, 11, 13, 16, 30, 40, 48, 51, 56, 59, 60, 65, 67, 70, 77, 92, 97, 98, 118n53, 131n8, 139n16, 141n38. *See also* diverted mothering; kinship: as resource; labor
Carlisle Indian Industrial School, 65. *See also* boarding schools
cemeteries: at Canton Asylum, 18, 19, 38, 43, 48, 64, 76, 77, 87–88, 102, 103, 104, 105, 108, 111, 150n68, 166n41, 169–70n1; Congressional Cemetery, 87, 157n39; family cemeteries, 36, 84, 98; as sites of contested memory, 18, 38, 64, 87, 98, 102, 103, 104–5, 106, 111, 130n95, 166n41; and St. Elizabeths Hospital, 87, 157n35
Cheyenne River Reservation, 32
children, institutionalized, 3, 8, 12–13, 15, 26, 41–42, 44–45, 58–59, 65, 72, 76–77, 111, 120n67, 140n27. *See also names of individuals*
Christopher, Clara, 50, 88, 137n70, 145n8, 157n40. *See also* staff, institutional
Clafflin, Peter, 68, 135n49
Cobb, Amanda J., 7, 82
Collier, John, 79–80, 152n84. *See also* staff, institutional
confinement. *See* containment; solitary confinement
containment, 3, 12, 30, 31, 36–37, 44, 55, 59, 76–78, 86–87, 88, 120n68, 130n4, 147n36, 153n2; and institutional patterns, 68–69, 70–72, 75, 82, 85, 86–87, 103, 144n4, 151n79. *See also* incarceration; institutionalization; solitary confinement; surveillance; transinstitutionalization; violence

Ickes, Harold, 79, 152n88
immigrants, 9, 33, 127n61
immigration. *See* immigrants
incarceration, 1–4, 16–17, 25, 30, 35–37, 46, 51, 55, 58, 59, 62, 67, 72, 106, 115n25, 125n46, 159n67; and death, 11, 17, 19, 20, 23, 36, 38, 43–44, 58, 64, 73, 74, 76–77, 84–87, 97–98, 102–4, 106, 111, 129, 134n31, 147 (nn30, 32), 150 (nn64, 66, 69, 70), 156n34, 157n39; and diagnosis, 7–9, 12, 13, 31–32, 42, 56–57, 63, 69–71, 75, 82, 84, 155n26; and removal, 16–17, 82, 91, 97, 103, 111, 134n38, 141n37. *See also* containment; institutionalization; labor; surveillance; *and names of individual carceral institutions*
Indian Asylum. *See* Canton Asylum
Indigenous systems of medicine, 8–9, 13, 28–30, 38, 54, 100, 108, 111, 114n18, 124n26, 169n1; and healers, 3, 53–55, 78, 84–85, 100, 108, 111. *See also* well-being
insanity, 1, 9, 12, 27, 28, 31–32, 34, 42, 45, 63, 125n46. *See also* diagnosis; pathology; sanism; settler ableism; Western biomedicine
inspections. *See* Canton Asylum: inspections of; Silk reports
institutionalization: and families and Native nations, 4, 10, 11, 12, 15–16, 22–25, 28–30, 35, 37, 39–42, 43–44, 45–47, 49, 51, 54, 55–56, 58–59, 64, 67, 84–85, 89, 92, 100–101, 105–6, 108, 142n49, 158n49; and lack of self-determination, 4, 5, 6, 11, 14, 16–17, 30, 36–37, 45, 46, 48, 49, 55, 56, 63, 86, 90, 97, 104–5; and life expectancy, 5, 12–13, 35, 42, 43, 44, 57, 58, 71, 76–77, 87, 134n31; sustained, 2, 4, 8–9, 16–17, 20, 25, 37, 43, 45–48, 57, 63–64, 77–78, 79, 80–81, 84, 106, 140n27. *See also* containment; incarceration; transinstitutionalization; violence
institutions. *See* institutionalization; transinstitutionalization; *and names of individual institutions*

intelligence, 28, 34, 40, 43, 46, 125n46, 135n51. *See also* settler ableism
Iron Shield, Harold, 17, 18, 42, 102, *103*, 103–4, 106, 165n39

Jensen, Francis, 82–85, *83*, 100
Jensen, Jack, 98–99, 100–102, *101*
Judah, Lavanah Smith, 38, 104
Juel, William, 74–75, 149n58. *See also* staff, institutional

Kampeska, Nellie, 12, 60–63, 74–75, 97, 142n48, 166n42
Kellyville, Creek Nation, 71
Kiger-St Clair, Caroline Jean, 93, 94, 162 (nn87, 95)
kinship: as resource, 1, 12, 13, 15, 23, 30, 39, 48, 58, 59–63, 77, 90; sustaining survivance, 6, 10, 13–15, 17, 20, 55, 58–60, 65, 67, 92, 104–7, 111; as target, 11–12, 23, 29, 39–40, 41, 43–46, 47, 55, 57, 63, 77, 89, 103, 131n8
Kitch-Kum-Me. *See* Jensen, Francis
Knox, Katie, 64. *See also* staff, institutional

labor, 4, 15, 27, 36, 48–51, 69–70, 87, 89, 96, 134n32, 137n74, 146n21, 156n29, 158 (nn44, 46). *See also* caregiving; diverted mothering
Lake Traverse Reservation. *See* Sisseton Reservation
land, 1–2, 13, 22, 37–38, 71, 88, 92, 100, 102; and settler colonialism, 2, 4, 5, 16, 18, 22, 26, 27, 29, 33, 37–38, 41. *See also* place
Landis, Ione, 50, 51, 137n72. *See also* staff, institutional
language, 6, 7, 8, 29, 30, 75, 79; and identity, 7, 14, 27, 59, 60, 63, 66–67, 98, 142n45, 170n13; as resource, 26–27, 57, 60–61, 63, 73, 122n12, 123n18, 148n47; as target, 7, 9, 37, 49, 53, 63, 66–67, 78

Nin-Hoon, 30
Noble, John S., 1

Office of Indian Affairs. *See*
Bureau of Indian Affairs
Oglala Lakota Nation, 13, 141n36,
143–44n66, 156n34, 166n42
O'Neil, Cora Winona. *See* Faribault, Cora
Winona
O'Neil, Faith, 17, 19–20, *19*, 64–65, 67,
94–95, 96–98, 108–11, *109*, 140n26,
143n60, 163 (nn96, 101) (chap. 5),
163n2 (chap. 6), 164n19
oral traditions, 13, 32. *See also* storytelling
orphanages, 16, 25, 95, 104, 120n68,
140n29, 158n49. *See also* institutionalization; Good Shepherd Mission Orphanage; transinstitutionalization
Ortley, South Dakota, 61
outing system, 15, 65, 88, 89, 90, 158n46,
159n60
O-Zoush-Quah, 53–56, *54*, 77–79, 80, 82–
85, 98–101, 138n1, 139 (nn9, 15), 154n4,
155n23, 164n26, 165n31

Pah-Kish-Ko-Quah, 99–101
pathology, 6, 8–11, 12, 27–31, 37, 39–40,
45, 55, 63, 75, 76, 84, 134n32, 149n56.
See also diagnosis; settler ableism;
Western biomedicine
patients. *See names of individuals*
Peatwatuck. *See* Jensen, Jack
persistent harm, 70–75, 84
personhood, 10, 14, 29, 58, 63, 75, 111
Pettigrew, Richard, 32, 35
Phoenix, Arizona, 15, 90, 91–93, 159n60,
161n86
Pine Ridge, South Dakota, 67, 141n36,
166n42
Pipestone Indian School, Pipestone,
Minnesota, 60, 80, 166n42. *See also*
boarding schools
place, 3–4, 5, 7, 33, 34, 37, 38, 43, 45,
50, 74, 85, 88, 98, 102, 103, 106; and
Indigenous identity, 3, 5, 13, 22, 25,

30, 35, 37, 38, 53, 55, 82, 85, 92, 98,
102, 103
political-relational theory of disability,
139n13
Potawatomi Reservation, 13, 35, 78, 82,
84, 99, 138n2
Prairie Band Potawatomi Nation, 13, 35,
37, 38, 53, 84, 99, 101
Prairie Band Potawatomi Nation Reservation. *See* Potawatomi Reservation
pregnancy. *See* reproduction
presence. *See* absence and presence
psychiatry. *See* Western biomedicine
Public Service Hospitals: Fort Worth,
Texas, 36, 85, 86–87, 88, 155 (nn23, 26),
156n34; Lexington, Kentucky, 36, 85,
87, 88, 155n23, 156 (nn33, 34). *See also*
asylums; *and names of institutionalized
people and their kin*

Rabon, Joe, 14, 85–88
racism. *See* eugenics; scientific racism;
settler ableism; settler colonialism
rape. *See* sexual assault
Reaume, Geoffrey, 10
reciprocity, 15, 20, 24, 39, 60–61, 77, 98,
100, 102, 106, 108–12, 118n48
reclamation, 64, 104, 109, 165n39, 167n53
Red Owl, Amos, 143n66
Red Owl, Lizzie, 13, 65–67, 89, 97
refusal, 25, 31, 32, 84, 86–87, 90, 97, 100,
154n14
remembering, 2, 3, 8, 20–21, 25, 17,
94–95, 102, 109–11; as act of kinship,
2, 3, 13–14, 20–21, 25, 38, 59, 63–65, 85,
88, 93–95, 96–98, 99–102, 104–7; as
component of healing, 20–21, 22, 85,
93, 98–102, 103–6, 109–12, 170n13; and
decolonization, 2–3, 13–14, 18, 20–21,
25, 32, 96–97, 102–7, 109–12, 170n13;
as form of self-determination, 2,
13–14, 18, 22, 32, 38, 88, 96–97, 102–7,
109–12. *See also* decolonizing practices;
survivance
Renville, Rose D., 57

Wam-Te-Go-She-Quah, 35

wardship, 5, 25, 32, 34, 38, 43

Washington, D.C., 2, 27, 31, 36–37, 77, 78–79, 81, 82, 85–88, 152n85

Wauketch, Seymour, 68

well-being, 13, 30, 38, 54. See also Indigenous systems of medicine

Werner, Charles, 12, 41–42, 132n15. See also staff, institutional

Western biomedicine, 2, 3, 32, 34, 35, 37, 55, 58, 77, 84, 100, 124n26, 125n46, 150–51n73; values of, 5, 6, 8–11, 12, 16, 27–29, 39–40, 43–44, 47, 70, 79–80, 133n26. See also diagnosis; Indigenous systems of medicine; institutionalization; pathology; settler ableism; settler colonialism

Window Rock, Arizona. See Tségháhoodzání

Wishecoby, Susan, 68, 148n46

Wong, Sau-ling C., 48

work. See labor

Yellow Bird, Pemina, 3, 29, 64, 104, 106, 112

Yun-nin. See Moss, Ruby

Zihkanakoyake, 26, 29–30, 64, 122n11